# Nurses of
# Passchendaele

# Nurses of Passchendaele

## Caring for the Wounded of the Ypres Campaigns 1914–1918

Christine E. Hallett

PEN & SWORD
HISTORY

First published in Great Britain in 2017 and reprinted in 2022 by
Pen & Sword History
an imprint of
Pen & Sword Books Ltd
47 Church Street
Barnsley
South Yorkshire
S70 2AS

ISBN 978 1 52670 288 3

Printed and bound in the UK by CPI Group (UK) Ltd, Croydon, CRO 4YY

Pen & Sword Books Ltd incorporates the Imprints of Pen & Sword Books
Archaeology, Atlas, Aviation, Battleground, Discovery, Family History, History,
Maritime, Military, Naval, Politics, Railways, Select, Transport, True Crime,
Fiction, Frontline Books, Leo Cooper, Praetorian Press, Seaforth Publishing,
Wharncliffe and White Owl.

For a complete list of Pen & Sword titles please contact
PEN & SWORD BOOKS LIMITED
47 Church Street, Barnsley, South Yorkshire, S70 2AS, England
E-mail: enquiries@pen-and-sword.co.uk
Website: www.pen-and-sword.co.uk

For Keith

Helen Fairchild.

# Contents

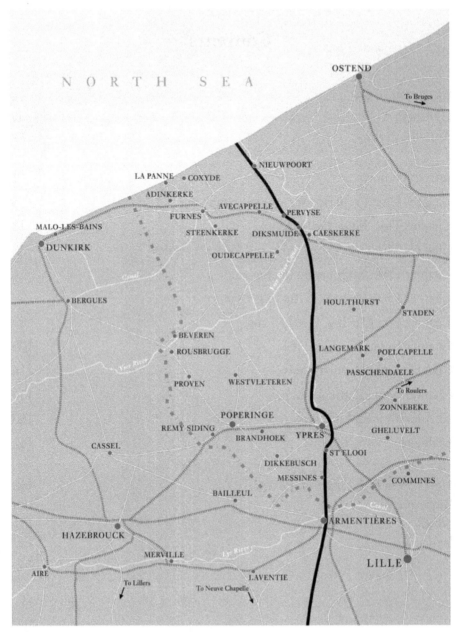

Map 1: The Ypres Front.

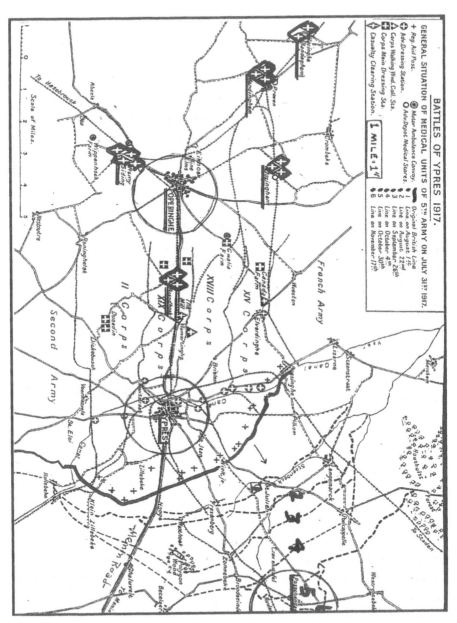

Map 2: Locations of Casualty Clearing Stations behind the Ypres Salient. (Reproduced by kind permission of Nelle Rote, from her book *Nurse Helen Fairchild*.)

# List of Illustrations

Front cover: Portrait of Helen Fairchild. (Image appears by courtesy of Nelle Rote and the Women in Military Service for America Memorial Foundation, Inc.). Background images from Pen & Sword Books' own collection

Back cover: Mobile Surgical No. 1. (Reproduced by kind permission of the Provincial Archives of Alberta (PR1986.0054.0012.0001))

Image 1: Portrait of Kate Luard as a young woman. (Image appears by kind courtesy of Caroline Stevens)

Image 2: Portrait of Sister Kate Luard seated outside her home, Birch Rectory, Essex, while on leave during the war. (Image appears by kind courtesy of Caroline Stevens)

Image 3: Portrait of Sister Kate Luard. (Image appears by kind courtesy of Caroline Stevens)

Image 4: Interior of Hospital Train No. 16. (Reproduced by kind courtesy of the Wills family and with the assistance of the National Railway Museum)

Image 5: Photograph taken in a treatment area at L'Hôpital de l'Océan's Vinkem site. (© The Belgian Red Cross Archives, Brussels; reproduced with their permission)

Image 6: Exterior view of No. 8 British General Hospital at Rouen. (From the collection of Kate Maxey; reproduced by kind permission of the Defty and Varley families)

Image 7: Interior of a ward at No. 1 British General Hospital, Étretat. (From the collection of Kate Maxey; reproduced by kind permission of the Defty and Varley families)

Image 8: A nursing sister with a group of 'walking wounded' patients. (From the collection of Kate Maxey; reproduced by kind permission of the Defty and Varley families)

Image 9: Wound irrigation being performed by surgeon and nurses at L'Hôpital de l'Océan, La Panne. (© The Belgian Red Cross Archives, Brussels; reproduced with their permission)

# Glossary

| | |
|---|---|
| AANS | Australian Army Nursing Service |
| ANZAC | Australian and New Zealand Army Corps |
| FFNC | French Flag Nursing Corps |
| NZANS | New Zealand Army Nursing Service |
| RAMC | Royal Army Medical Corps |
| TFNS | Territorial Force Nursing Service |
| QAIMNS | Queen Alexandra's Imperial Military Nursing Service |
| QAIMNSR | Queen Alexandra's Imperial Military Nursing Service (Reserve) |
| VAD | Voluntary Aid Detachment |

# Author's Note

When I embarked on this project, I had many doubts. I was not sure how I could do justice to the work of the women who saved so many lives on the Ypres Front during the First World War. Yet when I visited the 'Salient' I felt its powerful emotional pull. I had a sense of how fierce had been the experience of everyone who served in this small, compact geographical area. I also had a sense of how important the nurses of all nations had been to the survival and recovery of the wounded. It seemed to me that the work they had done in Flanders somehow epitomized the best of what they had achieved and the worst of what they had endured in the First World War as a whole. Here, in villages such as Rouesbrugge, Proven, Westvleteren and Brandhoek, their enduring influence can still be felt – but their work is still not really understood, and their contribution has still not been fully recognized.

When I first visited the Ypres area, I was struck by its tranquillity. As I wandered sites of former hospitals in 'rest areas' behind the lines – now fertile, arable fields and luxuriant pastures – I could see very few signs of the deep, traumatic scars the war had left a hundred years ago. In fact, I was often bewildered by the apparent calm and serenity of the area – particularly in the former 'zone of the armies'.

The peace that pervades the Ypres region seems somehow, in itself, a testament to the work of the nurses and other medical workers. Because, if you look carefully enough, you *can* still find signs that, here, in these fields, desperate battles took place – not between soldiers of opposing sides, but, as one nurse of the time said: between 'the science of destroying' and the 'science of healing'. The marks of trauma are well hidden. All that is left on the surface is a handful of museums and visitor centres – carefully designed to respect the humanity of those who died – and a huge number of simple, aesthetically beautiful monuments. It is as if the people of this region decided, long ago, to defy war by creating, in its direct wake, a perfect sense of peace and harmony.

A century ago, only a few miles away from these places – on the battlefields around Messines, Zonnebeke, St Julien, Langemark, Poelcapelle and Passchendaele – men were ploughing across no-man's land, sinking up to their knees, thighs, waists, shoulders, some actually drowning, in the foul mud created by constant shelling and toxic chemicals. And, as they floundered in the mire, their bodies were being shattered by bullets and shrapnel, their lungs seared by poison gas. If they survived long enough to reach hospitals behind the lines, a new struggle began. As they were carried into the reception areas of casualty clearing stations and field hospitals, invisible forces were dragging them to their deaths, just as the physical mud of the battlefield had dragged their bodies into the ground. The processes of physiological and emotional disintegration were like gravity – irrevocable unless countered by human strength. So a new fight began – between the fierce grip of death and the skilled artistry of the nurse. And even as nurses were putting all their strength into saving their patients, they were, themselves, in danger from aerial bombardment, long-range artillery and gas. Little is known about those battles. And the project of bringing them to the world's attention is far from over.

Because this book became such a personal project, I came to regard many of the people who helped me with it as personal friends. Of all my books, this is the one that has accumulated the greatest number of debts. I owe much to the generosity of people from all over the world, who have given freely of their time, enthusiasm and expertise to help me bring the work to fruition.

Relatives of former First World War nurses have been particularly kind. Many forwarded valuable material, memorabilia and images, and granted me permission to reproduce these. Nelle Rote, the niece of Helen Fairchild, gave me permission to reproduce text from her aunt's letters and a map of the locations of casualty clearing stations behind the Ypres Salient, all of which appear in her book *Nurse Helen Fairchild*. I also benefitted greatly from Nelle's deep insights into her aunt's experiences in France and Belgium. John and Caroline Stevens gave me permission to reproduce material relating to, and written by, Kate Luard: photographs and text from *Unknown Warriors*. Richard Thurstan and Jill Hunt gave me permission to reproduce a photograph of their great-aunt, Violetta Thurstan. They also spent a lot of time with me offering very valuable insights into Violetta's life and work. Maureen and Barbara Defty, along with their cousin, Elizabeth Varley, were very generous, welcoming me to their home and permitting me to reproduce text from several of their great-aunt Kate Maxey's private papers, and also to reproduce several photographs from the Maxey Collection. Marilyn McInnes was an inspiration, offering me insights into Sidney Beldam's experiences and giving me permission to reproduce photographs of him and of her grandmother,

Winifred Winkworth. I owe a debt to Caroline Williams who rescued the letters written by Ellen La Motte to Amy Wesselhoeft von Erdberg from a damp and decaying barn in Germany and deposited them in the Alan Mason Chesney Medical Archives of the Johns Hopkins Medical Institutions and who kindly gave me permission to reproduce material from those letters.

Archivists across the world helped me access research material for this book. I would, in particular, like to thank staffs of the Alan Mason Chesney Medical Archives of the Johns Hopkins Medical Institutions, Baltimore, USA; the National Archives, Kew, UK; the Nottinghamshire Archives, Nottingham, UK; the Liddle Collection; the Brotherton Library, University of Leeds, UK; the National Railway Museum, York, UK; the Australian War Memorial, Canberra, Australia; the Provincial Archives of Alberta, Edmonton, Canada; the Archives of the Lijssenthoek Cemetery Visitor Centre, Poperinge, Belgium and the Archives of Talbot House, Poperinge Belgium. Particular thanks are due to a number of individual archivists who gave very freely of their time. Marjorie Kehoe, of the Alan Mason Chesney Archives, was, as always, a joy to work with. She was kind enough to notify me of the Archive's receipt of the letters of Ellen La Motte, and to support me in obtaining access to these materials. Melissa Hardie-Budden, of the Hypatia Trust, was hugely supportive of my research on the life and work of Violetta Thurstan. Dona Bickerdyke, of the Nottinghamshire Archives, UK, supported me in obtaining copies of the letters of Annie Wright. Robin Wallace, of the Provincial Archives of Alberta, in Edmonton, Canada, enabled me to obtain copies of material relating to Madeleine Jaffray. Annemie Morisse forwarded me a photograph of Nellie Spindler. Jan Louagie forwarded me photographs held at the Archives of the Talbot House Visitor Centre. Fiona Bourne, of the Royal College of Nursing Archives, very kindly assisted me in accessing oral history material which offered valuable insights into the work of British nurses. Alison Kay, of the National Railway Museum, York, UK, assisted me in obtaining material relating to the work of nurses on ambulance trains. For permission to reproduce text and images, I thank:

- The Alan Mason Chesney Medical Archives of the Johns Hopkins Medical Institutions, Baltimore, USA, for granting permission (along with Caroline Williams) to reproduce material from the letters of Ellen La Motte.
- The Nottinghamshire Archives, Nottingham, UK, for permission to reproduce material from the letters of Annie Wright to the parents of Glynne Morris.

- The Australian War Memorial, Canberra, for providing a full scan of Hilda Loxton's Diary (2DRL/1172); and for permission to reproduce photographs held in their collection (orders 8350116; 8390823; 8519651).
- The Archives of the Hypatia Trust, Penzance, UK, for permission to reproduce material relating to Violetta Thurstan.
- The Archives of the Lijssenthoek Cemetery Visitor Centre, Belgium, for permission to reproduce a photograph of Nellie Spindler.
- The Archives of Talbot House, Poperinge, Belgium, for permission to reproduce material relating to Talbot House and photographs relating to L'Hôpital de l'Océan.
- The Archives of the Belgian Red Cross, for permission to reproduce photographs of L'Hôpital de l'Océan.

For a full list of photographic credits, please see 'List of Illustrations and Maps'.

Short extracts from the published memoirs of nurses and volunteer nurses have greatly enhanced this book. Brief excerpts from the following texts have been quoted: Catherine Black, *King's Nurse – Beggar's Nurse* (London, Hurst and Blackett, 1939), Baroness de T'Serclaes, *Flanders and Other Fields* (London, George Harrap and Co. Ltd., 1964), Mary Borden, *The Forbidden Zone* (London, William Heinemann, 1929), Ellen La Motte, *The Backwash of War* (New York, G. P. Putnam's Sons, The Knickerbocker Press, 1916), Anonymous [Agnes Warner], *My Beloved Poilus* (Saint John, New Brunswick, N. B. Barnes, 1917), Maud Mortimer, *A Green Tent in Flanders* (New York, Doubleday, Page & Co., 1918), Anonymous [Kate Luard], *Diary of a Nursing Sister on the Western Front* (Edinburgh, William Blackwood & Sons, 1915), Kate Luard, *Unknown Warriors* (London, Chatto & Windus, 1930). An excellent new edition of *Unknown Warriors* has been published by John and Caroline Stevens: *Unknown Warriors: The Letters of Kate Luard, RRC and Bar, Nursing Sister in France 1914–1918* (Stroud, The History Press, 2014). Quotations from two doctors' memoirs also added significantly to the book: George Crile, *An Autobiography* (Philadelphia & New York, J.B. Lippincott Co., 1947) and Harvey Cushing, *From a Surgeon's Journal, 1915-1918* (Boston, Little, Brown & Co., 1936).

The memoir of May Tilton (*The Grey Battalion*, Angus & Robertson Ltd., 1933) and the diary of Hilda Loxton (Documents 2DRL/1172; Australian War Memorial, Canberra) were of great importance in enabling me to understand the experience of nurses close to the front lines during the Third Ypres campaign. This book retells Tilton's and Loxton's stories and, in order to give voice to the writers themselves, it also offers a number of quotations. Despite extensive searches, no copyright holders have been found for these texts, and I, along with Pen & Sword Books, would be very grateful for any information that would enable us to contact them.

I have received generous help from a number of historians, guides and other individuals. Dirk Claerhout, of Beveren-Ijzer, Belgium drew my attention to the information on individual patients at L'Hôpital Chirurgical Mobile No. 1 (Mobile Surgical No. 1) from the French websites, *Memoirs des Hommes* and *MemorialGenWeb*. He also contacted the French Archives Nationales at Pierrefitte-sur-Seine. I am deeply indebted to Dirk not only for his invaluable assistance in accessing records that enabled me to identify patients at the hospital, but also for advising me on the whereabouts of archival materials relating to Australian nurse Hilda Loxton. Thanks are also due to Leo Bonte and Karien Becuwe, of Alveringem, Belgium.

Andrea McKenzie, of York University, Canada, went to a great deal of trouble to enable me to access source materials relating to Madeleine Jaffray at the Provincial Archives of Alberta, Edmonton, Canada. John Banham forwarded me information relating to Kate Maxey's career and connections in Leeds, and corrected errors in an early draft of my work on her. Jeremy Banning drew my attention to the letters written by Annie Wright to the parents of Glynne Morris, and sent me copies of these. Claire Chatterton was instrumental in drawing my attention to the significance of the work of Minnie Wood and Catherine Black. Sue Light, who died tragically before this work was completed, was always a source of enormous help and support. I miss her very much.

I am very grateful to Luc Inion for creating the memorial plaque to Helen Fairchild close to the War Graves Cemetery at Dozinghem – and thereby drawing my attention to her story; and also for sharing his insights into the work of casualty clearing stations in the Westvleteren area. Luc de Munck provided me with valuable information on L'Hôpital de l'Océan, and forwarded me photographs that are included in this book with the permission of the Belgian Red Cross Archives. Jan and Simon Louagie were both very generous with their time, providing me with important information relating to the Passchendaele campaign. Jan also forwarded material from the Archives at Talbot House, Poperinge, and checked and corrected a first draft of the section in this book relating to the work of the Everyman's Club. I would like, also, to express my gratitude to Lionel Roosemont of Frontline Tours for his remarkable insights into all aspects of the Ypres campaigns and for being the first person to take me to the site of L'Hôpital Chirurgical Mobile No. 1.

Many thanks to Claire Hopkins and Chris Cocks of Pen and Sword Books for their generous support and for the meticulous care with which they have corrected and improved this text.

As always, my most heartfelt thanks go to my family not only for appreciating my work but also for providing some welcome distractions from it. Very special thanks to Margaret Hallett for countless acts of kindness, and to Keith Brindle for his generosity and for always being with me as I ploughed across the battlefields.

# Introduction

The professional nurses of the early twentieth century were a unique group. Hiding tough practicality beneath a genteel, feminine appearance, they spent long hours performing heavy physical work. Yet, to any outsider visiting their hospital wards, they would have seemed calm and unruffled: the refined ladies of their 'households'. Most were from middle-class backgrounds, and combined a ladylike upbringing with financial need. Others were from working-class families; nursing offered them an alternative to domestic service, but its strong association with gentility also gave them a chance to better themselves. It had not always been this way. In 1836, when wealthy English gentlewoman Florence Nightingale had declared her intention to devote her life to nursing, her family had been appalled: in the mid-nineteenth century the care of the sick had been an occupation for women of the lowest possible class. In hospitals, where the medical treatment and support of the destitute were paid for by the philanthropy of wealthy donors, nursing was performed by women of the servant class. They were assumed to be mere drudges with neither education nor character. There *were* nurses who combined a high level of skill with a genuine sense of devotion to their patients; but they lacked authority and their efforts were too often invisible amid the hubbub and chaos of the nineteenth-century hospital.

Nightingale's expedition to Scutari to nurse the wounded of the Crimean War in 1854 changed everything. From then onwards, nursing, though still regarded by wealthy parents as an unworthy pursuit for their own daughters, was infused with a heroic light. It offered meaningful work to women who would otherwise have been socially and financially dependent upon their families. 'Ladies' of higher social status began to take a deep interest in it; and they brought into the hospital a sense of female authority – a belief in women's right to govern the domestic sphere.

At the end of the nineteenth century large hospitals in cities such as London, Philadelphia, Melbourne, Toronto and Wellington had their own schools of nursing. In these carefully controlled institutions young women lived sequestered lives in comfortable seclusion. The profession had flourished in the last four decades of the nineteenth century, and its leaders were dedicated to enhancing its reputation and throwing off the lingering taint of its nineteenth-century reputation. The training was highly practical. Young probationers mastered the complexities of their work on the wards, under the close scrutiny of 'sisters' or 'head nurses'. They listened carefully to lectures given by hospital doctors, taking notes which were scrutinized and corrected by a 'home sister'. Many were deeply interested in medical science, but they were warned by their 'lady superintendents' against assuming that their work was similar to medicine. Nursing, they were informed, was entirely unique: its own art. Although nurses owed deference to medical science, their own duties were to offer comfort and care to patients, to maintain a high moral 'tone' within their wards and to implement a range of treatments. And if these duties sometimes came into conflict – if, for example, a medical regimen made a patient deeply uncomfortable and seemed, at first, to worsen his condition – it was understood that the art of nursing lay in resolving these conflicts. The nurse was, above all, the arbiter of order, cleanliness and morality within the walls of the hospital. She provided the safe environment within which patients could be given the best chance of survival and recovery.

By the end of the nineteenth century nursing training was testing and physically demanding. Hospital schools had very high attrition rates. Young women entered with enthusiasm only to find that the work involved much more than soothing fevered brows. The emotional demands of caring for patients with life-threatening infectious diseases and healing the damage caused by industrial accidents took more energy and stamina than they believed they could muster. Most reached a point in their probationary period – their introductory training – when exhaustion threatened to overwhelm the will to continue. Many found new reserves of energy, but some became ill and had to leave.

The hospital routine was gruelling. Nurses were awake well before 6 a.m. and were on their wards by seven. The probationer's first duties were to sweep the floors, dust the bedside lockers, clean out the grates and lay new fires. Not all probationers were used in this way. 'Ladies' of the higher social classes paid fees to become 'special probationers'; as such, they escaped much of the drudgery imposed upon their working-class counterparts. Yet the maintenance of order and cleanliness was an important lesson for everyone. Not only did it instil discipline and stoicism, it also built physical strength and stamina. In an era when the British 'stiff upper lip' was highly valued, nurses were taught that they – above all others – must acquire it to a high level of refinement. They would be exposed to sights no gentlewoman could expect to witness: men and women writhing in agony from typhoid fever, losing control of bowel and bladder, lying in their own sweat and excrement; children dying of suffocation as diphtheria closed their throats; working-class people of all ages with limbs torn off by industrial machinery. Nursing was not for the faint-hearted. The work of cleaning the ward offered new probationers time to adjust to the hospital's atmosphere of fear and distress and to become part of a workforce that replaced that atmosphere with one of calm. They could only do so if they could learn how to harness their own emotions; their compassion depended upon self-control.

Only when a probationer was ready would the sister permit her to care for patients – teaching her the techniques of moving and handling their bodies, gently bathing and positioning them to protect skin and joints, feeding them, removing and disposing of excreta. If she survived all this without resigning, succumbing to an infectious fever or simply becoming worn-down, the probationer would be taught the more technical elements of nursing work: the administration of medications, the performance of complex dressings, the application of bandages and splints, the giving of enemata, bowel and bladder washouts, the management of saline infusions.

By the turn of the century, the trained nurses of most developed countries were highly respected professionals. Their image was one of purity and self-control, but their practice was not well understood. Their work was intimate and dangerous, and they had found ways to screen and protect themselves and their patients from public view. The hospital wards of the early nineteenth century had been places into which patients' relatives, medical students and interested members of the public had come and gone at will. The clamour, noise and occasional rowdiness of the typical hospital ward did not lend itself to healing. But by the first years of the twentieth century, these same hospitals had become closed and sequestered places of order and calm, and their nurses presented an outward face of serenity, concealing the drama and ugliness of the struggles with disease and death that took place behind carefully positioned bed screens. This is not to say that nurses had gained control of the spaces within which they worked. Hospital governors and medical doctors were still in command. But nurses were, increasingly, seen as vital to the smooth running of the work – and their presence was, almost everywhere, accepted by medical men.

Only one bastion of male medical control continued to hold out against the full acceptance of female nurses. The Royal Army Medical Corps (RAMC), founded in 1898, considered the care of soldiers to be an entirely unsuitable job for women of any class. Many of its senior members still regarded women who 'followed' armies and tended their wounded as little more than prostitutes. Although a small professional Army Nursing Service had been founded in the 1860s – inspired by Florence Nightingale's example and supported by her patronage – it had, by the 1890s, still gained only a slight foothold within the work of the RAMC. Most military nursing care was still offered by medical orderlies – men who were soldiers first and nurses second. The Second Anglo-Boer War (1899–1902) revealed the inadequacies of that system.

When hospital units were taken to South Africa in 1899 to care for the wounded very few female nurses went with them. The conditions produced by the South African War gave rise to epidemics of serious infectious diseases such as dysentery and typhoid fever, and when journalists brought home the scandalous news that thousands of apparently unnecessary deaths were occurring in military hospitals, their reports triggered national outrage. The scandal permitted military nurses to argue for the expansion of their service, and in 1902 a new elite army nursing corps – the Queen Alexandra's Imperial Military Nursing Service (QAIMNS) – was founded.

Over the course of the next ten years, the governments and populations of European nations became increasingly aware that their rivalries and alliances made war possible – even likely. The more concerned they became, the more they engaged in political and diplomatic manoeuvring. And war moved inexorably nearer. In Britain two powerful imperatives were emerging: the preparation of men for fighting and of women for military nursing. The Territorial Force Nursing Service (TFNS) was created in 1908, and over the following six years about 8,000 nurses entered their names onto its register, indicating their willingness to serve in time of war. The Voluntary Aid Detachments (VADs) were created in 1909 as part of the Haldane Reforms, a series of measures designed to place Britain in a state of war-readiness. The VADs enlisted semi-trained volunteers who would support the health and welfare of soldiers on the home front. In reality, their members had very little training of any kind. So-called VAD nurses attended classes run by fully trained professional nurses, and undertook voluntary work in local civilian hospitals; many became adept 'probationer nurses'. Still, their experience was slight. No one could have anticipated the demanding and dangerous work they would eventually perform on many war fronts.

*Chapter One*

# Preparing for War Nursing

As war edged nearer, professional nurses began to view themselves as fortunate: their skill would enable them to fulfil a vital function in time of conflict, and their fellow citizens would view them with respect – even with envy. Violetta Thurstan, the daughter of a doctor, was one of those who keenly anticipated war. She had worked at a fever hospital in Guernsey and at a children's hospital in Shadwell, before entering the London Hospital School of Nursing in December 1900 as a 'paying' or 'special' probationer. Her training school had a reputation for treating its trainees harshly, and the death of a number of probationers during the 1880s had resulted in a House of Lords inquiry. Violetta herself was taken ill several times during her training and was identified by her matron, Eva Luckes, as a danger to the hospital's reputation: 'We could never rely upon her to remain well for long,' wrote Matron Luckes in Violetta's personal file. But Violetta went on to surprise everyone by successfully completing her training and going on to become the Lady Superintendent of the West Riding District Nursing Association and a member of the Matrons' Council.

Violetta had been born in 1879 in Hastings on the south coast of England, and christened Anna Violet. Educated at Guernsey Ladies' College and at boarding school in Germany, she had acquired both a powerful gift for imaginative writing and an impressive mastery of several European languages, including German, French and Spanish. In 1914, she completed a correspondence course at St Andrews University and acquired the title 'Lady Literate in the Arts'. It was to fully trained professional nurses like Violetta that many Voluntary Aid Detachments (VADs) turned to provide training for their volunteers. About a year before the outbreak of the First World War, Violetta had joined the Westminster 146 VAD of the British Red Cross, helping to train its enthusiastic volunteers in the arts of first aid, bandaging and sick cookery. The whole country was preparing for war and Violetta spent a large part of the summer camping and drilling in the southern English countryside and engaging in avid discussions about the political situation in Europe and the possibility of war.

Like Violetta, professional nurse Kate Luard was anxious to serve her
country. One of eleven children of an Essex clergyman, Kate had worked as
a governess for about a year in order to save enough money to pay her way
through training as a 'special probationer' at University College Hospital
in London. She had been a highly successful student nurse, who went on
to serve with the Army Nursing Service during the Second Anglo–Boer
War and then to become matron of a tuberculosis sanatorium. She joined
the Queen Alexandra's Imperial Military Nursing Service (QAIMNS) as
a Reserve Sister on 6 August 1914 and was mobilized three days later as a
member of the No. 1 British General Hospital.

Not everyone could train as a special probationer. Unlike Kate Luard
and Violetta Thurstan, Nellie Spindler, a young woman from the north
of England, had not been able to afford such elite training. She was born
on 10 August 1891, the daughter of a police sergeant in Wakefield, a small
Yorkshire city with an unusual history dating back to Anglo–Saxon times
and probably beyond. In the Middle Ages, it had been a thriving centre of
the wool trade, and its castle was the site of one of the most important battles
of the Wars of the Roses. As a city, though, it was young: in the nineteenth
century, its cathedral had been restored from a neglected parish church by
proud Victorians determined to raise the status of their home town. When
Nellie was born, it was one of the most important coal mining centres in
Britain, with over twenty pits and all of the health risks associated with the
mining industry: lung diseases, industrial accidents, and poverty. Nellie's
father was promoted to police inspector, an office which required the family
to live within the city boundary, and Nellie was brought up at 104 Stanley
Road, and educated at the Eastmoor Council School. She was the oldest
of four children; when, at the age of 21, she decided to pursue a career as
a nurse, her sisters Lillie and May were 16 and 8, while brother George
Edward was ten. Entering the nursing profession was probably both a means
to earn some money to help support the family and an escape route from a
fairly crowded household.

Nellie's route into nursing was a typical one for a young woman of her
time who came from a family that was 'respectable', yet far from wealthy.
In 1910, at the age of 21, she entered the City of Wakefield Fever Hospital,
where she spent two years living in the nurses' home, working on the
wards and drawing a small salary as an untrained nurse. She was caring for
patients with infectious diseases ranging from dysentery and typhoid fever
to meningitis and influenza. In an era before antibiotics, such work was very
dangerous, but provided a nurse survived it – and the majority did – she

usually emerged with enhanced immunity to a range of common infections. Following a brief period of service at Barnes Nursing Home in Scarborough, Nellie entered the Township Infirmary at Leeds, as an 'ordinary' nurse probationer, moving from ward to ward, learning from experienced nursing sisters, and providing nursing care in exchange for a salary and theoretical instruction in anatomy, physiology, pathology and the principles of nursing care. While she was there the war began, and she enlisted with the Queen Alexandra's Imperial Military Nursing Service Reserve.

As soon as she had completed her training, in early November 1915, Nellie signed two forms of agreement indicating her 'willingness to serve', passed a medical examination, declared herself 'fit' and was posted, at the age of 25, to the Whittington Military Hospital in Lichfield. From lowly employee in a Fever Hospital, through 'ordinary probationer' to fully qualified military 'reserve nurse', Nellie had embarked on what she must have anticipated would be a highly successful and rewarding career.

The early life and career of Minnie Wood – another Wakefield nurse – was a little more comfortable than that of Nellie Spindler. She was born in Batley on 14 October 1880. Her father was a music teacher, and the family moved to Agbrigg Road, near Sandal Cricket Club in Wakefield, while she was still a child. She was educated at the fashionable – though not expensive – school of Miss Sandbach in Hull, and began training as a nurse in July 1905 at the age of 24 at the Salford Royal Infirmary in Lancashire. She enjoyed working on men's surgical wards, and, once she had successfully qualified, she spent most of the next three years perfecting her skills as a surgical nurse, rising rapidly to the role of sister. Already certain that she wanted to move into military nursing work, where her expertise in surgical care could be further challenged and perfected, she applied to join the QAIMNS in November 1911 at the age of thirty-one. Following a rigorous entry procedure, she was accepted into the regular army nursing service in February 1912, and when war began she was one of the first army staff nurses to be sent to France, embarking on 17 August, 1914.

Kate Maxey – another nurse from the north of England – had decided long before the summer of 1914 that she would serve her country in the event of a war. Born on 17 December 1876, at 30 Clyde Terrace, Spennymoor, a small but then prosperous industrial town in the Durham Coalfield, Kate was the youngest daughter of Walter and Jane Maxey, the owners of a large shop on High Street. Walter, a self-declared 'wholesale jeweller, cutler, and general hardware merchant, importer of French and German toys, china, Bohemian glass [and] wholesale Draper', was ambitious and diligent. He was also a forward-thinking man. Recognizing that Spennymoor provided few opportunities for the employment of middle-class women, by 1891 he made arrangements for the two youngest girls, Kate and Amelia, to live with an uncle and aunt in the city of Leeds. Social attitudes were changing rapidly and, although marriage was still seen as the most desirable future for a young woman, the opportunity to support herself financially – perhaps throughout her life – was coming to be recognized as almost equally important. Kate's and Amelia's uncle and aunt, George and Catherine McKane, were well established within the middle classes of the thriving city of Leeds – George being a physician with a medical practice. The Maxey family's plan for furthering the girls' prospects was successful: Amelia trained as a milliner and Kate pursued a career as a nurse. She entered the Leeds General Infirmary in 1900, qualifying in 1903, and remaining at the hospital for several years before moving to work at a nursing home at 22 Clarendon Road. In January 1912, recognizing that war was possible, she volunteered to join the Territorial Force Nursing Service (TFNS) as a member of the 2nd Northern General Hospital, a unit that was holding itself in readiness to create a military hospital if needed.

Kate was well acquainted with the Leeds surgeon, Sir Berkeley Moynihan, who had an important role in setting up the 2nd Northern General. In August 1914, Moynihan oversaw the unit's development for 'active-service'. In the earliest weeks of the war, it took over a newly built teacher training college at Beckett's Park in Leeds, creating a large military hospital of well over 2,000 beds. Kate was formally enrolled into the unit as a member of the TFNS on 30 September. As an experienced ward nurse, she was seen as a valuable asset and was posted to France on 9 October, one of the earliest Territorial Force nurses to serve overseas. Margaret Brander, another Territorial Force nurse, had been assistant matron at the Arbroath Infirmary, and a member of the 1st Scottish General Hospital, Aberdeen, when war was declared. She was called up for duty on 11 August, and travelled to France on 28 October, where she was initially attached to No. 14 British General Hospital.

When war began many citizens of Britain's self-governing Dominions – countries such as Australia, New Zealand, Canada and South Africa – saw themselves as honour-bound to join the 'mother country' in what was seen as a struggle to save the world from German imperialism. The Australian Army Nursing Service (AANS) was formed rapidly, creating units which travelled to the Eastern Mediterranean in the autumn of 1914. Nurses such as Emma Cuthbert, who had trained at the Children's Hospital in Melbourne, and Ellen McClelland from the Coast Hospital, Sydney, saw it as their duty to leave civilian nursing practice and join the AANS. For over a year, they worked in the hostile and difficult environments of the Eastern Mediterranean, and risked their lives caring for patients in transit from Gallipoli to base hospitals in Lemnos, Malta and Egypt on board hospital ships. May Tilton, a young nurse from Melbourne, enlisted for active service overseas almost as soon as war was declared. Her brother had, at the age of only 17, joined the Australian Expeditionary Force, and May believed that it was impossible for her to stand by and watch as he travelled overseas. She wanted to be part of the services that would care for 'boys' like him.

The New Zealand Army Nursing Service (NZANS) was formed with great difficulty. Its matron-in-chief, Hester Maclean, had to argue vigorously for the right to take a corps of nurses to serve in the so-called 'European War'. Her first unit reached the Eastern Mediterranean in the spring of 1915 and its members found themselves plunged into the unfolding Gallipoli crisis.

Like Australians and New Zealanders, Canadian nurses served with general hospitals belonging to units from their own country. Their distinctive uniform, with its military cut and brass buttons, distinguished them from other Allied nurses, and they were proud of the fact that they were the only professional nurses on the continent with military officer status. But not all nurses served with official military units. Agnes Warner was the daughter of a former American general; her family was one of the most highly respected and influential in the small city of Saint John in New Brunswick. Although a Canadian citizen, she, like many of her compatriots, had chosen to train in the USA. After studying natural sciences at McGill University, Montreal, she had become a nurse probationer at the influential Presbyterian Hospital in New York City. When war broke out in Europe she was travelling as a private nurse in France. She helped to establish – and eventually to lead – a small hospital in the spa town of Divonne-les-Bains, before moving to military hospitals, first in Paris and then in Belgium.

Madeleine Jaffray – another Canadian nurse – would also, eventually, find her way to the tiny strip of Belgium that remained in Allied hands. Madeleine was born in August 1889 in Chicago, Illinois, the daughter of James Jaffray, an immigration agent for the Canadian government. Her childhood was spent in Galt, Ontario, but she then decided to return to the USA to train as a nurse. She found a place at the Clifton Springs Sanatorium Clinic in New York. Soon after completing her probationary period, she moved to the St Elizabeth Hospital, North Yakahami, where she spent much of her time caring for miners and lumbermen with traumatic industrial injuries. She was in her early twenties when the war began and, as a Canadian nurse with extensive clinical experience, was able to enrol in the so-called 'French Flag Nursing Corps' (FFNC). She sailed from Saint John, New Brunswick, on Christmas Day, 1915, one of a group of nine nurses, under the leadership of Helen McMurrich, whose eighty-year-old mother had 'braved the wet and slush' to see them off at the North Parkdale Station, Toronto, several days earlier.

In the USA most nurses watched from a distance as Europe was plunged into the crisis of what was soon to be called the 'Great War'. But they soon realized that this could become their war too. Helen Fairchild, a young ward nurse at the Pennsylvania Hospital in Philadelphia was one of those who was already taking an interest. Helen had been born in Turbot Township, Milton, Pennsylvania, and had spent her childhood as a farm girl at Griffey Farm near Allenwood, before deciding to train as a nurse. She had graduated from the Pennsylvania Hospital in 1913, and was to join the U.S. Army Nurse Corps Reserve in 1916, as a still-neutral USA was beginning to prepare itself for involvement in the war.

Ninety miles from the Pennsylvania Hospital and a world away from Griffey Farm, Ellen La Motte, an influential public health nurse in Baltimore, was considering a new career move: she wanted to be a writer. She had recently drafted a book about the care of tuberculosis patients, but was searching for a more likely outlet for her writing talents. By 1913, she was living a Bohemian life in Paris, editing her book and sending back articles for publication in American nursing journals. She appears to have decided to move to Europe after a succession of frustrating experiences in her home city of Baltimore. Her work as a tuberculosis nurse was bringing her into dispute with other prominent public health nurses in the USA. She argued vehemently for a hard-line approach to the segregation of tuberculosis patients – to protect the rest of the population. But this appears to have alienated her from other nurse leaders such as Lavinia Dock and Lillian Wald. At the end of 1911 she experienced personal disappointment when a close female friend refused to leave Baltimore and begin a new life with her. She had written to another friend, Amy Wesselhoeft von Erdberg: 'I told [Louise] I was ready to go with her – anywhere – to give up my work and all here, and together we would find work and freedom beyond the reach of anyone. She did not want to … I'm unhappy and it all hurts so.' Her political views were changing. Earlier that month, she had written: 'Outwardly I'm a good Socialist, and speak at meetings and all that, but inwardly I'm a free Anarchist – free – free … It is a lot more fun.' Ellen was one of a tiny minority of American middle-class women – a number of whom joined the nursing profession – for whom political radicalism and liberty from conventional social relationships were part of a deliberate choice. Moderately wealthy herself (by the standards of her time), she disdained 'the idle rich' and campaigned vigorously for female suffrage and for legal limits to the working hours of women and children.

By October 1913, Ellen was living in a pension at 166 Boulevard Montparnasse in Paris, and already had a new circle of friends, among them the philosopher Gertrude Stein who had invited her to 'lunch and dinner and tea' and given her copies of her books. In fact, she was finding that her new friends took up 'more of my time and energy and nervous force than I want to give', and so she decided to move to a small apartment in a poorer quarter of Paris – 'The Island of St. Louis' – where she hoped no one would find her. She had discovered 'a perfect little ancient rat-hole. Three rooms, with sloping oak floors; lop sided windows, looking out on the Seine, and walls as thick as prison walls'. From her window there was a view of the morgue at Notre Dame, which she felt suited her 'blue' mood. But she soon discovered that other aspects of life in the 'IVeme Quartier' did not suit her. The chimney of her apartment smoked and there were no restaurants nearby. She was her landlady's 'pure victim', paying exorbitant prices for meals based on horse meat. She returned to the pension on the Boulevard Montparnasse and became absorbed, once more, in the life of a small Parisian intellectual elite – experimenting in gymnastics, vegetarianism and weaving.

By April 1914, Ellen had completed work on her book, *The Tuberculosis Nurse*. She was depressed. In a letter to Amy she wrote:

> [I]t seems so inadequate and worthless and badly written and badly expressed … such mechanical, uphill work … After I get a little rested and changed in my mind, then I shall begin on the sort of work that I want to do – the sort of writing that I feel perhaps I can make good at – at any rate I am eager to try, and shall feel some spontaneity in writing of that sort.

When war began, Ellen searched for military hospital work, knowing that such work would enable her both to support the Allied war effort and to experience events and challenges that people would want to read about. Her plan was to nurse in a military hospital, and then to write about her work.

American nurses had plenty of time to consider whether they wanted to get involved in the First World War. But for British units the war – although not unexpected – came quickly. Volunteers were needed urgently. Within just a few weeks of the outbreak of war many thousands of British and Dominion nurses enlisted. The ability to perform one's patriotic duty was a significant part of the identity of early-twentieth-century western peoples. But identity was also a matter of social class and status. Aristocratic and upper-middle-class ladies took it for granted that they were needed by the nation – even though they had no occupations. Their 'breeding' – their superior birth and their delicate upbringing – conferred on them, they believed, the ability to perform the most valuable national service. Yet their options were restricted. It would be unthinkable for those from the very highest social classes to fight or, indeed, to perform any function seen to be, in any way, masculine. Just as the social order was fixed, so too was the order between the sexes. Men worked outside the home; women were its guardians – the 'angels' who protected the domestic space, providing a safe and comfortable haven to which the man could return from his worldly achievements. Ladies were not permitted to work for a living. Indeed, to perform such work was to admit that one was operating at the level of the 'working class'. For aristocratic and upper-middle-class women the solution was clear: they would serve their country voluntarily by nursing its wounded and becoming the 'mothers of the nation'. The Voluntary Aid Detachments provided an outlet for the talents and desires of many. But, for the really enthusiastic, only the creation of their own hospital units was sufficient. Millicent, Duchess of Sutherland, was one such woman. Born Lady Millicent St Clair-Erskine in 1867, she had married into the British aristocracy in 1884. In the summer of 1914, as war drew nearer, she began to take a deep interest in the creation of a war hospital. In many ways, she belonged to another, earlier time. During the Second Anglo-Boer War private hospitals had provided a significant amount of the care for sick and wounded soldiers, but they had also come under scrutiny at the war's end when senior doctors and nurses began to recognize the need for a more formal and organized partnership between professional military medical and nursing services.

Within just a few weeks of the outbreak of the First World War, British nurses had travelled to the continent in their hundreds, most heading for Belgium, the place where they saw the earliest dramas of the conflict unfolding. Members of the official nursing services – the QAIMNS, its Reserve and the TFNS – were, at first, frustrated to find that wealthy volunteers were moving to the main 'centres of action' ahead of them. Even those who travelled to France with official military hospitals were, at first, placed well away from the war zone. This was soon to change, as the war was transformed from a mobile conflict to one of entrenchment, and a static 'Western Front' began to emerge.

*Chapter Two*

# Fight for Freedom

When, on 4 August 1914, the British government declared war on Germany, its action was met with both anxiety and approval by the majority of British people. Most believed that the government's cause was just and that it was the duty of every citizen to take a stand against 'Prussianism'. But few people had more than the vaguest notion of why Germany, a nation that had for centuries been an ally, had become 'Prussian' and their enemy. They had a sense – fuelled by propaganda – that a new characteristic had invaded the German mentality like a disease, and that it must be opposed. Most were convinced that Prussianism was a particularly offensive form of aggressive militarism which would always be coupled with an imperialistic desire to expand and conquer. They failed to make any connection between their own vast empire spanning the entire globe and German territorial expansionism. To them the British Empire was, of course, an inherently good thing – a civilizing influence. Prussianism, on the other hand, was a destructive force which crushed the weak under its heartless, unthinking heel, a power that was purely aggressive. And it was undeniable that one of the earliest actions of what was to become a global conflict was the blatant and destructive invasion of a neutral country – Belgium.

Histories of the First World War generally agree that the conflict was triggered by the assassination of Franz Ferdinand, the heir to the Hapsburg Austro-Hungarian Empire in Sarajevo on 28 June 1914. But they also accept that Britain was drawn into the conflict by the German invasion of Belgium. The phrase 'poor little Belgium' came to be repeated so often in newspaper articles, letters and diaries that it became almost like a mantra for the British people. And it had a powerful appeal for professional nurses – women who had consciously decided to devote their lives to the care of the vulnerable and weak. Many had already indicated their willingness to work as military nurses in the event of a war. About 2,000 had joined the register of the Queen Alexandra's Imperial Military Nursing Service Reserve (QAIMNSR). Another 8,000 had joined the Territorial Force Nursing Service (TFNS), ready to staff general military hospitals at home in the event of war. As a powerful sense of the need to defend 'poor little Belgium' began to take hold of the British mentality, and men enlisted in their hundreds of thousands to fight the 'invading hordes', women across the nation began to ask themselves how they could help. For many the answer seemed obvious: by nursing the wounded; by nurturing and caring for these national heroes; by restoring them to health so that they could return to the fight. Few understood what nursing work really involved.

In the summer of 1914, the city of Ypres was one of the most peaceful and prosperous in Western Europe. Its Catholic cathedral stood alongside its protestant churches. Once – 400 years previously – it had formed part of a Catholic Hapsburg Empire, ruled from Spain, but the area's self-governing states and cities had retained a spirit of independence and Belgium had, by the nineteenth century, emerged as a proud and independent nation composed of recognized provinces. Flanders, in the west, was a flourishing region of agriculture and trade, and Ypres, one of its major cities, was an admired centre of commerce and culture. Its status as an epicentre of civilization and prosperity was advertised to the world by its magnificent Cloth Hall, a wonder of Gothic architecture which dominated the main square and proclaimed the public spirit and shared wealth of its people. No one could have predicted that, by the end of the year, Ypres would be a scene of utter devastation.

In August 1914 when the German Kaiser, Wilhelm II, decided to support his Hapsburg cousin, the Emperor of Austria-Hungary, against the Serbs, he must have been fairly certain that he was also making a choice to go to war with Serbia's protector: Russia. And because Russia, France and Britain had, in 1907, formed the so-called Triple Entente, he also knew that his actions would probably destabilize Europe, bringing two power blocks, the Triple Entente and the Central Powers, into open conflict. Germany and France had been rivals for centuries – a rivalry that had been heightened by the Franco-Prussian War of 1870–71. But the Kaiser hoped that the British government, whose head of state was his cousin, King George V, would remain neutral. This hope was not entirely misplaced: neutrality was, indeed, one possible option for the British. But the Kaiser had forgotten about the British national character: the 'bulldog' spirit that had been honed over centuries of exploration, empire-building and insularity. Britain's recent past had not cultivated a spirit of restraint or neutrality.

In late July, the German army put into action a plan its high command had devised over eight years previously: the so-called Schlieffen Plan. Its main objective was the capture of Paris; its essence was speed. German strategists were aware that, in the event of war, the 'entente' between France and Russia would solidify into a more formal alliance, but they also believed that it would take the Russian army at least six weeks to mobilize. If France could be defeated in that time, and brought to peace terms, the German army could turn to face the Russians on its eastern border; defeating one nation at a time was the crux of the strategy. But the entire plan was dependent upon Belgian compliance, and the German high command had completely misjudged the Belgian people. The Schlieffen Plan required the German army to outflank the French by moving through Belgian territory and taking control of Paris from the north. But when the Kaiser asked the Belgian government to permit his troops to march through its territory, his request was refused. So the Germans marched into Belgium as a conquering force and the Belgians immediately became, in the eyes of the British, both the victims and the plucky heroes of the war.

When, on 4 August, Britain declared war, it was to eastern and central Belgium that all eyes were turned. By 26 August shocking reports were being sent back to Britain of the sacking of Louvain, and the destruction of its world-renowned university library. Days later, the city of Antwerp was being bombarded with high-explosive shells. Refugees were flocking to the coast. Boarding any vessel that would give them passage, they crossed the North Sea to Britain, where they recounted horrific stories of German brutality. One of the first tasks of Britain's War Propaganda Bureau, established in early September, was to amplify these narratives. Rumours of the raping of nuns, the bayoneting of babies and the mass killing of peaceful citizens spread rapidly throughout the British Dominions and were, by the end of August, being told as far afield as the USA. There was a kernel of truth in them: desperate to meet their strictly timetabled objectives, German officers were ordering their soldiers to implement harsh reprisals against citizens who impeded the advance. Troops were told that their lives were in immediate danger from Belgian snipers firing from the upper windows of houses. And, although such guerrilla tactics were probably rare, it was true that the Belgians, inspired by the resolution of their government and the open defiance of their head of state, King Albert, were fighting back. The resistance of their tiny professional army against an invading force of tens of thousands exceeded everyone's expectations. Although unable to hold back the German army entirely, they slowed its progress.

By mid-August, the British regular army had mobilized and was ready to face the Germans at Mons. Defeated, it regrouped and joined forces with its French allies close to the River Marne. Here, almost within reach of Paris, the German army was turned back. Further north, more and more Belgian territory was being overrun, but Ypres was soon to emerge as one of the last bulwarks of freedom and resistance.

Faced with the ruin of its Schlieffen Plan and an end to its rapid, decisive western advance, the German high command recognized that it had no alternative but to fight on two fronts. Now its focus was on securing the best possible positions in the west. Its leaders in the field turned their sights to the Channel ports: Calais, Dunkirk, Ostend and Zeebrugge. Racing towards these new objectives, the German army threw itself against the Allied forces in a series of indecisive battles. Eventually, still twenty-five miles from the coast, it reached the gently rolling countryside of Flanders just east of Ypres. Here among quiet, rural villages like Zonnebeke, St Julien and Pilckem, it dug in, creating a series of deep trenches and earthworks, pushing forwards from these in an attempt to take the strategic city of Ypres itself.

Just to the east, well behind the German front lines, was a quiet, rural village situated on a modest rise which no one would, in peacetime, have called a ridge. This was Passchendaele. Because it lay to the east of the Wytschaete Ridge and was positioned on slightly higher ground than neighbouring settlements, it would eventually become an important Allied objective. The distance from Ypres to Passchendaele is eight miles. Stretching across a wide territory extending from Messines in the south to well beyond Langemark in the north was a terrain that would become, in the next four years, the graveyard of hundreds of thousands of men – and the ground from which enormous numbers of desperately wounded soldiers would be brought back to military hospitals behind the lines. And as early as September 1914 the first few of those hospitals were being established in centres such as Furnes, a small town north-east of Ypres. But these earliest field hospitals were not the highly professional and carefully equipped units of the Royal Army Medical Corps; they were the makeshift, freelance hospitals of volunteers.

On 9 August, just five days after her government's declaration of war, Millicent, Duchess of Sutherland travelled to Paris and offered her services as a volunteer nurse. But her real intention had always been to create her own hospital. She knew that, as an untrained nurse, she could achieve very little, so, using her social influence, she negotiated with Antoine Depage, head of the Belgian Red Cross, to fund a hospital unit and bring it to Belgium. She acted fast: by mid-August she had enlisted nine fully trained nurses from Guy's Hospital in London, and had paid their passage to Belgium. With their expert assistance, she established a hospital at the Convent of the Soeurs de Notre Dame in Namur. But in mid-August the advancing

German army began to bombard the city and patients and nurses were forced to shelter in underground cellars.

Millicent was not unique. In the early months of the war, dozens of volunteer units travelled to Belgium, anticipating that they could help to secure a rapid Allied victory. The eccentric and highly energetic Hector Munro, a convinced feminist, took his 'Flying Ambulance Corps' to Belgium in August. Among its number were two spirited young women, Elsie Knocker and Mairi Chisholm, who had met through their common interest in motorcycling. Daring and deliberately reckless, Elsie and Mairi had ridden their motorcycles to London and had enlisted with Munro's unit as ambulance drivers. Elsie's desire to do significant work close to the battlefield was the main force behind their exploits. Orphaned as a baby, Elsie had been brought up by adoptive parents who had really wanted a boy. Her childhood experiences had made her tough and resourceful: 'I had to mould my upper lip to keep it stiff through a life of misunderstanding,' she was to write later in her memoir, *Flanders and Other Fields*.[1] She had married young – to an abusive man who she soon divorced – and she had a young son, Kenneth. As a single parent, she had needed to find some means to make a living, so, leaving Kenneth with her adoptive parents, she had travelled to London to train as a midwife and nurse.

When the war began Elsie's training seemed like a passport to the frontlines. Taking Mairi Chisholm with her, she volunteered to serve Munro's unit, and was one of the first trained nurses to reach Belgium. Munro accepted with alacrity her application to work as an ambulance driver – after all, she had both nursing and driving skills, as well as being able to take apart and repair an engine. Elsie spent the first weeks of the war driving along shell-scarred roads through bombed-out villages conveying Belgian wounded to Munro's makeshift hospital at the Flandria Palace Hotel in Ghent.

In the early autumn of 1914, many volunteer units like Munro's were created. Most established themselves close enough to the rapidly moving front lines of the war to be heavily bombarded by long-range artillery. By September these 'ambulance units' were among the thousands of refugees choking the Belgian roads, fleeing towards Ostend in the hope of gaining a passage on board one of the ships sailing for England and safety. In October the German advance across Belgium was halted and Munro was able to stabilize his unit in the small Belgian town of Furnes, north-west of Ypres. Here, it cared mainly for Belgian wounded being brought from the newly created line of demarcation that was already known as the 'Western Front'.

Hospital units like Millicent's and Munro's have come to be seen as both enterprising and reckless. But such judgements have been made with the benefit of hindsight. In the autumn of 1914, the war was a great national enterprise. Whole peoples responded to it with a determined sense of duty. The vast majority of citizens resolved to 'do their bit' for whichever nation or empire they belonged to, but, for some, doing one's duty was not so simple. Americans living in Europe were presented with a daunting choice. Should they return to the safety of their neutral country, or become a part of the Allied cause? For Chicagoan millionaire, Mary Borden Turner, the decision was simple. She had married a British missionary in 1908 and was pregnant with their third child. A popular London socialite, she identified closely with the upper classes of her adopted home. Within months of her daughter, Mary's, birth, she had travelled to the continent, offered her services as a volunteer nurse to the French Red Cross, and been taken on to work in a converted casino on the north coast caring for desperately ill men with typhoid fever. Mary found the casino a depressing place. Yet, as an aspiring author, she also discovered that her experiences fuelled a particularly urgent and candid form of writing. She was later to put down her thoughts about the casino, in a piece entitled *The Beach*:

> Rows of beds under the big crystal chandeliers, rows of beds under the big gilt mirrors, and the skating rink is full of beds, too. The sun blazes down through the glass roof. It's like a hot house in Kew Gardens. There's that dank smell of a rotting swamp, the smell of gas gangrene. Men with gas gangrene turn green, you know, like rotting plants … Behind the windows of the casino, under the great crystal chandeliers, men lie in narrow beds. They lie in queer postures with their greenish faces turned up. Their white bandages are reflected in the sombre gilt mirrors.[2]

In the summer of 1914, American nurse Ellen La Motte had been dividing her time between Paris and London. When Germany declared war on France on 3 August, she hesitated, but then, in late October, decided to settle in France – the home of her Huguenot ancestors. French women were volunteering in their thousands to nurse the wounded, and Ellen assumed that her professional nursing services would be valued by her adopted country. But everywhere she went, she was viewed with suspicion – a neutral American whose allegiances were not clear. Much later, on 14 March 1915, she was to write to her close friend, Amy Wesselhoeft von

Erdberg – who was herself having a difficult time as an American, married to a Latvian and living in Germany:

> I came over the last of October, trying to place my valuable services where they were needed, but there is an enormous difference between being needed and wanted, and in spite of all sorts of influence, I have now spent four months being told that as a neutral I am not eligible for anything! Yet there is great and appalling need, and to my trained eye and trained senses, the thing is monstrous. All that, however, will have to come later. So now after making between twenty-five and thirty attempts to get work – real work, my generous disposition is a bit gone off. So be it. Europe is intensely interesting just now, and I am going to settle down and write. I have tried hard to be altruistic, now I shall be egotistic for a change![3]

By this time, she was living near the Boulevard St Germain in a 'most delightful little apartment, in one of the old parts of the city … A private hotel, dating from the seventeenth century'. Although she had only three rooms, she had given up her Bohemian lifestyle and was living quite comfortably. Emotionally, she was in turmoil, declaring that 'the things I did believe in are all busted up, blown over, torn down … War has reduced me to a bad plight!' But relations with Amy – an American of German ancestry living near Berlin – were becoming strained, and letters reached Germany via a tortuous route, having to pass first through neutral America.

In Britain, qualified professional nurses of the QAIMNSR had mobilized within days of the declaration of war. Catherine Black, an experienced Irish nurse from Donegal, who was working as a private nurse for The London Hospital, was asked by her matron, Eva Luckes, to fill a vacancy at the Cambridge Military Hospital in Aldershot. Well before the end of August, many other members of the QA Reserve were already in northern France, working alongside the RAMC to establish general hospitals. But then, for several weeks, they found themselves waiting for the wounded to arrive. The earliest hospital units had been posted some distance from the battlefields and men were dying for want of skilled medical and nursing attention. The so-called 'lines of evacuation' were operating far too slowly. Men wounded in places such as Mons and the Marne died in horse-drawn ambulances before they could reach the care of nurses. As September began, Sister Kate Luard, of the QAIMNSR, was waiting at the 1st British General Hospital near Le Havre. She and her colleagues had an inkling, from the newspaper reports filtering through to their part of France, that the fighting was fierce. But where, they wondered, were the wounded? 'This is a first rate war for waiting,' she wrote to her family from her hospital in a boggy hay field.[4]

Elsewhere, freer, more independent, yet unqualified and inexperienced women were following the example of Millicent, Duchess of Sutherland, and Hector Munro. They were making directly for the place where they saw the drama of the war unfolding: 'poor little Belgium'. Wealthy women who could finance their own hospital units acted with astonishing rapidity. Like many of their fellow citizens, they had been anticipating war for at least six years – since the Haldane Reforms had created the respected Voluntary Aid Detachments in 1909. Mabel St Clair Stobart was one of the best prepared. She had been drilling the volunteers of her 'Women's Sick and Wounded Convoy Corps' on the cliffs above Studland, her Dorset home, for many years, and had taken a unit to support the wounded of the 1912 Balkan War. Now, she gathered together her nurses – both trained and volunteer – her orderlies, her women doctors and her ambulance drivers, and headed for Brussels.

Volunteer units were converging on Belgium, even as the German army was pouring across its eastern frontier. Although they were established and run by volunteers, they needed fully trained nurses. Some professional nurses soon came to view these units as their best possible means of getting close to the 'hottest' part of the war zone. Anxious to use their skills and to be part of the Allied force that would halt the German advance, many fully trained professional nurses signed up with unofficial units and headed for Belgium. A few wrote about their experiences, though most elected to remain anonymous. One trained nurse from the north of England joined the first unit she could find. She and her fellow nurses, realizing that the lady with whose 'ambulance' they had enlisted had experience of neither hospital work nor strategic leadership, were so nervous that each carried a lethal dose of morphine to be taken in the event of capture by 'the enemy'. In the event, 'the enemy' did not capture them. It did, however, subject them to the most terrifying experience of their lives – by shelling them from a distance with heavy artillery.

Having set up a hospital in a beautiful glass-roofed former ducal palace on the Boulevard Leopold in Antwerp, the unit was forced to shelter in a cellar, as high-explosive shell after high-explosive shell landed nearby and their glamorous hospital wards began to shatter and fragment around them.[5] As they admitted wounded Belgian and British soldiers, the nurses realized that they were encountering a new type of warfare. They had never seen anything like these wounds. Some had treated injuries caused by rifle bullets; they knew that you had to look for two wounds: one small and neat, where the bullet had entered the body, and one larger and more ragged – the exit wound. But none had ever seen the multiple traumatic injuries created by machine-gun fire which blasted its way into the body, tearing through muscle and bone, embedding bullets and debris. Nor had they witnessed the injuries created by modern shells: patients were arriving with huge areas of lacerated flesh, limbs blasted completely away or hanging from threads of muscle and tendon, cracked skulls held together only by dirty bandages, deep gaping cavities in abdomens and chests. Every shrapnel shell was packed with thousands of steel balls, and was fired from an artillery gun at high velocity. It was typically timed to explode in the air on its approach towards the ground, at which point its lethal load along with jagged, burning pieces of metal casing would be forced downwards. If the pieces hit the ground, they threw up swirling clouds of earth. If they hit a human being, they sliced into and through his body. Other shells exploded on landing, blasting their contents upwards, causing untold damage to chests, jaws and faces. Their randomness was horrific. Even more destructive than these were the high-explosive shells fired from howitzers. If a man were on the receiving end of one of those he would probably never even make it to a hospital ward. His body would be completely fragmented so that nothing was left, or blasted into a handful of pieces that could be gathered into a small sack. In the face of such horror, survivors began to take on the appearance of ghosts – shock etched into their faces, their dreams haunted by the sights they had witnessed, their nerves shattered.

It was the work of nurses to somehow heal these traumatized men. Professional nurses' civilian training had given them ways of coping with emergency situations. Faced with a severely injured patient, the nurse began by carefully assessing his wounds, checking his pulse and blood pressure, watching and listening to his respirations. The first priorities were to stop any bleeding and stabilize the patient's circulation; without that, he would die very quickly as his vital organs were robbed of oxygen and nutrients. Many patients had been in poor condition – malnourished and dehydrated – even before they had been wounded. The trauma and bleeding of their injuries further robbed their bodies of fluid, sending them into severe physiological shock, a condition in which small arteries, veins and capillaries contract, drawing blood into the body's core to protect the vital organs. If this condition was left untreated, tissues would, eventually, be irreversibly damaged. The only way to halt it was to infuse fluid into patients' bodies as quickly as possible.

But many were unconscious and even those capable of drinking were likely to require surgical treatment under a general anaesthetic; if they filled their stomachs with fluid they might vomit and choke later when they emerged from ether or chloroform. Ingenious ways of pumping fluid into men's bodies were found: through wide-bore needles into the tissues of the armpits and groin, or through rubber tubing into the rectum.

Once his condition was stable, a patient was taken as quickly as possible to the operating theatre where bullets, shell fragments, pieces of uniform and other debris were removed from his body and any infected tissue was sliced away. On his return to the ward, a nurse would check his wounds, assess his general condition at fifteen-minute intervals, and care for him through the nausea, vomiting and disorientation that accompanied the regaining of consciousness. As soon as it was safe to do so, she would begin to rebuild his strength with nutritious food and fluids.

All of this was complicated enough, but when the work was performed in a badly lit cellar, with inadequate equipment and resources, and a shortage of food and water it became almost impossible. To make matters worse, the shelling of the town was becoming more intense; a warning had been sent from the officers commanding the German forces that it would become still worse: civilians must leave. In September a brigade of Royal Marines had been sent to support the Belgian defence of Antwerp and other strategic cities. They had reached the battlefield using an unusual mode of transport: a fleet of London buses. Now, with Antwerp crumbling around it, the hospital unit on the Boulevard Leopold managed to commandeer five of those buses and pack its patients into them, the critically wounded inside, the less severe cases on the open tops. The journey from Antwerp to Ostend took fourteen hours, and when the morphine ran out, nurses dosed their patients with whisky and soda they had 'liberated' from a fashionable Antwerp neighbourhood.

Some British units were trapped in Belgium and overtaken by the German advance. Millicent Sutherland's first effort to establish an Allied hospital was overrun by the rapidly advancing German army. She and her staff were taken prisoner and were eventually escorted across the border to the Netherlands, from where they returned home. Undaunted, Millicent began work to recreate her unit. In October, following in the wake of the official army medical services, she took her second hospital to France, where it was established in the Hotel Belle Vue at Malo-les-Bains near Calais.

Not all volunteer leaders were wealthy and underqualified. Experienced professional nurse Violetta Thurstan had persuaded her employer, the

National Union of Trained Nurses, which had only recently taken her on as its Organizing Secretary, to permit her to lead a unit of fully trained professional nurses to Belgium on behalf of the Order of St John of Jerusalem. Alongside the British Society of the Red Cross, the Order saw itself as responsible for providing essential treatment and care to the sick and wounded. There was, in fact, a significant degree of rivalry between the two organizations, which only came to be resolved when, in the autumn of 1914, they agreed to work together under a 'Joint Committee'. In reality, both organizations were remnants of an earlier age. Military medical care was already becoming a highly professional, militaristic and disciplined project. Yet service with the Red Cross and Order of St John of Jerusalem appealed to nurses with a desire for personal and professional freedom.

Even though she was a fully trained nurse, Violetta Thurstan had joined neither the QA Reserve nor the TFNS in 1914. In many respects she was caught between the old world and the new. She had been a member of the Westminster 146 VAD since 1913, but had written a somewhat scathing article about the 'drilling and marching' tendencies of such units. When war was declared she chose independence over professional military service, and, acting in a freelance capacity, took her group of nurses to Brussels under the auspices of the Order of St John, without the direct support or involvement of the official army medical or nursing services.

Violetta was in charge of over forty trained nurses. As the invading German army approached Brussels and the mayor advised citizens to lay down their arms, Violetta decided to remain at her post to care for the Belgian and British wounded who continued to pour into the city. But she and her nurses were soon taken prisoner and ordered by their captors to spend their time in a specialist unit, caring for the feet of German soldiers – feet that were filthy and often horribly damaged by weeks of marching across Belgian territory. Violetta soon came into conflict with the commanding officer of the hospital, who, upon finding out that two of her brothers were serving with the Royal Navy, took great pleasure in recounting the worrying (and, as it proved, inaccurate) news of a great German naval victory in the North Sea. Rescue came in the form of an invitation from the Mayor of Charleroi: he needed nurses for a small hospital that was caring for both French and German wounded. Violetta and another nurse were allowed to go.

Arriving at their new assignment, the two nurses found chaos: the hospital was staffed entirely by Red Cross volunteers who knew almost nothing about hygiene, or about the treatment of wounds. Soon after their arrival, their French patients – even those still in dangerous conditions – were put into motorized waggons and removed to imprisonment in Germany. Violetta and her colleague decided to walk back to Brussels, but the territory over which they were travelling was under German military rule and they risked capture as spies. Using her impeccable German, Violetta convinced the patrols they met that she and her companion were German Red Cross nursing sisters. They reached Brussels, but soon after their arrival they and their colleagues were packed into a train along with hundreds of other volunteer medical workers and transported to neutral Denmark. From there Violetta negotiated a posting with the Russian Red Cross and travelled via Sweden and Finland to Petrograd, where she joined a flying column, and travelled to Poland to support the Russian army on the Eastern Front.

On 19 August, the day Violetta Thurstan's party of nurses left Charing Cross station to catch the boat-train to the continent, another unit of highly experienced professional nurses joined the same train. Vocal campaigner for British nurse registration, Ethel Gordon Fenwick had received a request from Dr Marcelle, Director of the Hospital of St John at Brussels. Marcelle was a keen supporter of the professionalization of nursing, and had, in happier times, attended a meeting of the International Congress of Nurses in Cologne in 1912. Now, he needed the support of fully trained British nurses to help his own nursing colleagues meet the pressures of caring for tens of thousands of wounded soldiers, along with massive numbers of sick and homeless civilian refugees. The Order of St John offered to finance a mission, which would consist of thirty nurses, to be sent immediately to Brussels. Among their party was Annie Mildred Hanning, a thirty-seven-year-old, highly experienced professional nurse, who had trained at the Sunderland Royal Infirmary between 1900 and 1903. Annie had been born in Mauritius, in County Durham, but had settled in the south of England after having completed her training, working first in Walthamstow and then, as the sister-in-charge, at a private nursing home at Bexhill in East Sussex. Annie was among the hundreds of medical workers who were taken prisoner by the advancing German army and then deported from Belgium to neutral Denmark.

Like Violetta Thurstan and Annie Hanning, wealthy volunteer nurse Mabel St Clair Stobart was trapped behind enemy lines in the late summer of 1914. Unlike them, however, her party was obliged to walk to the Dutch border, from where they managed to reach Rotterdam and secure a passage to Britain. Mabel, like Violetta, decided to move eastwards. She travelled, with her Sick and Wounded Convoy Corps to support the war effort on the Serbian Front. But some volunteer medical units regrouped in England

and returned to 'active service' in Belgium. Others were never captured, having successfully retreated to the small strip of Belgian territory – barely twenty miles wide – that remained in Allied hands. Among these was Hector Munro's Flying Ambulance Corps, with its intrepid 'lady-motorcyclists', Elsie Knocker and Mairi Chisholm. Elsie was unusual. Although she had enlisted for an ambulance corps, and was prepared to use her skills as both driver and mechanic, she was also a fully trained professional nurse, with the skills and knowledge required to provide a sophisticated degree of first aid to sick and wounded soldiers.

In Paris, the so-called 'American Colony', a community of expatriates living permanently in the city, began looking at ways in which they might expand the 'American Hospital of Paris', an organization that had been established in 1910. With the support of the American Chamber of Commerce they were able to extend their hospital and donate it to the French government for use as a war hospital. In return, the government offered them the magnificent Lycée Pasteur at Neuilly-sur-Seine, just outside Paris. The renamed 'American Ambulance' was rapidly fitted out; fourteen U.S. cities offered direct financial assistance, and Henry Ford shipped motors to Paris to be used as ambulances. The first patients arrived on 6 September, by which time the hospital staff consisted of fifteen doctors, seventy-five trained nurses and about 170 Red Cross assistants. Among the first to respond to the call for medical staff were George Crile, a prestigious surgeon from Cleveland, Ohio, and talented Boston neurosurgeon, Harvey Cushing, who arrived in April 1915, with the 'Harvard Unit'. Trained nurses were scarce, and a unit of British nurses was sent out by the Order of St John of Jerusalem to support the work of the few trained U.S. nurses at the hospital.

There were many U.S. citizens in France in August 1914. At a time when travel was seen as a luxury, wealthy Americans spent extended periods touring Europe. Many had a particular affinity for France, seeing it as one of their country's oldest allies. That summer, Agnes Warner, a Canadian citizen, whose father had served as a general in the Union Army during the American Civil War was travelling Europe as the private nurse to a wealthy Long Island couple, Mr and Mrs Roswell Eldridge. When war was declared her party was staying in the spa town of Divonne-les-Bains. Immediately, Agnes – a highly trained nurse – offered to help the local committee of the Red Cross to establish a military hospital. As it became clear that the war was not going to be over by Christmas, she accompanied the Eldridges back to the safety of New York State, before returning alone to Divonne.

Agnes had graduated from the New York Presbyterian Hospital in 1902 and already had extensive experience of running a hospital ward. Now, at Divonne, she was invited to manage an entire hospital. It would not be long before her talents brought her to the attention of Mary Borden and earned her a place in one of the most active hospitals behind the French lines in Belgium.

On 19 October 1914, just to the east of Ypres, the British and German armies fired the opening bombardments in an encounter that was to set the pattern for the so-called 'battles' of the First World War. The First Battle of Ypres was bloody and unrelenting. Both sides used heavy artillery, creating sweeping storms of jagged metal into which they sent men with bayonets fixed ready for combat. But both sides were already learning about the near-impossibility of crossing the lethal expanse of ground between enemy lines that was beginning to be called 'no man's land'. After two months of exhausting mobile warfare, neither side was in any doubt about the devastating effectiveness of modern industrial weaponry. Men still carried the bolt action rifles that had been the staple weapons of the Second Anglo-Boer War (1899–1902) and the Russo-Japanese War (1904–5). But now they were also manoeuvring heavy machine guns across the battlefield, and were using horse-drawn limbers to drag massive field artillery guns into positions from which they could fire on their enemies from a distance of several miles. By November 1914 the cavalry charges and marching formations of the nineteenth century had been replaced by the lumbering gun-teams and concrete bunkers of a new era. The industrial warfare of the twentieth century was born at 'First Ypres'.

As the battle thundered through the last weeks of October and most of November the Ypres Front began to take on a strange appearance. The British lines were becoming fixed in the shape of an unwieldy bulge around the north, east and south of the city – a bulge which came to be known as the Ypres Salient. The longer the British army held onto the Salient the more determined it became to defend the city, which was rapidly becoming an allied symbol of the fight for Belgian freedom against Prussian imperialism. But British troops, in their shallow trenches, provided easy targets for heavy artillery fired from sophisticated concrete emplacements and bunkers on the high ground of the Messines–Wytschaete Ridge to the south, the lower Pilckem Ridge to the east and the flatter ground to the north. The British decision to defend Ypres, rather than give up the city and create a straighter, safer frontline just behind it probably cost tens of thousands of lives. But its propaganda value was incalculable: Ypres was seen as the place where the

British stood their ground and refused to let the might of the German army pass. The fact that it was also rapidly becoming a place of dread for British soldiers escaped the notice of most citizens on the 'home front'. Among the few non-combatants to understand the true nature of the Salient were the nurses who listened to the stories of the shocked and wounded men who were brought back to military hospitals. Those stories were part of an outpouring of horror and relief expressed by many of those who escaped their near-death experiences to reach the safety of a field hospital. Nurses – the people who were at their bedsides during the early days of their recovery – were their witnesses.

On Sunday 20 September, Kate Luard's 'waiting game' had ended. She had been posted to a railway station in northern France. Every train that arrived from the east was loaded with wounded men packed into cattle trucks, lying on straw and in terrible conditions. Their wounds were protected only by dirty field-dressings and most had had nothing to eat or drink since leaving the battlefield. Kate and her colleagues were the first female nurses they encountered since being wounded days earlier. In the little time that was available before the train had to move off, the nurses climbed into the trucks with trays of dressings. They cleaned up and dressed their patients wounds as best they could, offered what food and water were available and then watched as the train moved off towards bases that were still many miles away.

It was clear that a more efficient system for the evacuation of the wounded was desperately needed. Already the army medical services had determined that there was a need for small field hospitals close to where the fighting was taking place. They also recognized the ineffectiveness of horse-drawn ambulances, and were calling for the transport of large numbers of motor ambulances to France and Belgium.

As the 'Western Front' began to take shape so too did its lines of evacuation. The inefficient process that had transferred wounded men by horse-drawn ambulance to cattle-trucks on French railways was beginning to give way to the smoother operation of motor ambulances and specially converted trains. No one had anticipated that armies would 'dig in' as determinedly as they did, creating semi-permanent bulwarks extending for 450 miles from the North Sea to the Swiss border. But the stability of the Western Front meant that stable lines of evacuation could also be developed. By the end of 1914 the transport of wounded from the battlefields to well-established hospitals in safe areas had reached an unprecedented level of efficiency. Transport services like these had never been seen in any previous war – but then, no previous war had produced such desperately wounded men in such large numbers.

The first treatment offered to a wounded soldier was likely to be given by stretcher-bearers – or even by himself. Every man had a 'first field dressing' sewn into the lining of his jacket. This was a well-padded, iodine-impregnated dressing to which was attached a long length of cotton bandage. This could be wrapped around a damaged limb or used to hold an abdominal, chest or head wound together. Stretcher-bearers then carried the man to his regimental aid post, where he was rapidly assessed and given emergency treatment by his unit's own medical officer. A label was attached to his lapel detailing the nature of his wound, the urgency of his condition and whether or not he had received morphine or any other drugs. He was then transferred to a motor ambulance.

One of the most important innovations of autumn 1914 was the creation of casualty clearing stations (CCSs). The earliest of these (known as 'casualty clearing hospitals') were established in October 1914. All were within ten miles of the fighting lines, and there was some debate at senior levels about whether female nurses should be posted to them. Medical men knew that the success of modern surgery depended on nurses, whose work in preparing patients for operation then monitoring and supporting them as they emerged from the toxic effects of the anaesthesia, was vital. But, at first, senior medical officers were unwilling to sanction the presence of women close to the front lines of battle. It was only as a result of the insistence of Matron-in-Chief, Ethel Hope Becher, and her deputy in France and Flanders, Maud McCarthy, that nurses were allowed to move forward from base hospitals to CCSs. Soon, a system was established that allowed senior nurses to move staff temporarily from general hospitals in bases such as Boulogne, Etaples, Le Havre and Rouen to CCSs close to the front lines for periods ranging from six weeks to six months. Most nurses were eager to accept such postings, but all were obliged to sign disclaimers stating that they were, indeed, volunteers. In October, Territorial Force nurse Kate Maxey was moved up the line from the No. 8 British General Hospital at Rouen, to serve with the No. 58 Casualty Clearing Station – better known as the 'West Riding Casualty Clearing Station' – one of the first Territorial CCSs to be established on the Western Front.

Some of the earliest British CCSs were established, along with French and Belgian field hospitals, in or close to Poperinge, a small town just under eight miles from Ypres. Poperinge, seemed, at first, to be an ideal location for such small hospitals. It was close enough to the Salient to permit the rapid evacuation of wounded; but it was also far enough away to permit the continuation of something close to 'normal life'. Soldiers spent time there during rest periods, buying necessities in its shops and frequenting its many *estaminets* (small café bars). By the end of the year, however, it was becoming clear that the town, within easy range of German artillery, was likely to become a target. The railway line known as 'Line 69' ran from Kortrijk in the east, through Ypres and Poperinge, and then on to Hazebrouck in France. The war had cut it in two. Its western section was used by the Allies to bring men, supplies and ammunition to Ypres. This made it – and every town along its tracks – vulnerable to shelling. CCSs located in or close to the town were soon relocated. British CCS No. 4 was established in Poperinge on 21 October 1914, but moved south to Lillers in December that year.

The significance of CCSs soon became clear. Not only were many of the wounds inflicted by modern industrial weaponry both deep and extensive, they were also contaminated by dirt and debris from the heavily manured agricultural fields of France and Flanders. When a bullet, shrapnel ball or piece of shell casing entered a man's body, the so-called 'anaerobic' microorganizms harboured by these and other pieces of debris were pushed inwards – into a dark, moist and airless environment in which they could thrive. They multiplied rapidly, causing rampant infections which destroyed large swathes of tissue. Such infections could kill with terrifying rapidity. A patient with even a small wound could be dead within days of the wound becoming infected with anaerobes.

Surgeons and nurses diagnosed one of the most common types of infection – gas gangrene – by pressing the skin and muscle around the wound, feeling for the crackling sensation created by the movement of the trapped gas bubbles produced by the bacteria. These gas-producing bugs were the most lethal they had ever encountered. But even more distressing was the horrific disease, tetanus, caused by another anaerobic bacterium, which caused spasm of the muscles until the patient's back arched and his mouth pulled back into the horrible rictus grin from which the disease gained its popular nickname: 'lockjaw'. Such patients often died of exhaustion before their immune systems could begin to counteract the disease. The only way to prevent muscle spasms was to keep patients quiet and relaxed, and the only way to build the strength patients needed to withstand the attacks was to feed them slowly and carefully – often from a teaspoon.

Confronted with such horrors, surgeons and nurses in CCSs struggled to find solutions. At best, they received patients five or six hours after wounding. Their priority was to remove contaminated tissue quickly before anaerobic infections had a chance to take hold. Each time they received a convoy from the front, they got to work: preparing their patients for theatre and operating on them, removing not only bullets, shrapnel and debris but also large swathes of tissue from around the wounds, creating larger, cleaner cavities which could be treated with antiseptics to kill any lingering bacteria.

Even as CCSs were being established, new ambulance trains were also being built to replace the goods trains – like the ones met by Kate Luard in early September – that had proved so ineffective in transporting wounded men. If the lines of evacuation were to work at all, the wounded had to be moved out of CCSs as soon as they were stable, to create space for new casualties. The process of casualty evacuation would only work if it could be kept moving. Base hospitals were anything from thirty to eighty miles from the front lines and there was a danger that men would be lost – from uncontrolled bleeding or wound infection – before they reached safety. The long journey from a CCS to a general hospital at a military base could take between six and thirty-six hours depending on rail traffic. Ambulance trains were always given the lowest priority in the train schedules.

The earliest of the new type of train were French passenger locomotives. Each carriage was fitted with rows of bunks and converted into something resembling a hospital ward. Eleven such trains were converted, and were numbered 1 to 11. Then, in November the earliest purpose-built trains were shipped from Britain. Many were manufactured with the help of donations from wealthy philanthropists. Number 15, for example, was the 'Princess Christian Ambulance Train'.

At the end of September, Kate Luard was posted to one of these early ambulance trains. 'Did you ever know such luck?' she wrote home to her family. She knew that the work of nurses on ambulance trains would mean the difference between life and death for many men. On board these trains, dressings could be changed, antiseptic wound treatments could be administered and patients could be made comfortable in bunks or, for the more lightly wounded, on seats.

Obtaining sufficient food and water for the hundreds of patients on board her ambulance train was one of Kate's greatest challenges. She knew that good nutrition and hydration could make the difference between wounds that festered and those that healed. Fortunately, Belgian and French citizens often donated fresh food, handing bowls of soup and porridge, and boxes of fruit and vegetables in through the doors and windows of carriages as the train paused or moved slowly through railway stations. Even then, Kate wrote to her family, feeding patients with facial injuries was a 'stupendous business' requiring careful food preparation, lengths of sterile rubber tubing and infinite patience.

In Furnes, Elsie Knocker was becoming impatient. Hector Munro's volunteer hospital was makeshift and ill-equipped. Patients were dying for lack of adequate attention – not because the hospital staff did not care about them, but because there were simply not enough nurses. Besides this, she also believed that many men were dying needlessly before they even reached the hospital. She was to write later in her memoir:

> I wanted to set up a first-aid station (or Advanced Dressing Station, as it was called) where the wounded could rest and recuperate before being jolted over the roads to the operating table. I noticed how many of them died of superficial hurts, a broken arm, perhaps, or a gash. They 'died on the way to hospital' or on the pavements or the floors, and I knew why this happened. They were the victims of shock – the greatest killer of them all.[6]

Elsie was unable to gain support for her scheme either from Munro or from the British military medical services. So – with her friend, Mairi Chisholm – she simply went ahead. A Belgian army doctor, Dr Van der Ghinst, found her a house in the tiny ruined village of Pervyse, with a 'deep, damp but safe cellar'. Soon she and Mairi had established a close camaraderie with a Belgian unit in the front lines at Pervyse, which provided them with furniture and security, in exchange for first-aid services ranging from the taking of cups of hot soup and coffee to men on sentry duty in the trenches, through the cleaning and dressing of minor injuries and the extraction of teeth, to the treatment of patients with deep and extensive injuries whose care offered ample opportunity for Elsie to prove the value of her theory that wound shock should be treated as close to the front lines as possible. Reports on the work being done by the two women soon won them fame on the British 'home front', earning them the soubriquet 'The Heroines of Pervyse'. The British Red Cross began to support them with equipment, and eventually the British Army itself began to tolerate their presence on the front lines – albeit serving Belgian, not British, troops. Eventually – because of their strategic position – the Royal Flying Corps would issue them with binoculars and ask them to act as 'spotters', reporting on the movement of British aeroplanes across the front lines.

That autumn, the Belgian army established a base at La Panne, a small seaside town which had, before the war, been a popular holiday resort for wealthier Belgians. King Albert and Queen Elisabeth set up home there in a small villa close to the beach, and every morning they could be seen taking the air on the seafront. Their presence was calculated to provide a morale boost to military units passing through the base. The head of the Belgian Red Cross, highly experienced doctor Antoine Depage established a huge hospital – L'Hôpital de l'Océan – in a hotel just behind the beach with the financial and practical help of Elisabeth, who dressed in a nurse's uniform and accompanied him on some of his hospital rounds, offering moral support and encouragement to the wounded. At times she visited the wards and assisted in the dressing of patients' wounds. Her appearance in a flowing, romantic – yet still somehow clinical – snow-white dress, white heeled shoes and a stylish white turban was a deliberate and calculated display of daring, and Elisabeth's courage and compassion became a symbol of hope for the Belgian people. On a more practical note, Depage also brought trained, professional nurses from Britain and France to his hospital. Before the war he had taken a great interest in nursing education and had, with his wife, Marie, employed Edith Cavell to establish a formal nursing school to support his hospital, the Berkendaele Institute, in Brussels. L'Hôpital de l'Océan soon became a beacon of clinical competence on the north coast – the largest and most advanced Belgian military hospital ever created. It spread outwards from the hotel at its core to take over a vast area of the surrounding sand dunes, which were transformed into a city of huts.

In November 1914 the Germans launched a powerful bombardment of the city of Ypres, perhaps to show its 'defenders' that, however determined they were to hold onto it, they could not prevent its demolition. On 22 November the famous Cloth Hall suffered several direct hits and was totally burned out. From the end of November onwards, the Ypres Salient protected not a living city but a desolate, bombed-out ruin, its Cloth Hall reduced to a series of gaunt fingers of stone reaching into a cordite-filled sky. Relentless artillery bombardment from both sides had destroyed the drainage systems of the fields surrounding the city, turning large parts of the Salient into a quagmire of mud and slush that froze in winter and dried out only temporarily during the hottest months of summer. The defence of that morass was to be the mission of British and Dominion soldiers for the next three and a half years. Saving the lives of those soldiers was to be the mission of Allied nurses.

## Chapter Three

# 'Second Ypres' and Other Assaults

In base hospitals behind the Western Front, New Year 'celebrations' for 1915 were muted by feelings of dismay. The war which was supposed to have been over by Christmas seemed to be digging itself deeper into the muddy heartlands of Flanders and north-eastern France. It was spreading, too, like a disease. On the Eastern Front terrible battles had been fought at Tannenberg and the Masurian Lakes in the north, and Galicia in the south. In Serbia – the place where it had all started – there was stalemate, but the German and Bulgarian armies were poised to push the Sebians back towards the mountains and the sea.

The Allies were setting their sights on the Turkish peninsula of Gallipoli – a narrow piece of land controlling the Dardanelles and the entrance to the all-important Bosphorus straits, gateway to the Black Sea. Strategically, this was an excellent idea: maps seemed to show how easy it would be to encircle the Central Powers by taking control of the Dardanelles. But no one had taken the trouble to research the terrain over which they would be sending men to fight. When, in April, Allied troops – including large numbers of Australians and New Zealanders – landed on Cape Helles and below the rugged cliffs at what was later to be named Anzac Cove they found themselves pinned down on tiny beachheads from which they spent the next eight months battling their way yard by bloody yard towards the Turkish positions on the Gallipoli heights. That spring members of the army nursing services of Britain, Australia and New Zealand were sent to base hospitals in Egypt to care for the tens of thousands of wounded men pouring from the peninsula. As it became clear that the Gallipoli campaign was just another entrenched and bitter battle of attrition, nurses were deployed closer to where they were needed: on hospital ships and on the island of Lemnos just over thirty miles from the Dardanelles.

On the Western Front, Allied military medical and nursing services were still grappling with the appalling wounds created by modern military weaponry and contaminated by ancient species of microbe. Casualties were arriving at regimental aid posts with such extensive and badly infected wounds that new ways had to be found to contain the damage before a patient collapsed from shock, blood loss or infection. The wounded were moved as quickly as possible – ideally within a few hours – to casualty clearing stations which were better organized than the early units of 1914, their staff now more adequately prepared for the horrors they were witnessing.

As mentioned, some of the earliest CCSs had been established as 'casualty clearing hospitals', alongside French field hospitals in the small town of Poperinge, on the railway line from Ypres to the Belgian–French border. By the spring of 1915 it was becoming increasingly clear that the town was not a good location for hospitals. Because its railway station was a frequent final stop for troops on their way to the front lines – who disembarked and made the remainder of the journey on foot – the area around the station was a target for German long-range artillery. On 12 March 1915 three shells exploded in the market square. Hospital units began to look for safer locations in smaller, less conspicuous settlements.

On 5 May, Frederic Bompaire, the commanding officer of Hôpital d'Évacuation 15 visited a small farm just under two miles from the French border. The 'Ferme Remi' named after its owner, Remi Quaghebeur – who had died only weeks before – was later to become the site of one of the largest complexes of casualty clearing stations on the Western Front. Bompaire persuaded Quaghebeur's widow, Marie, to lease the farm buildings and land to the French Service de Santé des Armées. Its location was perfect. It was sufficiently far from Poperinge to make it safe – for the time being – from bombardment, and it lay just in front of the main railway line running between Poperinge and Brandhoek, permitting the easy transfer of patients. The first nurses were billeted in its farm buildings just a few days later; all were French, many with a full professional training – a rare thing in France at that time. Within a month the Royal Engineers had built a raised platform next to the rail tracks to permit the easy loading of wounded. The first British CCS – No. 10 – arrived in July, and was joined, in August, by No. 17. The 'Ferme Remi' had become became 'Remy Siding', an international complex of forward field hospitals.

Typically, seven fully trained nurses were now deployed to each CCS under the supervision of a 'head sister'. They worked closely with military medical orderlies, whose training was not nearly as extensive as their own, but whose approach to their work was often highly adaptive and whose skills had been honed by experience. Although orderlies were, formally, under the control of the Royal Army Medical Corps, they were usually willing to recognize the authority of sisters on their hospital wards, and the two groups cooperated well together. Orderlies were responsible for the infrastructure of the hospital: for pitching tents, digging latrines and laying duckboards. They also cleaned and maintained order within the wards: sweeping floors, dusting lockers and maintaining gas and coal-fired heaters. Beyond this, they did a great deal of nursing work: offering fundamental care to patients – washing, feeding and toileting them – and engaging in more technical work, such as applying splints and bandages.

Patients were moved as quickly as possible 'down the line' to general hospitals in northern France, some in large cities such as Rouen, others in small seaside towns such as Boulogne and Etaples. By the beginning of 1915, whole stretches of coastline were covered with hospitals, resembling huge encampments, or makeshift shanty-towns. For the first five months of 1915, Margaret Brander, with the 1st Scottish General Hospital, was stationed at Wimereux, near Boulogne. In the winter the work was heavy; large numbers of patients were coming in with frostbitten feet. Their blisters were treated with iodine and turpentine. The condition was later to be recognized as 'trench foot', and would come to be treated as a commonplace of the war. Infectious diseases – brought on by the cold, damp and overcrowding of the trenches – were rife, and included dangerous, life-threatening conditions such as typhoid, pneumonia and rheumatic fever. On 17 January, Margaret commented in her diary: 'We are working under great difficulties at present – no gas – electric most uncertain up and down and the coke stove no use whatever – the wind simply blowing down the pipe. And it is so cold.'[1] Many of the hospital's very sick patients also had severe wounds. Margaret wrote that one of her new patients 'has had an injury to the eye by the head of another man being blown against his face'. Two days later, the patient underwent an operation in which the surgeon removed a hair, two small pieces of bone and a piece of shrapnel from inside the eye.

Medical officers were still searching for ways to solve the problem of anaerobic wound infections. Journals such as the *Lancet* and the *British Medical Journal* carried research papers in which the doctors reported their 'trial and error' findings. Nursing journals, such as the *British Journal of Nursing*, the *Nursing Times* and the *Nursing Mirror* kept a close eye on these findings, sometimes re-publishing medical papers and sometimes including commentary or essay competitions in their pages in order to keep their readers informed about new approaches. Controversy was rife. Powerful senior military medical officers (many of whom had served in the Anglo-Boer War) debated a range of treatments for war wounds. Sir Anthony Bowlby, consulting surgeon with the British Expeditionary Force, argued for the radical and stringent use of chemical antiseptics. Everyone knew that these chemicals – compounds such as iodoform, sodium hypochlorite, hydrogen peroxide and perchloride of mercury – were potentially toxic and could damage a patient's liver and kidneys. Yet it seemed worth the risk if it meant the difference between his rapid death and his longer-term survival. But other voices urged different measures. Some continued to argue for the conservative treatment – the application of dry antiseptic dressings which were then left undisturbed. Others, led by H. M. W. Gray, recommended the surgical removal of large swathes of tissue around the wound to 'carry away' the infection, leaving only healthy tissue and putting a stop to any inflammation. Sir Almroth Wright, an eccentric yet highly respected surgeon who was later to conduct important research on devices to prevent gas poisoning, argued for the use of 'hypertonic saline solution'. At first this seemed a rational solution to the problem of wound infection. Wright had noticed that the serum which seeped out of an infected wound possessed healing and antiseptic properties. His aim was to mobilize the body's own defences by encouraging this process. So he used high concentrations of salt, dissolved in sterile water, to draw high volumes of serum – by osmosis – through the infected tissues around the wound. He argued that this process would leach bacteria out of the wound and, if used meticulously enough, would eventually draw all poison from it. To a certain extent the hypertonic saline solution must have worked well – the constant dripping of sterile saline solution through a wound would have helped clean its base and margins and encouraged the growth of healthy new cells. But salt water was no match for anaerobes.

Nurses were called upon to implement a range of wound-care measures. They never appeared to take part in decisions about which treatments were to be used. But they took an enormous interest – and they were well-placed to observe the effects of wound-care measures ranging from the application of dry dressings; through the pouring of antiseptics into wound cavities and the packing of gaping wounds with gauze swabs dripping with chemicals; to the syringing of wounds with saline. Their carefully made and assiduously reported observations could have significant influence: sometimes providing a surgeon with the confidence to continue a treatment, at other times gently steering him onto a new course. Women of their time, the professional nurses of the First World War were deferential to medical science, recognizing firm boundaries between their work and that of the surgeon. They never knowingly crossed those boundaries. And yet they were the individuals who were at the patient's bedside, observing his every reaction – both physiological and emotional. They knew what worked and what didn't and their scientific knowledge, built up through three years of training gave them a clear sense of not only *whether* a treatment was successful, but also *why*. Although some surgeons had highly chauvinistic attitudes towards female nurses, most appreciated their work, valuing their intelligent decision-making, their meticulous attention to detail, their capacity for observation, their ability to offer comfort and support to patients and their calming influence on an entire ward. Most worked in close partnership with nurses and valued their knowledge and views on the efficacy of treatments.

Eventually, by the late spring of 1915, a new approach emerged – one which almost everyone agreed was highly effective: the 'Carrel-Dakin' treatment. Henry Dakin, a British scientist working at the University of Leeds, had demonstrated the efficacy of the powerful antiseptic, sodium hypochlorite, in cleaning up heavily infected wounds. Another group of scientists at Edinburgh University had also 'discovered' it at about the same time, and had named it EUSOL, an acronym for 'Edinburgh University Solution of Lime'. But it was 'Dakin's Solution' that came to be used on every war front. Dakin teamed up with a French surgeon, Alexis Carrel, who was working for the American Rockefeller Foundation, and who discovered an ingenious means of delivering the solution into the beds of deep wounds, using lengths of rubber and glass tubing. The two men conducted research at a military hospital in Compiègne, and discovered that they could eradicate a large proportion of the wound infections coming into the hospital. Their work was soon widely recognized and emulated by surgeons in other military hospitals. It became the staple treatment for infected wounds. Although highly cumbersome, a Carrel-Dakin apparatus applied in a CCS would often be left in place as the patient receiving treatment was loaded onto a hospital train, and then also as he was transferred by ambulance to a base hospital in northern France.

The Carrel-Dakin treatment could not have worked without the intelligent dedication of trained nurses, who made themselves responsible for its safe and effective application. Pushing chemical solutions of any kind through open wounds carried its own risks, and nurses ensured that the glass and rubber apparatus used was completely sterile, that solutions were carefully prepared and that dressings were loose enough for the irrigation technique to work, yet firm enough to protect the wound.

The lines of evacuation were beginning to crystallize into an efficient and effective series of networks along which the wounded were moved as rapidly as possible. From the battlefield, they were carried by stretcher-bearers to their regimental aid posts; most were moved on to advanced dressing stations, and all were then loaded into motor ambulances that took them to the nearest CCS. Once treated and stabilized they were put onto ambulance trains or barges, which conveyed them to base hospitals. Here, they were assessed to see whether they should be returned to a rest camp and then back to the front lines, or given a much-desired 'Blighty ticket': a passport home to Britain.

In Wimereux, Margaret Brander was receiving patients with a range of infectious diseases. Nurses working closely with such patients and living in cold, draughty environments were, themselves, vulnerable to infection. On 19 February, Margaret recorded in her diary that 'a great depression has been cast over us all. Sister Cole has contracted cerebro-spinal meningitis. Matron found her lying on the floor this morning. She was a nice quiet girl, rather of the old-world style.' Sister Cole died at 6.30 a.m. two days later, without regaining consciousness.

In February 1915, Kate Luard was still on Hospital Train No. 10, taking wounded from a region just south of the Ypres Salient. Kate described in a letter home to her family how, on 18 February, she and colleagues loaded a large convoy of wounded men at Bailleul. Among them was a sergeant with 'a fearful wound in his thigh, which [had] gone wrong'. During infantry assaults, soldiers were given clear orders: they must always continue to advance. If a comrade was wounded next to them, they must not stop to help him but must keep moving, leaving his unit's own stretcher-bearers to rescue him. But men often lay wounded in no man's land for many hours until recovered to a regimental aid post. Kate described the sergeant's story:

> They were getting out of the trench for a bayonet charge, and he had just collected his men when he was hit; so the officer "shook hands with him" and went on with the charge, leaving him and another man, wounded in the leg, in the trench. They stayed there several hours with no dressings on, sinking into the mud (can you wonder it has gone wrong?)[2]

Kate's patient undoubtedly had a severe anaerobic infection. He had received anti-tetanus serum at his regimental aid post, but gas gangrene was still a serious risk. Alongside him was another seriously injured soldier: 'a lad of 24 with both eyes destroyed by a bullet'. She added that he 'has not the slightest idea that he's got no eyes, and who is going to tell him? The pain is bad, and he has to have a lot of morphia, with a cigarette in between.'

In the spring of 1915, the British and French lines stabilized along the northern part of the Western Front. Some of the fiercest battles of 1915 were fought over the ruins of what had once been French villages close to the Belgian border. In March, just twenty-three miles from Ypres, the battle of Neuve Chappelle brought thousands of badly wounded men into CCSs around Bethune and Lillers. British forces had successfully taken the village of Neuve Chappelle, and the earliest casualties arrived in CCSs in high spirits, despite their injuries, recounting tales of success and 'breakthrough'. But they were unable to sustain their planned advance onto the strategically important Aubers Ridge. Mistakes were made; at times, troops came under bombardment from their own artillery, and infantry battalions ran out of ammunition before they could reach their objectives. Soon the mood in the CCSs turned from excitement and jubilation to shock and deep frustration. Neuve Chappelle was to set the pattern for the attritional battles of the next three years, in which both sides devised more and more ingenious ways of achieving 'breakthrough', only to repeatedly learn the same lesson: early-twentieth-century trench systems and industrial weaponry favoured defenders, not attackers. No matter how determinedly an army tried to break through an opposing trench system, and no matter how furiously it bombarded its opponents before commencing its attack, defenders could always sit tight in their heavily defended bunkers and concrete 'pillboxes' waiting for the storm of metal to clear and the vulnerable bodies of their human attackers to move into the wide open space of no man's land protected only by woollen khaki uniforms and peaked caps (later helmets). Then it required a period of careful concentration and resolute determination to mow down the advancing force – almost to a man – with a hail of machine-gun bullets supported by a barrage of shrapnel and high-explosive shells from artillery behind the lines. Nurses in CCSs often commented in their diaries that these battles were 'murder not warfare'.

On 13 March 1915, a man was loaded onto No. 10 Ambulance Train with a 'shattered' head. He had received brain surgery in the CCS, and had been put onto the train the next morning. Kate was delighted to be able to write to her family that he actually recovered during the journey to the base hospital, 'enough to remark, as if he were doing a French exercise, "You-are-a-good-Nurse!"'. Two days later, on Monday, 15 March, she woke in her bunk at 2.30 a.m., just as the train arrived back at Bailleul, to the noise of an 'incessant cannonade'. Reaching for her writing paper, she attempted to capture in words the sights and sounds around her: 'The sky is continually lit up with the flashes from the guns – it is a pitch-dark night – and you can hear the roar of the howitzers above the thud-thud of the others ... Must try and sleep now, as we shall have a heavy day to-day, but it is no lullaby.'[3]

Hours later the train was completely packed with wounded men. CCSs were under intense strain, with hospitals intended for 300 men typically receiving 800 in each convoy. To relieve pressure, as many patients as possible were put onto the trains. All bunks were filled; patients who should, ideally, have been lying down became 'sitting cases', and stretchers were placed on the floors down the middle of carriages. But one of the things that struck Kate the most was the patience and gratitude of her patients. One, a youngster of 22, with both legs amputated, was 'dazed and white, and wants shifting very often. Each time you fix him up he says, "That's champion."'.[4]

On 17 March, the train loaded up again at Merville, still taking wounded from the Neuve Chapelle 'push'. Many of Kate's patients were Canadians. There were also eight German prisoners of war, one of whom insisted on kissing her hand in gratitude, 'much to the orderlies' amusement'.

Back at the base in Wimereux, on the north coast of France, Margaret Brander was on night duty, receiving many of Neuve Chapelle's worst cases. At the beginning of that month, she and her colleagues had been moved into new billets, at the Hotel Regina, which was 'very swell', but also very noisy. Margaret's room was right opposite the bathroom and, as far as she could tell, there were people bathing 'all day long'. There was no lock on the door, and she was frequently disturbed, until she put a sign on her bedroom door. She commented in her diary: 'I pity the next one who wakes me from my sleep.' When, on 15 March, the wounded began 'pouring in', she was already exhausted. She was shocked by the condition of the men who were unloaded from the queuing ambulances at the doors of the hospital. The wounds were 'ghastly' and many of the men were 'frightfully mangled'. Wards and corridors were filled with stretchers, leaving only a narrow pathway for stretcher-bearers to negotiate. The English chaplain pitched in to help the nurses and orderlies undress the patients. Somehow they coped without calling up the day staff. Margaret's diary seems to have been a useful outlet for the impressions of those mid-March days:

> Some of the cases are really dreadful. Fractured femurs, many of the men having face wounds, fractures of the arms etc. One man I may give as an example. His nose was broken, his humerus compound fracture, femur fracture compound, penis shattered. And not a grumble from him only gratitude. Another in the other corner [compound] fracture femur, bullet wound of anus, bullet probably lodged in pelvis. Another both eyes shot out and part of brain bulging out from forehead. Yet another huge wound head and

one huge one extending shoulder to shoulder. A little boy of 19 years has wound of rt. shoulder, hip and leg. Fracture [compound] of arm and wound of hand. Bullet also in abdomen. To-night he has all the symptoms of peritonitis. The head cases are innumerable. One has died tonight, he only came this afternoon, never has been conscious. Many more are dying. There are many bad chest cases. Trephining and amputations are continuous. Words can never describe this scene.[5]

Later that month, all night work had to be done in total darkness, as Zeppelins hovered over the coast, ready to drop their bombs on any obviously inhabited site. The patient with the head wound and both eyes shot out, soon came to be referred to as Margaret's 'head boy'. He was often delirious and had to be sedated with hyosin and morphine. On 29 March, Margaret commented that he had been 'most pathetic calling out for his mother, and singing Rock of Ages! He is such a nice boy.' But three weeks later, Margaret's courage and strength began to run out and her matron, noticing her haggard appearance, sent her to recuperate at the Princess Louise's Convalescent Home for nurses at Hardelot. Margaret was relieved, yet anxious. The home – expertly run by Lady Gifford, who brought nurses' breakfasts to them on trays every morning – was 'truly a home of rest'; but a few days among the tranquil forest and sand dunes of Hardelot made it difficult to return to the rigours of active service.

In April 1915 the war took a new and even bleaker turn. On the morning of the 22nd, specialist engineers in the German lines, wearing thick, protective overalls and masks opened the valves on 6,000 cylinders of chlorine gas, allowing their greenish yellow contents to drift slowly on the easterly breeze across no man's land towards their enemy's trenches. Unsure of what was happening, the French and Algerian soldiers in the trenches watched as the strange, ghostly phenomenon approached them, recognizing its destructive purpose, but knowing that if they ran for their lives they would be shot for desertion. As it reached them their irresolution turned to panic and they did run – but not before approximately 1,000 had been killed. The German infantry advanced rapidly behind the gas cloud, easily taking the French trenches. But they were unable to press home their advantage. As the air began to clear newly arrived Canadian troops, alongside British Territorials, held their ground, and then counter-attacked in an action that was to become part of the Canadian legend of the war. They retook the conceded trenches. This action opened not only the bloody Second Battle of Ypres but also a new era in warfare. From then onwards the forces of both Allies and Central Powers were to use increasingly destructive poison compounds, and they were to deliver these into their enemies' trenches in increasingly ingenious ways, including, from mid-1916 onwards via 'gas shells'.

It was one of the earliest 'arms races' of the modern period: scientists on both sides struggled to find means to protect their troops while more effectively destroying their enemies. Even as experts were designing more and more lethal chemical compounds, they were also vying with each other to devise increasingly ingenious gas masks. The earliest attempts were primitive, to say the least. Lieutenant John Smythe of the 15th Ludhiana Sikhs was later to describe to historian, Peter Liddle, how the Indian Corps was marched thirty miles to reinforce the beleaguered troops at Ypres. 'We had no idea what we were getting into at all,' he declared before describing how he and his men were told to dip their handkerchiefs into buckets of chemical liquids before advancing to the front lines. If they encountered gas they were to clap these handkerchiefs over their noses and mouths. Smythe's analysis of the situation was that his survival was a matter of good fortune. He received only a 'whiff' of the gas and was careful not to swallow any.[6]

On that day – 22 April – and in the weeks that followed doctors and nurses in field hospitals and casualty clearing stations within ten miles of the front lines found themselves overwhelmed by 'rushes' of patients who all appeared to be suffering from either bronchitis or pneumonia: they were choking and gasping for breath. Many had collapsed completely and had to be stretchered into the hospital units. Most were also blind; the gas had inflamed the delicate tissues of their eyes to the extent that they were swollen, closed and agonizingly painful. Trained nurses on triage duty – receiving patients into reception tents, assessing them and making decisions about their treatments – knew at once that these choking and blinded men were not simple cases of chest infection. Their clothes and hair were impregnated with some strange-smelling substance. Just being near to them made nurses and orderlies cough and their eyes smart and sting. They acted quickly, stripping men of their uniforms and washing the chemicals from their bodies. Nurses knew, from their experiences with pneumonia and tuberculosis patients, how to treat patients with damaged chests. Normally, they must be kept warm, and should be nursed upright in a sitting position. But these men's lungs seemed to be full of liquid, as if they were drowning in their own body fluids – which, indeed, they were. As the chlorine had seeped into their airways – trachea, bronchi and bronchioles – it had burned and scarred the delicate membranes. The tissues had reacted by producing lymph – a fluid that normally would have permitted healing by combating infection and moistening the airways. But the overwhelming nature of the chemical damage meant that vast quantities of lymph were being produced, swamping patients' lungs. They had to be nursed horizontally, on their sides, to drain the fluid from the lungs; and they were given morphine for their pain and reassurance to alleviate their panic – which would, otherwise, worsen their physical condition. Because such severe damage to lungs was likely to cause rapid heart failure, doctors prescribed powerful stimulants, such as strychnine and camphor oil – dangerous chemicals that had to be given in carefully calibrated doses.

One trained British nurse serving the Belgian Red Cross was based in a makeshift hospital in an old alms house in Hoogestadt, on the Furnes-to-Ypres road, close to where the British and Belgian lines met. Her unit received some of the first gas-injured patients from Second Ypres. She described how

> We flew from man to man, inserting hypodermic needles, giving saline injections by the dozen. In the X-ray department we were cutting off their clothes as they lay on their stretchers. Soon a mountain of clothes lay outside the back door – British, Belgian and German uniforms. Gas had been used in the trenches for the first time that day. There they lay, fully sensible, choking, suffocating, dying in horrible agonies. We did what we could, but the best treatment for such cases had yet to be discovered and we felt almost powerless.[7]

Men who survived the first few hours of their poisoning were likely to become more stable and begin to recover. Within a few days, however, they would invariably relapse: the damage to their lungs meant that infection was quick to set in and most began to develop severe bronchitis. At this stage they were nursed in an upright position, supported on many pillows (if these were available). Their still-painful eyes were swabbed – ideally every two hours – with sodium bicarbonate, to neutralize the acid produced by the gas and to prevent potentially damaging infections. Most of those who survived the gas also recovered their sight after about ten days. But during their time in the wards of the CCS, in hospital trains and then for their first few weeks at a base hospital, they were so breathless, sightless and debilitated that they required 'total nursing care': their every need, from cleansing and comforting to feeding and toileting, was met by nurses and orderlies.

Margaret Brander, now serving on Ambulance Train No. 12 was working long shifts. Her first journey was to Bailleul, 'where the guns were going steadily'. Two hundred and sixty-five cases were loaded; more than half of these were gas-poisoned. Passing Saint-Omer, Hazebrouck and Calais, the train arrived at Boulogne eight hours later, where the worst cases were unloaded, before the train continued to Étretat – not arriving until the afternoon of the next day. Margaret wrote about the routine of ambulance train work in her diary:

> After loading up and starting, we immediately took temps, and made a slip of paper out for each patient pinning it on his pillow. We put on it what patient suffered from, his temp, diet and treatment and, when unloaded, each pt. had this slip pinned on him. Then we started dressing those that had not been done at the CCS and any that were soaked through. If time permitted and we had water to spare, we washed faces and hands and that was the thing they were all so grateful for. When it was absolutely necessary we changed shirts but all except very bad cases had to lie with clothes on. We managed to give them a good meal, with soup and meat, plenty of bread. Next morning the cleaning had to be started all paint work being washed inside and outside windows cleaned and brasses polished.[8]

Second Ypres was the most significant of all the failed assaults of 1915. It was one of the few large-scale German attempts to break through the Allied lines and, because of the surprise element introduced by the use of chlorine gas, it almost succeeded. It was also the second devastatingly destructive large-scale battle at Ypres, fixing the reputation of that city in the minds of Allied soldiers as a place of dread.

In late May, just over twenty-five miles away at Festubert, the Allies threw their men against the Western Front in a desperate attempt to break the German lines. They were thrown back, suffering thousands of casualties. Now working in a CCS, Kate Luard described how she had 'just admitted a gunner suffering from shock alone – no wound – completely knocked out; he can't tell you his name, or stand, or even sit up, but just shivers and shudders. Now he is warm in bed, he can say "Thank you." I wonder what exactly did it.'[9] The next day, casualties began to stream into the CCs at 3.30 a.m., until the unit was 'full to bursting'. All the patients were 'sopping wet with blood or mud or both'. There followed several nights of 'horrors', in which staff took in 'a long whirl of stretchers, and pitiful heaps on them'.

Patient after patient died and even the kitchen boy stayed up all night to help. At 1 a.m. on 18 May, three days after the first convoys arrived, Kate got to bed and wrote to her family:

> It has been about the worst night of all the worst nights. I found the wards packed with bad cases, the boy of 18 dead, and the other boy died half an hour after I came on. Two more died during the night, two lots were evacuated, and had to be dug out of their fixings-up in bed and settled on stretchers, and all night they brought fresh ones in, drenched and soaked with clayey mud in spadefuls, and clammy with cold.[10]

No. 12 Ambulance Train was still moving between CCSs at Bailleul and a range of base hospitals. The work was becoming increasingly dangerous, and Margaret Brander was now exhausted from continuous night duty. On 16 May, the day after the opening of the battle of Festubert, the train moved up to Bethune, just eight miles from the front lines. The loading of patients took many hours, and was not completed until 4.30 a.m. By 2.30 p.m. the next day, the patients had been unloaded at Boulogne, and the train was en route back to Bethune. Margaret took the opportunity to write up her diary, recording the surreal nature of her experience at the front:

> The guns were going at it like a cannonade and you heard the nightingales singing too. I shall never forget that loading. The men who came all told us we had big successes and that we were bombarding up till 5 a.m. Then there was to be an advance. We were not far from our fighters and the din of the guns was awful. Flare after Flare of the shells went up. The stars were shining peacefully, the heavens were the only peaceful spots and the nightingales knew nothing of it. As we listened to the cannonade it sounded death everywhere.[11]

For the next two days and nights, the train made two journeys between Merville and Boulogne. At Merville, shells were passing directly over the train. The work was 'heavy' and the rain was almost continuous. Margaret's diary is a telling record of the intense pressure of work on No. 12 Ambulance Train. An entry for 21 May describes how:

> Last night at 12 midnight we loaded up at Bailleul. For an hour we watched the star shells. Everything was one continuous flash and

the train shook again when some of the guns went off. We carried down 285. Stretchers 70. Sitting 215, the worse cases being taken off at Boulogne, and we unloaded between 1 and 2 a.m. at Versailles on the 22nd. Loaded again at 7.30 a.m. there and unloading at Le Havre at 11 p.m. Total 232. Officers 8. Stretchers 91. Sitting 133.[12]

With only two professional nurses on each ambulance train, the work was unremitting. It was also deeply distressing. On 26 May, the load was particularly 'heavy': 'Men unconscious tied on stretchers, gas gangrene smells awful. One man died ½ hr. from Boulogne. Wounds dreadful. 249 total. 30 walking 219 stretchers.'[13] On 31 May 1915, Margaret was mentioned in Sir John French's despatches 'for gallant and distinguished service in the field'.

Many of the volunteer hospitals that had raced to Belgium at the outbreak of war were brought under the auspices of the French Red Cross Societies or the French Service de Santé des Armées during the early months of 1915. Millicent, Duchess of Sutherland established her hospital at the Hotel Belle Vue in Malo-les-Bains. In the summer of 1915, it came under heavy shellfire and was moved to Bourboug, near Calais. Here, its staff and patients became the subjects of a series of paintings by Victor Tardieu, winning recognition as 'The Hospital in the Oatfield'. On 15 October, the unit was taken over by the British Red Cross and was attached to No. 35 General Hospital near Calais.

Over seventy miles from the front, life in Paris was continuing almost as normal, but inhabitants knew that a German breakthrough would threaten their city within just a few days. Ellen La Motte managed to obtain work as a volunteer at the American Ambulance at Neuilly, a suburb just outside the city, in the spring of 1915. The 'Ambulance' had been much praised in the nursing press as an important centre for the treatment of French wounded, but Ellen found the work disappointing. The hospital was, in her opinion, too far from the front to be really useful. It seemed to have become a haven for American and French volunteers with very little training, who simply wanted to be able to say that they had participated in the war effort. Ellen was now using her contacts in Parisian society – among them the novelist Gertrude Stein – to search for a posting closer to the front lines.

That year, recognizing the need for a better organized 'nursing department', the directors of the American Ambulance invited Margaret Dunlop, Directress of Nurses at the Pennsylvania Hospital in Philadelphia, to take charge. Margaret was able to obtain a leave of absence, and travelled to Neuilly with three of her most trusted colleagues, Helen Grace McClelland,

Mary Mallon and Agnes Guerin. Arriving at the 'Ambulance', they began to develop the clinical practice of the nursing staff, working closely with American and French surgeons to improve nursing care practices and implement the latest wound-care techniques.

Canadian nurse, Agnes Warner had returned to France, and had been persuaded to support the work of the Ambulance. In mid-February, she wrote a letter home:

> Oh mother, it is awful to see the sad things that have happened. In some cases there are only pieces of men left. One young chap, twenty-one years old, has lost both legs. At first he did not want to live, but now he is beginning to take an interest in things and is being fitted for wooden legs ... The dental department has done wonderful work. They build up the frame work of the face and jaws and then the surgeons finish the work done by making new noses and lips and eyelids. I thought I had seen a good many wonderful things, but I did not believe it possible to make any thing human out of some of the pieces of faces that were left.[14]

American millionaire Mary Borden was, by this time, living in Paris, and, as an influential member of the so-called 'American Colony', she took an interest in the American Ambulance and became well-acquainted with several of its nurses, including Ellen La Motte and Agnes Warner. When she had been serving as a volunteer nurse in a military hospital on the French coast, she had, in spite of her lack of experience, seen clearly that her unit was ill-equipped, under-resourced and staffed with inadequately trained nurses. In France, professional nurse training had not advanced so rapidly as in Britain or the USA. There were only three secular, professional nurse-training schools for the entire country, and most care was offered by nuns. Although the vast majority of these religious nurses were compassionate and highly experienced, their training was under the control of the Catholic Church and was likely to emphasize spiritual redemption to the same extent as, or sometimes beyond, physical and emotional care. Mary was frustrated, and became determined to use her wealth, influence and persuasive power to find a more effective way of helping the French military nursing services. She met with General Joffre, commander-in-chief of the French army, and persuaded him to allow her to create her own hospital unit. Unlike the British Army Medical Services, the French Service de Santé des Armées was only too happy to accept the help of dynamic and wealthy women like Mary

Borden. By July 1915 she was firmly installed as the *Directrice* of L'Hôpital Chirurgical Mobile No. 1 (Mobile Surgical No. 1), a 160-bed hospital in Beveren (modern-day Beveren-Ijzer), about a mile from the Belgian–French frontier to the north-west of Poperinge, close to the Belgian lines and within twenty kilometres of Ypres, the city that was already both a devastated ruin and an Allied symbol of hope and determination.

Mary had complete control of the nursing care within the hospital. She worked closely with the French *médecin chef*, surgeons and orderlies. Her nurses were British, Canadian, Australian and American, and she was able to persuade Ellen La Motte and Agnes Warner to each take charge of a ward. Many of Mary's sisters were fully trained professional nurses who had volunteered their services with the so-called 'French Flag Nursing Corps', a unit created by Englishwoman Grace Ellison. Grace, like Mary, had offered to serve as a volunteer nurse in the French Service de Santé, only to discover that the work was too difficult for her. Realizing that she could offer the best support to the French by using her organizational talents to mobilize fully trained nurses, she created her corps by recruiting British and Dominion nurses, many of whom had been turned away by their own country's official army nursing services. Among those who found their way to Mobile Surgical No. 1 over the following months were British nurses, Annie Hanning and Mabel Jones, and Canadian nurses, Madeleine Jaffray and Helen McMurrich. She was also able to arrange for the New South Wales branch of the Australian Red Cross to send several Australian nurses, among them Sisters Hilda Loxton, Lynette Crozier and Minnie Hough. The Australian nurses were sponsored by the New South Wales Jockey Club and were given uniforms consisting of a blue dress and a white apron, earning them the nickname 'Bluebirds'. They began the long journey to Western Europe in the summer of 1915.

Ellen La Motte's much shorter journey from Paris to Beveren was a dramatic one. She and a group of colleagues arrived at Dunkirk, in the so-called 'zone of the armies', only to discover that their hospital was not yet ready, and that they must spend several nights in a hotel in nearby Malo-les-Bains. On the night of 20 June, they watched from their balcony as Dunkirk was bombarded by long-range guns located twenty miles away beyond Diksmuide. The sight was terrifying. As shells blasted their way through buildings, citizens could be seen running to the beach for safety like swarms of tiny ants. On the morning of the 22nd a German Taube aircraft dropped a bomb just outside the hotel. Yet Ellen was hungry for experience; she wanted something to write about. In the late morning, with nothing else to do, she and a colleague travelled into town to view the ruins; but the bombardment recommenced unexpectedly, and she discovered at first hand the terror of being shelled. This was certainly more experience than she had bargained for. Soon she discovered that there was a forty-minute time-lapse between each shell, as the German artillerymen waited for their gun to cool. Knowing that they could not escape the town before the next blast, she and her colleague searched desperately for shelter, finding it eventually in the cellar of a kindly Belgian family. Ellen was to write about this experience in a highly successful article for the popular American journal *Atlantic Monthly*. She described the fascination of watching a bombardment from a distance, the dread of experiencing it at first hand and the relief of eventual escape:

> In all directions we could see shattered houses, streets and sidewalks littered with broken glass, fallen bricks and rubbish, gaping walls open to the heavens. It was terrible to pass through those hot streets, wondering, as we walked, whether we should reach Malo before the guns began again. It was like walking in a nightmare, dragging leaden legs, with the terror that comes with dreams.[15]

Eventually, Ellen and her group reached Beveren. In peace-time it had been a tranquil and verdant agricultural town. Now, in the summer of 1915 – with contingents of soldiers churning up its narrow main street as they marched in formation towards the front lines of war – it was a grim and dreary place. The German advance had been halted just five miles to the east during the desperate fighting of late October 1914. A strip of land covering approximately 300 square miles was all that was left of free Belgium, and nurses who came to Beveren commented that this place felt like the end of the world. During the Battle of the Yser, Belgian forces had opened sluices at Nieuwpoort, far to the north, during a period of high tides in late October, creating a flooded region that was about a mile wide. Flood plains around the villages of Beveren and Rousbrugge (modern-day Roesbrugge) became lakes and swamps during the wet season, but the villages themselves – and the fields immediately surrounding them – remained dry, like islands in a vast swamp. Mobile Surgical No. 1 was in one of these higher fields just outside Beveren. It was surrounded by a dense, impassable hawthorn hedge, and in its highest corner there was a large, impressive, timber gateway and sentry-box. The war seemed very close. From the hospital, Mary commented that you can hear cataracts of iron pouring down channels in the sodden land, and you feel the earth trembling … There is nothing but mud all about, and a soft fine rain coming down to make more mud – mud with a broken fragment of a nation lolling in it.[16]

That summer young men were passing through Beveren in their tens of thousands. Nurses in the hospital could hear the purposeful tramping of their feet, passing from the French border just a mile away, past the hedge at the foot of the hospital. Days later, these same men returned as the shattered remnants of human beings. Many never returned at all. That autumn, Mary Borden noticed that they were being replaced by Territorial regiments of older men. Many were only in their forties, but, when survivors among them returned from the trenches for periods of rest, she noticed that they looked like elderly men. They seemed to be infused with a terrible resignation:

they knew that they were not going home, and they knew that they were condemned to death. They knew this; they had always known. They understood and they did not complain. France was at war. They were old men. Their sons had been killed. They were taking the place of their sons.[17]

These 'old men' were to form a large part of the patient population in Mobile Surgical No. 1 for the rest of the autumn.

Queen Elisabeth of the Belgians took a great interest in the work of the hospital. Mary was impressed by this gentle yet formidable woman, whose tireless work supporting military hospitals belied her fragile appearance. Yet Mary was also discomfited by the incongruity of the queen's presence in the zone of the armies – just as she was disturbed by her own presence there. One day, after viewing Elisabeth at a medal ceremony in Beveren-Ijzer town square, she wrote of her fascination with this 'queen-nurse': 'She was a beautiful animal, dressed as a nun and branded with a red cross … a strange fantastic thing, like a white peacock.'[18] Although Mary felt great admiration for Elisabeth, she also felt that, by watching the suffering of the men while remaining safe, the queen was also, somehow, 'insolent'.

There was much about what she saw at Mobile Surgical No. 1 that discomfited Mary. In her essay 'Moonlight' she wrote about her experiences the night after local farmers had cut the hay in a nearby field. Its 'sweet sickish scent' made her uncomfortable. It intruded upon the usual hospital smells of disinfectant, mud, blood and gangrene, reminding her that there was a life beyond the closed, confining hedges of Mobile Surgical No. 1.[19]

On 25 September 1915, a 'big push' began at Loos, just south of Lille. It was to be the last, and most ambitious, of the costly and unsuccessful attempts that year to break through the German lines in the northern sector of the Western Front. The West Riding Casualty Clearing Station (also known as the No. 58 CCS) was established in the small town of Lillers in October, to support the last and most desperate stages of the assault; Territorial Force nurse Sister Kate Maxey was one of its most experienced members.

Like so many military nurses, Kate had a strong sense of duty; in 1912, she had joined the staff of the 2nd Northern General Hospital – ready to be 'called up' to serve her country at twenty-four hours' notice in the event of a future war. As things turned out, global conflict had not been long in coming. Kate had been working at a nursing home in Leeds when her country declared war on Germany. By 9 October, she had been posted overseas to the No. 8 General Hospital in Rouen. From here, she was moved 'up the line' to Lillers, a posting she almost certainly would have welcomed, because of its proximity to the front lines.

Not even her extensive experience at the base in Rouen could have prepared Kate for the casualties pouring out of the scarred remains of what had once been the mining town of Loos and its surrounding villages. The German army had been well dug in and the capture of heavily fortified strongpoints such as the Hohenzollern Redoubt had produced thousands of casualties. By the time No. 58 CCS arrived, the campaign had reached its height and ambulances were streaming into Lillers. The staffs of the two CCSs already there were struggling to rescue the shattered remnants of men who arrived at their gates. But they were becoming more organized in their efforts. Around this time CCSs began to work in pairs, with one unit taking in approximately 300 patients before closing its doors and handing over to its neighbour. This allowed each CCS a period of time in which it could concentrate on supporting and treating its existing patients before beginning to 'take in' again.

Surgical and wound-care techniques were becoming more effective too. By now, well aware of the dangers of anaerobic wound infection, surgeons were becoming much bolder, removing vast areas of tissue, incorporating wide margins of apparently healthy flesh around the obviously infected skin and muscle in order to ensure that any infection was eradicated. This created huge workloads for nurses, who prepared their patients for the trauma of surgery, offered close and meticulous assistance in operating theatres, and then supported their patients' recovery in CCS wards. Surgery heightened the trauma of injury and sharpened the pain of wounding; nurses alleviated that trauma and blunted that pain. This was not only a matter of comfort, it was actually one of life and death. A patient whose trauma overwhelmed him could die of shock; one who haemorrhaged from a surgical wound site could die from blood loss; one who was not watched sufficiently carefully and given the correct treatment could die from the effects of toxic anaesthetics – ether and chloroform.

Controversies surrounding the treatment of infected wounds were settling. Even Sir Almroth Wright was beginning to recognize that hypertonic saline solution was not the only answer to wound infection. The Carrel-Dakin technique was becoming the treatment of choice in most CCSs, creating enormous amounts of work for nurses who cleaned, sterilized and maintained the equipment, mixed the Dakin's solution to carefully calibrated measures, managed the treatment regimes, and gave pain relief and emotional care to traumatized patients through whose raw and tender wounds these chemicals burned their course.

At Mobile Surgical No. 1 rivalries between surgeons were taking a disturbing course. In a field near to the hospital, a so-called *auto-chir* had been set up. A new invention of the French Service de Santé des Armées, the *auto-chir* was a truly mobile hospital that could travel quickly and easily to where it was needed. The problem was that this particular unit did not seem to be needed at all. The northern sector of the Western Front was quiet. The following February it became even quieter, as men and materials were moved south to serve the desperate defence taking place at Verdun. Then, in July, the failed Allied assault on the River Somme had forced the French high command to draw more troops from its northern sector. The line in the northern part of the Ypres Salient was now being held by *les vieux* – the 'old men' who were seen as the best for the job, remaining stubbornly in their trenches no matter how bad the conditions became. The superbly equipped *auto-chir* was standing idle, and its staff were beginning to ask why a volunteer unit run by a woman who was a British citizen by marriage was, effectively, taking its place. Mary Borden offered two of her wards to the *auto-chir*'s highly qualified staff, allowing them to take charge of these specialized units, but this only seemed to add to the tension, by creating two cliques of French staff within the hospital.

On the British 'home front', at the Cambridge Hospital in Aldershot, towards the end of 1915, Catherine Black was caring for some of those who had survived the journey 'home'. She was in charge of a ward 'crowded to the last bed with acute medical cases' – men suffering from heart failure, nephritis, rheumatism and infectious diseases. One day, a young New Zealand surgeon named Harold Gillies walked onto her ward and declared that it would be the perfect place for his 'jaw cases'. Catherine soon found herself specializing in the care of men with severe facial injuries, and participating in some of the earliest plastic surgery. One of her greatest difficulties was in keeping her patients' wounds free of anaerobic infections. If gangrene took hold in a face wound it was likely to be fatal. Another challenge was the feeding of these patients, who were suffering extreme and demoralizing pain. Tomato soup, egg flip, beef tea and coffee formed the staple diet. Above all, Catherine and her nurses were challenged by the emotional trauma of men 'condemned to lie week after week smothered in dressings and bandages, unable to talk, unable to taste, unable to even sleep without opiates because of the agony of lacerated nerves, and all the while knowing themselves to be appallingly disfigured'.[20] But challenges like these were already changing their practice. Forced to extend the clinical skills they had learned in training and honed during years of experience, the nurses of the First World War were expanding their practice into realms they had never ventured into before, becoming experts in trauma-care and minor surgery.

By the end of 1915 most nurses knew that this war – already being referred to as the 'Great War' – would not end soon. It had already yielded far more casualties than they had ever thought possible, and they were beginning to realize that the two entrenched sides facing each other across no man's land were trapped in a self-reinforcing and increasingly destructive process.

*Chapter Four*

# Supporting the Salient

In the summer of 1915, CCSs on the Ypres front had struggled to cope with overwhelming numbers of wounded. Working in such crowded environments with huge numbers of casualties meant that nurses sometimes found themselves unable to give all the care they thought necessary. It was difficult to know which patients to prioritize: those who were dying and needed immediate comfort – a chance that would never recur – or those who, if treated immediately, might be saved. Such ethical dilemmas caused great stress – even anguish – for many nurses.

Ideally, the severest wounds should have been dressed and treated with antiseptics more than once a day. But that summer, many patients had to be put onto ambulance trains following only cursory treatment. Margaret Brander, on No. 12 Hospital Train, commented on the desperate condition of some of the wounded taken on at Remy Siding on 22 July:

> Some of the cases were so bad they should have never been put on. Suppurating appendices without any tubes, abdominal cases with middle line incisions sutured up with silkworm gut, no tubes, binder undone found one mass of pus and faecal matter. Appendix case died, and we thought a few more would too. Altogether it was a ghastly load.[1]

The relentless shelling of the Ypres Salient disrupted water drainage systems, creating huge craters and transforming the region into a muddy morass which turned to slush and ice as the temperature dropped in the late autumn. The winter that followed was a harsh one, the poor conditions in the trenches giving rise to a range of diseases, including the louse-borne 'trench fever', a life-threatening illness which debilitated large numbers of men. 'Trench foot', a condition caused by a failure of circulation to the feet resulting in tissue death and wound infection, was also rife. Many patients suffered such severe damage that amputation of the foot or leg was necessary to save their lives. CCSs in the region close to the villages of Proven and Westvleteren behind the Salient were kept busy with large numbers of sick men. Their staff soon gave them humorous names such as Mendinghem ('mending-em'), Dozinghem ('dosing-em') and Bandagehem ('bandaging-em') which soon became the names by which they were officially recognized.

Sisters with both the QA and the TFNS were moved frequently between base hospitals and casualty clearing stations, gaining experience and developing their skills in leadership. After a brief spell at No. 14 General Hospital in Wimereux in late October and November 1915, Kate Maxey was moved to the No. 1 British General Hospital at Étretat on 20 November. Here, she met and befriended QA Reserve Sister Edith Appleton. The two women probably worked together at the Étretat Casino; their billet was the grand Hotel Blanquet.[2]

On 17 October 1915 Kate Luard was posted to No. 6 British Casualty Clearing Station as sister-in-charge. She was to remain with the unit until 11 November the following year when it was located in Lillers. The CCS was housed in several different buildings: the main unit was close to the 'Grand Place' (Grand Square) in a school, while the separate officers' hospital was in an orphanage located up a 'cobbly slum'. During the battle of Loos, even though the CCS was 'taking turns' to receive casualties with two other units, one in Bethune and another in Choques, the hospital 'overflowed' with wounded, and many men had to be nursed in the town's backyards and in the square itself. Kate and another sister stayed up all night for several nights caring for helpless stretcher-cases. On 21 October, she described how

> I happened to go into the Infant School this morning, just in time to see a delirious boy, with a bad head-wound, with a large brain hernia tear off his dressings and throw a handful of his brains on to the floor. This is literally true, and he was talking all the time we re-dressed the hole in his head. Then we picked up the handful of brains, and the boy was quiet for a little while. He is very delirious and will not get better.[3]

A week later, she wrote of a young boy whose arm had been blown 'clean off'. 'Mustn't make a fuss about trifles,' he said to her. She and the commanding officer kept him in the hospital for as long as they could, to make sure that his stump had healed, before putting him on an ambulance train to Le Havre. But, on 13 November, she received a letter from a sister at the base hospital. The train had taken thirty hours to reach its destination, and soon after the 'boy's' arrival he had suffered a severe haemorrhage from his stump, losing so much blood that he died the next day.

British volunteer hospitals in the areas around Furnes and Dunkirk continued to struggle with large rushes of casualties. The British war correspondent, Philip Gibbs, was to describe the sights and sounds of the 'moribund ward' – the ward where dying patients were taken – at the unit served by Dr Munro's Flying Ambulance Corps in his book *The Soul of the War*. He had been asked to help remove the body of a dead man from one of the wards:

> It was a moral test almost greater than my strength of will to enter that large room where the wounded lay, and to approach a dead man through a lane of dying ... The smell of wet and muddy clothes, coagulated blood and gangrened limbs, of iodine and chloroform, sickness and sweat of agony, made a stench which struck one's senses with a foul blow. I used to try to close my nostrils to it, holding my breath lest I should vomit ... Bearded soldier faces lay here in tranquillity that told of coming death. They were dying before their time, conscious, some of them, that death was near, so that weak tears dropped upon their beards, and in their eyes was great fear and anguish ... The corpse I had to carry out lay pinned up in a sheet. The work had been very neatly done by the nurse, and she whispered to me as I stood to one side of the bed, with a friend on the other side: 'Be careful ... He might fall in half.'[4]

Elsie Knocker and Mairi Chisholm had established an advanced dressing station in the Cellar House at Pervyse on the Belgian front lines towards the end of 1915. Elsie began to develop her specialist work with patients suffering from physiological shock. Her theory that shocked patients must be stabilized before being moved to a base hospital later came to be recognized as part of accepted trauma practice.

The winter of 1915/16 was bitterly cold. At No. 20 British General Hospital, Dannes-Camiers, Margaret Brander was having a 'weary' time. Tented wards were heated only with braziers, and it was a winter of 'high winds, snow, rain and cold, tents being blown down, wet walls, everything damp'. Still, she had good relationships with her medical colleagues, and her VAD volunteers were 'little gems'. At Christmas she created something resembling a banquet for her patients, amplifying hospital rations with gifts of food sent from her home town of Huntly. An Aberdonian piper marched around the camp, playing in every ward. On returning from her last leave, she had brought flower seeds with her from Scotland and, in the spring, she and her orderlies planted these outside her tents. She was delighted when the orderlies won the first prize for 'best kept wards inside and outside'.

The winter of 1915/16 was a busy time for Mary Borden's Mobile Surgical No. 1, which took in large numbers of French casualties from the Western Front. Even though the most significant campaigns were taking place far to the south of Belgium, in Verdun and on the Somme, the northern part of the Western Front remained active, and the hospital was full of wounded, sick and dying men. From time to time, it also took in civilian casualties. An elderly Belgian civilian, possibly a refugee, who had been left destitute was brought in to the hospital to die. A small boy who had been hit by a shell fragment at his parents' estaminet near Ypres also died in one of the hospital's wards.

That winter was a particularly cold and uncomfortable one. The hospital was within sound of the front-line artillery of both sides, but the nurses had become used to the constant roar of the guns. Mary Borden even wrote of it as her 'lullaby', adding, 'If it stopped I could not sleep.' The nurses' quarters were wooden huts with leaking roofs and rattling windows, heated by iron stoves. On rainy nights their occupants pulled mackintosh sheets over their beds and put up umbrellas over their heads to protect them from drips. At times the high winds that swept across the Flanders plains lifted their roofs a few inches, and they cowered under their mackintoshes, waiting to see whether the flimsy coverings would be swept right off. This did occasionally happen. Agnes Warner had arrived in September 1915, and had very quickly become one of Mary Borden's most trusted nurses. Towards the end of the month, she wrote to her mother:

> We have a man in our ward who had a piece of shrapnel the size of an egg in his abdomen; they had to take out about half a yard of intestines, which had been torn to pieces. He was also shot through the shoulder, in the arm and leg. As we got him within two hours after he was wounded there was no infection, and having a clever surgeon he is getting along famously.[5]

By the end of 1915, the hospital had become a well-organized unit. Each ward specialized in a particular form of surgery. There was a hut for patients with head injuries, and one in which men's fractured limbs were packed into splints and put into traction to straighten them while they healed. There was a special ward for abdominal injuries, one for 'chests' and one in which men with gangrenous wounds were given the latest antiseptic treatments. There was also a *salle des grands blessés* (ward for the critically wounded) where the most seriously injured men were sent.

In December 1915, an American friend of Mary Borden arrived to take charge of the hospital's reception hut and linen room. Maud Mortimer was later to write a memoir of her time at Mobile Surgical No. 1. She remains a mysterious figure. Although her book *A Green Tent in Flanders* recounts her experiences in detail, all names appear to have been altered. She offers a vivid description of the hospital. Arriving in mid-December 1915, 'past a high old windmill and our own private sentinel, we turn sharply into the hospital enclosure, the tricolour fluttering over its gate'.[6] The hospital was, essentially, a muddy enclosure, surrounded by a high hawthorn hedge and containing, at the time of her arrival, sixteen green-painted wooden huts, about half of which were hospital wards. Inside these huts, each wall was lined with beds, with only a yard or two between the foot of one row and that of the other. Some sisters took pleasure and satisfaction in giving their wards a particular appearance. Maud commented on the 'show ward' of a fully qualified French nurse to whom she gave the pseudonym '*La Basine*'. All of the blankets in this ward were red, and patients were clothed in red nightgowns. Along with the wards, the hospital also had an operating theatre, to which was attached a small X-ray hut, a *salle d'attente* (reception room) to which new patients were brought to be triaged, a pharmacy, a wash house, a linen room, a mortuary, a chapel and sleeping huts and tents for staff. Between the huts were 'narrow walks or *trottoirs* which thread quite picturesquely back and forth across our muddy enclosure'. Towards the lower end of the site was a pond on and near which lived a small colony of ducks.

Maud drew pen-portraits of many of her colleagues at Mobile Surgical No. 1. The doctors were, in her opinion, highly expert, and much loved by their patients. The hospital was inspected by two generals each week – one a member of the Service de Santé des Armées, the other a military man, who also made frequent visits to award medals: the Croix de Guerre for valour and the Médaille Militaire (an award which also carried a pension) for particularly heroic actions in the field. Many of the orderlies were Catholic priests – some of them conscientious objectors, whose religious beliefs prohibited killing. Some of these men were excellent nurses, and all were willing to don a cassock over their soldiers' uniforms, at a moment's notice, throwing off the manner and appearance of military orderly to give last orders to a dying patient. Much of the washing, mending and cleaning was done by Belgian women, many of them refugees from the eastern part of the country now under German occupation. Of the French nurses, only one was fully qualified, but the others had already attained so much experience of war service that they ran their wards with great confidence. One had already been awarded the Croix de Guerre for valour, for remaining at her post when her hospital in Poperinge was shelled the previous autumn.

Maud was a close observer of human nature, writing vivid descriptions of her patients. In December 1915, Francois Coquelin was brought into the hospital. He had been born on 22 May 1878, and conscripted into the 76th Territorial Infantry Regiment in his mid-thirties.[7] A 'strange unsoldierlike looking man', Francois had been cooking dinner for his colonel in a rest area behind the lines, when a shell, landing at his feet, had exploded and blown them both off. En route to the hospital he had suffered a severe haemorrhage and he arrived in a seriously weakened state. He was, said Maud, 'black-haired and plump, with a perfectly round head and face in which were set perfectly round, black eyes edged with short, black lashes'. He was very talkative and his nurses grew fond of him. When he went to the operating theatre to have both legs amputated, Maud wrote of how 'we keep his bed warm and peer again and again through the windows, across the pond … to the closed door of the operating room'. But Coquelin never woke from the anaesthetic.

In December 1915, the French sector to the north of the Ypres Salient had undergone an interesting change. One of the so-called 'Bataillons d'Afrique' had been placed there. Its members were very different from *les vieux* who had held the line that autumn. The Bataillons d'Afrique were France's penal units. In them were placed the army's troublemakers, alongside convicted criminals who had completed their terms of imprisonment in civilian institutions and were now performing their national military service. Normally, the *bataillons* served in Algeria, Morocco and Tunisia but, in these desperate times, three units were brought back to help man the Western Front. Here – in the belief that they had nothing to lose – they were often used as storm troops or placed in difficult or demanding sections of the line. Their members had acquired the nicknames: '*Joyeux*' – the 'joyous ones' – and '*Zephyrs*' or 'light breezes'. But lightness of spirit was only one of their reputed characteristics. They were also known for their wild, uncontrolled behaviour, their vulgarity, and their criminal tendencies. In reality they posed serious disciplinary problems for hospital units. Just before Christmas convoys of *Joyeux* began to roll into Mobile Surgical No. 1. The *médecin chef* insisted that – regardless of their injuries – they must be separated from each other. As they were admitted and assessed at the hospital's reception hut, the *salle d'attente*, they were carefully divided between the hospital wards – no more than two or three in each ward at any one time.

Mary Borden wrote of a group of twenty *Joyeux* – also known as 'Apaches': they were 'all handsome young men – these assassins, thieves, pimps and traffickers in drugs – with sleek elastic limbs, smooth polished skins and beautiful bones ... they went over the top when the signal was given like wolf-hounds suddenly unleashed ... Their arrival had created something of a sensation in the hospital.' Of one, in particular, to whom she referred as the '*Enfant de Malheur*', she wrote a disturbing short story, which she would later decide to include in her book, *The Forbidden Zone*.

Mary was not the only nurse at Mobile Surgical No. 1 to write of her encounters with the *Joyeux*. Maud Mortimer was helping in the *salle d'attente* the day Alexis Boitel, a young member of the Bataillon d'Afrique, was brought in. Alexis had been born on 16 July 1892 and was only twenty-three.[8] This was the second time he had been wounded. Moved by his cheerful courage, Maud gave him the pseudonym 'Louis' and included his story in her own memoir. She described her first impression of him: he was 'as gay as a cricket', even though he had 'only stumps for toes on one foot, frost-bitted during last winter's campaign ... a bullet wound under his arm, a torn ear, a scalp wound, and ominously bandaged thighs'. He was admitted on 20 December, but lived only nine more days. By 26 December the hospital staff were referring to him as 'your boy'. She knew he was not going to survive:

> His desperate gaiety cuts to the quick. The General has decorated him ... The price, these young lives, and the dear, boyish recklessness of their inexperience, are distorting my values ... He has suffered agony and begins to lose hold on his blithe good humour. Something of himself has already gone on, and he is growing irritable under the terrible strain. Gangrene draws a denser and denser screen around him, slowly severing him from life.[9]

It was quite common for nurses of Mobile Surgical No. 1 to become attached to individual Joyeux. To them, these 'boys' seemed desperately young, and they were often orphans. For 24-year-old Adrien Le Roux, the care of Canadian nurse Agnes Warner 'came nearer than a true mother's than anything this boy had ever known'. Adrien had been born on 29 March 1891 in Evreux,[10] and had begun to earn his living as an acrobat as a small child. Later becoming a waiter in a café, he had been convicted of a crime – no one knew what – and had been 'poured' into the punishment battalion. His nurse saw only his fragile vulnerability and battled for weeks to save him, buying his favourite foods from the market at Beveren and spending extra time with him, coaxing him to eat and drink. But there was a much darker side to Adrien's story. Ellen La Motte was convinced that his surgeon was keeping him alive unnecessarily, in order to practise new, experimental treatments on his wounds. She was certain that not only the surgeon, but also the *directrice* – Mary Borden herself – was aware that this boy's life could not be saved – only prolonged. Maud Mortimer commented that his patience in the face of such treatment made him the 'pet of the hospital'. Eventually, when he was close to death, Mary Borden wrote to the general. Adrien's, she argued, was an act of bravery as impressive as any that had ever taken place on a battlefield: he deserved to be decorated with the Croix de Guerre and the Médaille Militaire. It took several days to convince the general that a member of the Bataillon d'Afrique deserved such honour, and the delay meant that he arrived too late, reaching the hospital with the two medals just twenty minutes after Adrien's death.

Maud's favourite time at the hospital was during the February of 1916, when she was put on night duty to assist her favourite nurse, the 'Night Hawk'. Like all characters in her book, the 'Night Hawk' is almost certainly modelled on a real person – probably Agnes Warner. Maud idolized her trained colleague, who was 'all disinterestedness, all devotion and self-forgetfulness'.[11] Moving from ward to ward, watching the ducks asleep on the pond under the moonlight, the two women would put down their flickering lanterns at the door of each hut they entered, so that the orderly on duty at reception could find them if any new patients arrived. Some nights were uneventful: 'the men snore loudly, there is hardly a groan.' On others, the nurses worked desperately hard, receiving new convoys of wounded, offering pain relief and comfort to damaged and dying men. During the day, they shared a sleeping tent, pitched outside the perimeter hedge. It was reached by climbing through a small hole in the hedge: '[We] balance ourselves on a slippery plank – laid precariously across the ditch, and which under our weight generally slips into the slime – then across a space thickly set with thistles.'[12]

Mary Borden often joined the night staff at midnight for a cup of cocoa, which was enjoyed in the sterilizing room next to the operating theatre. She stood at a table with her staff, pushing aside the drums containing sterile dressings for the next day's work. During busy times, after rushes of patients, they also had to push aside dirty bandages, and throw cloth-wrapped severed limbs onto the floor.

Some of the most tragic cases to be brought into Mobile Surgical No. 1 were the attempted suicides, who were to be operated upon and nursed back to health in order that they could be court-martialled and shot for desertion. To view such a desperate act as a form of criminal behaviour seemed entirely wrong-headed to most of the nurses, who preferred to see these men as cases of temporary insanity, but they were assured by the *médecin chef* that to pardon such men would result in 'epidemics' of suicide in the trenches. The attempted suicides must be healed so that they could be made examples of. Mary Borden wrote of one such case – a man who had shot himself through the roof of his mouth. She was convinced that his suicide attempt had little to do with the war but had, in fact, been caused by the loss of a lover: 'Rosa' was the only word he ever spoke, and it became the pseudonym she gave him. His aim had failed: a bullet was removed from just inside his skull, and his head was carefully dressed. Every night he tore off the carefully applied gauze and bandages, exposing his wound to infection, and every night his nurse replaced them with new, sterile padding. Then, one night, Mary asked the nurse to leave the dressings off – to allow infection to take hold, and 'Rosa' was allowed to die in his hospital bed.

Ellen La Motte's perspective on everything related to the war was rapidly becoming tainted by a profound disillusionment. She wrote a scathingly ironic short story about a patient who had attempted suicide in December 1915. This man too had 'fired a revolver up through the roof of his mouth'. But, she added, he had 'made a mess of it. The ball tore out his left eye and then lodged somewhere under his skull.' The man was violent and hostile: 'he shouted and screamed and threw himself from side to side', deliberately spitting blood onto Mary Borden's pristine white uniform. The identity of La Motte's patient is unknown, but the archives of the French Ministère de la Défense contain a death certificate for one Charles Auguste Edouard Fauvel of the Bataillon d'Afrique, who had been born on 27 June 1888 at Saint-Lô and had died on 17 December 1915 at Mobile Surgical No. 1. Cause of death had been noted as '*blessé par balle de revolver*' ('wounded by a revolver bullet').

It was the boredom of working at Mobile Surgical No. 1 that Ellen found most trying. For her, it was a 'stagnant place' where 'much ugliness [was] churned up'. Extraordinary and dramatic incidents such as the treatment of the suicide case provided brief moments of drama in an otherwise monotonous routine. Unlike her colleagues, Ellen found little to admire in her patients. One, whom she referred to as 'Marius', had yelled in rage at his stretcher-bearers and ambulance drivers – calling them 'dirty cowards'.

He had been lying in no man's land with a severe abdominal wound for ten hours before anyone came to rescue him. He was right in thinking that the delay would kill him: it had permitted anaerobic bacteria to find a stable foothold in his abdominal walls, to multiply and to infect vast swathes of tissue. By the time he reached the hospital, his abdomen was probably infected by a wide range of microorganizms, and major organ failure was inevitable. Ellen wrote of him:

> In a field hospital, some ten kilometres behind the lines, Marius lay dying. For three days he had been dying and it was disturbing to the other patients. The stench of his wounds filled the air, his curses filled the ward ... His was a filthy death. He died after three days' cursing and raving. Before he died, that end of the ward smelled foully, and his foul words, shouted at the top of his delirious voice, echoed foully. Everyone was glad when it was over.[13]

Ellen had been working at Mobile Surgical No. 1 since the autumn of 1915. She was still writing to her friend Amy Wesselhoeft, an American living in Germany, but the tone of her letters was anxious. She was reassuring her friend that there was no 'gulf' between them. She pointed out that she had 'started out being very prejudicial and partisan', but now, in a carefully worded letter of 28 February 1916, she implied that her eyes had been opened to the propaganda peddled by what she ironically referred to as 'those pellucid wells of truth, the newspapers'. She declared that 1915 had been a 'tremendous' year for her. She had been 'rather fortunate' with her writing. Even the conservative *Atlantic Monthly* magazine had published her articles. She added: 'I am now planning another book – this time *my* book, me. The last one was not me.'

Ellen wrote a poignant yet still sharply cynical short story, taking as her subject Mathurin Marie Rochard, a thirty-nine-year-old gardener who, before the war, had been in charge of the gardens of the château at St Brieuc close to the Brittany coast in Finisterre.[14] Rochard was no soldier. He was said to have done his work well and conscientiously, and to have pleased the wealthy woman who owned the château. He had been born in Plessala on 15 November 1876,[15] had married a woman much younger than himself, fathered a son and then been widowed. He died alone behind a red screen in the corner of *Salle 1* (Ward 1) at Mobile Surgical No. 1 on 27 January 1916. It was his aloneness that angered Ellen the most. But it was only one of the many things about the hospital and the war itself that enraged her.

The short story Ellen went on to write placed the pride of the hospital medical staff, with their expert knowledge of infection and their 'beautiful, expensive' X-ray machinery', alongside the almost primeval suffering of their patient. It was not just that they were unable to relieve Rochard's agony, they actually seemed to have no regard for it. The medical students of the 'surgical school' at the hospital had found Rochard an 'interesting case', because gas gangrene had developed so quickly. In the theatre, they crowded around his anaesthetized body and pressed the flesh above his thigh wound, feeling the crackling sensation of the gas bubbles produced by thriving and multiplying anaerobic bacteria beneath. This was no ordinary wound: Mathurin Rochard's 'thigh, from knee to buttock, was torn out by a piece of German shell', and the wound extended into and through the hip joint, making amputation impossible. Digging the dead tissue from its base, the surgeon filled the yawning gap that remained with pads of gauze soaked in carbolic acid – a highly corrosive material. The acid burned into the remaining, healthy tissue of Rochard's thigh and buttock, and he woke from the anaesthetic in agony. His nurse spent much of the night turning him from side to side – knowing that there was no position in which he could find relief from his pain, yet wanting to offer him the emotional reassurance that she was there to help him. She called for the *médecin chef*, who instructed her to give Rochard morphine 'as often as she thought best', as well as injections of strychnine to keep his heart pumping. Ellen's writing deliberately masks any sense of who this nurse was – whether she herself, or a colleague. In addition to the thigh wound that was going to kill him, Rochard also had 'a full inch of German shell' inside his skull, which was distorting his sense of reality. Between his pain and his brain damage, Rochard was conscious only of his own suffering, crying out that his wounds burned. Ellen's verdict was that 'the science of healing stood baffled before the science of destroying'.

Rochard had been a hero – no one was quite sure exactly what he had done, but the day after his operation the general visited the ward and pinned a Médaille Militaire to the wall above his bed. Rochard was one of the few patients who seemed to evoke real pity in Ellen – a pity that she was willing to express in her otherwise almost entirely cynical and emotionless text:

> Little Rochard! Little man, gardener by trade, aged thirty-nine, widower, with one child! The piece of shell in his skull had made one eye blind. There had been a haemorrhage into the eyeball, which was all red and sunken, and the eyelid would not close over it, so the red eye stared and stared into space. And the other eye drooped and

drooped, and the white showed, and the eyelid drooped till nothing but the white showed, and that showed that he was dying.[16]

On the night of 26 January, the night nurse spent much of her time with Rochard, recognizing that he was likely to die soon. In the morning, she asked the day sister to allow her to remain with him, but the sister sent her to her tent to sleep – she would be needed the next night. Later that day, the sister instructed an orderly to remain with Rochard while she herself went for lunch. Returning 'after a short time', she 'hurried behind the flamboyant, red, cheerful screens that shut him off from the rest of the ward' only to find that Rochard was dead. The two ward orderlies were sitting at the other end of the ward, playing cards and drinking wine.

Ellen seems to have felt compelled to write about the starkness of Rochard's loneliness. But another member of Mobile Surgical No. 1 had also noticed him. Maud Mortimer devoted one of her chapters to a man to whom she gave the pseudonym 'Mathurin Godard'. Her description gives him an attractiveness that belies his almost-monstrous appearance in Ellen's text:

> He has a clean-cut face, rather wide than long, small, delicate features, and a fine skin, its whiteness pointed by the scarlet semi-circle of a half-closed, bloodshot eye. He is wounded in the head, and in the thigh too high up for amputation, and gas gangrene has set in. At first he is restless and complaining, but he allows himself to be soothed.[17]

In Maud's story, 'Godard' is kind and thoughtful to his nurses, and recovers sufficiently to dictate a letter home to his family:

> Dear Uncle and Aunt: I am here, wounded, though my wounds are much less serious than I at first feared. I am drinking orange juice as I write this by the hand of a nurse who is very good to me. Tell René his father has won the Croix de Guerre and the Médaille Militaire – he may be proud of him when he grows up. As to business matters, do not worry. After a year without me, you will know better what to do than I. Your affectionate nephew, Mathurin Godard.[18]

'The hospital is shocked by this man's death,' wrote Maud, emphasizing the fact that no one was indifferent to his suffering. In her version of his story, his aloneness was a matter more of misfortune than of negligence. Mathurin's aunt travelled from Brittany to see him, but arrived just a few hours after his death. She 'cried bitterly'. She was younger than 'Godard' himself, and was, clearly, deeply fond of him, although Maud shades her reaction to his death with a sense that she might also have been deeply dismayed at having been left with the responsibility of having to care for Mathurin's son:

> 'You tell me he was decorated and a hero? He certainly had character … He was honest, it is true, and never spared himself … René is with us now. He is a delicate little chap and needs care. One hundred francs a year pension goes with the Médaille, is that not so? Ah, only fifty when the decorated one dies? Only fifty francs. Well, even so you need not be afraid. René shall never want for a home, and I will tell him you say his father died a hero. Think of it, Mathurin a hero!'[19]

In March 1916, a report was compiled on the work of the hospital. 'We have only lost one man in every thirteen and – since, for the most part, only the worst cases are brought to us – the hospital may be proud of its record', commented Maud.[20] A few days later, she received a wire from her family in the USA, asking her to return home. On 22 March, just prior to her departure, Mary Borden gave her permission to take a trip to Poperinge with her great friend, Agnes Warner. Much of their time was spent seeking news of Agnes's nephew, Bayard Coster, who was serving with a Canadian regiment, somewhere in the Ypres region. Poperinge was desolate: 'There is a crushing sameness in destruction,' Maud commented. 'Most window spaces are boarded up, others are pasted over with Union Jack stars of paper to hold them firm through future shocks … the church is locked … the square and market place look deserted.' Yet the troops drilling in the square, waiting their turn to go to the front lines, were full of life – 'so rosy and so young'. Maud was no longer in any doubt about the immorality of war, declaring that 'the mutilated bodies and the lives of innumerable scapegoats are the highway along which we still irresponsibly chalk up a score'.[21]

In Bernay, a small French town well to the east of Paris, British nurse Annie Hanning was running 27th Temporary Hospital, as its head nurse, or *infirmière-major*. Annie had travelled to the continent with one of the first British volunteer units in August 1914. In Belgium, she had been captured by the Germans, and returned to Britain via Denmark – probably on the same train as Violetta Thurstan. For her work in Brussels, she had been awarded the Princess Marie José Medal for services to the Belgian nation. In 1915, anxious to return to the 'war effort', she had joined the French Flag Nursing Corps, and Bernay had been her first posting. In the late spring of 1916, she was redeployed to Mobile Surgical No. 1, becoming one of Mary Borden's most loyal and capable ward sisters. She arrived soon after Maud Mortimer's departure. Later that year, Canadian nurse Madeleine Jaffray also joined the unit. She and colleagues Helen McMurrich and Margaret McIntyre had spent several months at a huge French base hospital at Talence in the Gironde before being transferred to Belgium.

On a bright, cold July morning at the other side of the world, Hilda Loxton was boarding the hospital ship *Kanowna* – one of twenty-one fully trained professional nurses who had volunteered to serve France under the flag of the Australian Red Cross. Hilda had been born on 24 December 1879 and was living in Becroft, a suburb of Sydney, when war was declared. Unable to obtain a posting with the Australian Army Nursing Service, she decided that the Red Cross service was likely to provide the most direct route to the front lines. She was right: within a year of her departure, she would be at Mobile Surgical No. 1, within ten miles of the reserve trenches on one of the most dangerous parts of the Western Front.

During the six-week journey which took them to Southampton, via Suez, Cairo, Alexandria and Malta, the Australian Red Cross 'Bluebirds' earned the respect of their ship's captain, Lieutenant Colonel A. B. Brockway, who wrote to them on 22 August, two days before their arrival, declaring that 'for many years to come Australian women will be judged by you'.

Submarine activity in the English Channel kept the Australian nurses in London for over two weeks, during which time they were treated by the Vicomtesse de la Panouse, President of the French Flag Nursing Corps, to afternoon teas, visits to famous London sights and trips to the theatre. Soon, though, their work was to begin in earnest, as they were posted to an infectious diseases hospital at Palvas-les-Flots, a small fishing village on France's Mediterranean coast. Hilda, a keen diarist, made a note on arrival that this seemed to be 'a very small dirty looking little place'. Its first appearances did not deceive. The trained nurses found it difficult to create safe and sanitary environments within their wards. One nurse was put on night duty in charge of three floors with only a candle for light. Instruments were sterilized in a saucepan on a small stove, and the hospital's French orderlies – known as *infermièrs* – had almost no understanding of the need for cleanliness nor, it seemed, any desire to acquire it.

On 1 July, 1916, the 'big push' that was to be known as the battle of the Somme had begun. A joint British-French effort, it produced tens of thousands of casualties from both nations. That summer Mary Borden – always eager to be working in the 'hottest' part of the line – left Belgium to establish a new hospital at Bray-sur-Somme, supporting the French arm of the offensive. Agnes Warner was left in charge of Mobile Surgical No. 1.

In July, 1916, Ellen La Motte also left Belgium – for good. She landed in New York on 12 July, and took her book to the publisher, Putnam's, the next day. Within ten days, her editor had accepted her manuscript, and was planning to publish in September. But Ellen would not be in the USA to see the book's launch. She was already making preparations for a 'round the world' trip with close friend, Emily Chadbourne. They departed San Francisco for China on 26 August. They would find themselves so preoccupied by the exploitation of colonial peoples in the Far East that they would remain there for two years, during which time Ellen was to become a vigorous campaigner against the opium trade. As she prepared to embark for China, leaving both Europe and the USA far behind her, Ellen seemed, at last, to have found fulfilment. In a final letter to her old friend, Amy, who was still living in Germany, she wrote:

> I hope you will like it, Amy. You will like the style, I hope, and also see that in a measure I am finding myself, but as you say, I hope to do better ... Do you remember those long talks we used to have, about my finding myself etc? Well a good part of your predictions have come true. I seem to have had a complete change of ideas and aspirations since breaking off my rather strenuous career three years ago ... I want to tell you that ... I have never forgotten you ... and so have held fast to a faith due to my personal experience, and it has done everything for me. With such lots of love, dear, I am as ever, your same old Ellen.[22]

When Ellen's book appeared it caused a sensation. It was immediately suppressed by the official censor in Britain, but in the USA it gained an interested readership. Some were already arguing that their nation should side with the Allies and declare war on Germany – but a significant proportion of U.S. citizens were German immigrants, and an even larger proportion could see no reason why their nation should engage in what was seen as a purely European conflict. Nevertheless, by April 1916, a number of influential U.S. physicians were calling upon their medical colleagues to begin to prepare for war. George Crile, prestigious professor of surgery at Western Reserve University in Cleveland, Ohio, was among the most prominent of these. He proposed that the American Red Cross should support large hospitals in creating their own military units; these would travel to Europe where they would care for U.S. soldiers in the event of an American declaration of war.

That spring, Margaret Dunlop returned from her leave of absence at the American Ambulance in Neuilly, and resumed her supervision of the nursing services at Philadelphia's Pennsylvania Hospital. In November 1915, her senior medical colleague, Richard Harte, had travelled to Neuilly to observe the latest techniques of war surgery for himself. He too returned, in 1916, and was elected chairman of the Red Cross Committee in Philadelphia. He set to work, collaborating closely with the Pennsylvania Committee for National Preparedness and the Emergency Aid Committee to create a war-ready unit at the Pennsylvania Hospital. Already impressed with Margaret Dunlop's experience and abilities, he recommended that she be appointed chief nurse for the new unit.

Margaret was already closely involved with the work of the Head of the Red Cross Nursing Department, Jane Delano, who was creating a U.S. Army Reserve Corps. The official U.S. Army Nurse Corps had been established in 1901, but remained a small unit. The creation of its Reserve had been proceeding quietly for some years. In Philadelphia, Margaret had already selected and enrolled a number of current and former Pennsylvania Hospital nurses. Richard Harte was impressed with her choices, declaring later that these were 'young women of matured judgement and experience, many of whom were holding positions of great responsibility in other hospitals outside of Philadelphia', adding, 'It can readily be seen how fortunate we were in securing such an earnest, skilful and conscientious group of women, keenly alive to their work and to the interest and welfare of the patients who might be entrusted to their care.'[23]

Thirty-two-year-old Helen Fairchild was one of the first to respond to the call for 'Reserve Nurses'. She was working as a ward nurse at the Pennsylvania Hospital, travelling home to Griffey Farm on occasional leave, and spending much of her free time writing letters to her parents and her six siblings. She was particularly fond of her brother, Ned, who was twenty-five, and her sister, Christine who, at the age of fourteen, was writing a lot of 'crazy stuff' in her letters.[24]

Alongside these trained professional women was a remarkable group of orderlies – known as 'corpsmen'. Many were students at the University of Pennsylvania or at the Haverford College. Typically, they were young, enthusiastic and intelligent. They worked well with their slightly older female colleagues, the trained professional nurses for whom they clearly had great respect. Alongside them was a smaller group of older men, who were anxious to play a part in the war, and worried that they would be too old to be accepted into combatant units. Helen Fairchild was later to write home to her mother that she would 'not want to work with a finer bunch' adding, 'Gee, half of our enlisted men are millionaires or millionaires' sons'.[25]

By 1916, the large Belgian Red Cross Hospital in the 'Hôtel Océan' at La Panne was caring for thousands of patients. Its nursing staff was made up of fully trained Belgian and British nurses. Working alongside them were large numbers of British VADs, among them two cousins from Chester, Alison and Dorothea Macfie, who had been taken on earlier that year.

On 11 May 1916, Kate Luard, working with No. 6 CCS was transferred to Barlin, about twelve miles to the south-east. Here, they were close to the front lines. On 14 May an aerial bombardment of the village of Barlin brought four civilians into the hospital; two, a mother and step-daughter, died in the anaesthetic room before they could be treated. The remaining two, an elderly man with a piece of fractured bone protruding from his leg and a boy of nine with a piece of shrapnel in his head, were operated on and made comfortable in the wards. Wounded men from attacks on nearby Vimy Ridge poured into the hospital. Many had been lying for hours in no man's land before being rescued by stretcher-bearers. On 17 June, Kate wrote home to her family:

> I never told you about Bob, the very badly wounded boy from Yorkshire. He has a weary painful existence, but he dictated to me this letter to his mother: 'Dear Mother – This is to tell you I am doing grand – the wound in my side is healing fine [It isn't; it is a colostomy and also has a broken rib sticking out of it]. You are well looked after here – it is as good as being at home – bar kin – You live on the best of everything. I had chicken and jelly for dinner to-day. And there is a gramophone and the best of company. Tell Dad and Daisy not to worry about me at all. I hope I shall soon be with you all. Your loving son, Bob.' I said, 'Well, you've told her all the nice things, Bob, what about all the nasty things?' He looked me deliberately in the face and said, 'And what are the nasty things, Sister?' And he has very bad nights, a racking cough from the rib, a helpless right arm lying on a cushion, a septic wound through his cheek which gives him a horrible taste in his mouth, and the broken rib and the colostomy.[26]

About two weeks later, on 2 July, Kate wrote that 'poor Bob who asked me "And what are the bad things?" was 'going steadily downhill'. A day later, she brought his story to a close: 'He died to-day suddenly clutching my hand and saying, "Is it all right? Don't leave me."'[27]

In the Barlin Communal Cemetery Extension there is a white headstone standing among 1,092 others. The name R. W. Hunt is etched onto its surface. The young man lying beneath it was, in life, the son of Mr. and Mrs W. H. Hunt of 10, Louisa Street, Ormesby, and a private with the 13th Battalion of the Durham Light Infantry. He died on 3 July 1916 at the age of 23, clutching the hand of his nurse. After the war, his widow, M. H. Hunt, paid the Commonwealth War Graves Commission to have the following inscription etched onto his memorial stone: 'Only those who have loved and lost can understand war's bitter cost.' Yet the nurses who held the hands of shattered and dying men like Bob also understood. The apparently matter-of-fact tone of Kate Luard's letters home to her family overlays a counter-current of deep emotion. On 3 July, the day of Bob's death, she wrote:

> We have that ward full of abdominals in all stages, recovering, hovering, and going to die or dying. It is sometimes rather overwhelming to all our nerves. The Sister (Miss. D) who runs it is made of real gold of a quite rare kind, and was made especially for it, but it will wear her out in time.[28]

Towards the end of 1916, Kate was appointed head nurse of British Casualty Clearing Station No. 32, which was soon to be relocated to Brandhoek, a hamlet of Vlamertinghe, very close to Ypres and within three miles of the reserve trenches of the Salient.

The first Australian and New Zealand nurses arrived on the Western Front from the Eastern Mediterranean in the early summer of 1916. Nurses of the 1st and 2nd Australian General Hospitals landed at Marseilles and travelled by train directly to general hospitals in northern France. After serving at several stationary hospitals in Egypt and Palestine, May Tilton had been transferred to England, working in Brighton and Birmingham before being posted to France, where she served, for a time, with the 4th British General Hospital in Camiers. New Zealand nurse Ida Willis had arrived in the Eastern Mediterranean as head nurse of the hospital ship *Maheno* in the summer of 1915, and had spent several months in an Egyptian base hospital caring for wounded men returning from the disastrous Gallipoli campaign. In 1916 she and a large number of colleagues were moved to France where they were posted with the No. 1 New Zealand Stationary Hospital, at first near Amiens and then at Hazebrouck.

In June 1916, the French evacuation hospital at Remy Siding was transferred to Dunkirk; at around the same time two Canadian CCSs joined the British at Remy, providing thousands of beds for the rapid treatment and evacuation of the wounded from the Ypres Salient. British nurse Kate Maxey – who had been promoted to sister on 5 July 1916 – was once more with No. 58 British CCS in Lillers. She was mentioned in despatches for 'gallant and distinguished service in the field' on 25 November.

The year 1916 was a relatively quiet one behind the Ypres Salient. The great campaigns of that year took place at Verdun and the Somme. Yet CCSs in the region were busy with men suffering both from wounding and from the catastrophic illnesses associated with trench life. Ambulance trains frequently carried full loads down the line to bases and, in general hospitals, understaffed wards were at times full of patients who, in peacetime, would have been seen as deserving one-to-one nursing care. As 1916 drew to a close, workloads were increasing as yet another bitterly cold winter brought still-significant numbers of cases of wounding, along with thousands of cases of severe illnesses such as typhus, diphtheria and influenza into the lines of evacuation.

## Chapter Five

# Prelude to the 'Big Push'

A round the margins of the Ypres Salient, German forces continued to dominate the high ground: the Messines and Wytschaete Ridges in the south and the lower Pilckem Ridge and Gheluvelt Plateau further north. But, as early as July 1915, Sir Herbert Plumer, commander of the British Second Army, had begun to make plans for the demolition of these strongpoints. Tunnelling companies of the Royal Engineers had been ordered to dig deep passageways from just behind their own lines right under no man's land, towards positions beneath German fortifications on Messines and Wytschaete. The plan was to pack large quantities of the highly volatile explosive ammonal into chambers at the ends of these tunnels, which, when detonated, would destroy the German strongholds on the crest of the ridge. By the beginning of 1917 the tunnels were almost beneath the German front lines, and British commanders were anxious that they should be used before they were discovered.

Plumer was aware of how risky an attempted breakthrough in the Ypres Salient would be: when Haig sought his advice on an assault in the North, he counselled caution, recommending that the strongpoints of Messines and Wytschaete must be taken and carefully consolidated before any attempts were made to take control of the rest of the Salient. Haig was sceptical, preferring to plan for an all-out assault across the Ypres Salient, but even the most tentative plans for Ypres had to be put on hold by political developments of spring 1917.

David Lloyd George had taken over as British prime minister in December 1916. He was suspicious of Haig's willingness to sacrifice men to a war of attrition, and wanted to turn the focus of the Allied campaign further south. He supported a plan devised by the new French commander, General Robert Nivelle, for an offensive at the Chemin des Dames in the Aisne Department of France. Haig was appalled, convinced that his own plan was more strategically sound. Following lengthy – and at times acrimonious – negotiations, he was able to forge an agreement with the British government that, should the Nivelle Offensive fail, the Ypres campaign would be permitted to go ahead. He continued to plan – and Plumer's engineers continued to dig.

January 1917 was a bitterly cold month. In the CCSs behind the Ypres Salient water froze solid in bowls, patients were wrapped tightly in blankets with hot water bottles at their feet, and vials of drugs were carefully warmed before being injected. All winter, convoys of patients with trench foot had been brought in and amputations of toes, feet and legs had proceeded at an alarming rate. The experience of the previous winter had alerted officers to the dangers of this gruesome condition: failed circulation and fungal infections destroyed skin, exposing the underlying tissues to gangrene and other bacterial infections. Men on duty in the front lines had been issued with whale oil to rub onto their feet to insulate the skin and protect the circulation. Nevertheless, the freezing conditions in the front lines, where soldiers slept night after night curled up for protection in small holes cut into the sides of their trenches, never removing their socks or shoes or the puttees that were tightly wrapped around their ankles and lower legs, meant that trench foot was rife. So, too, was trench fever, a debilitating and life-threatening disease, transmitted by the lice that infested men's uniforms. Working closely as they did with their verminous patients, nurses could not prevent their own clothes from becoming infested, and many wrote in their diaries of spending long evenings searching the seams of their dresses and aprons for lice. In such circumstances, the frequent washing of uniforms – preferably in very hot water – was highly desirable and Belgian laundresses in the localities of CCSs were kept busy.

Soldiers were often brought into CCSs in states of near-collapse simply from the hardship of their lives in the front lines. Just marching into their forward positions carrying all of their kit on their backs was exhausting. Depending on his intended role in the planned assault, a man could be carrying over 100 pounds of kit, including rifle and bayonet, grenades, pouches and bandoliers of ammunition, food rations, water bottles, waterproof sheeting, gas mask, entrenching tool and steel helmet. Men with previously undiscovered diseases – heart valves damaged by childhood infections, or undiagnosed cases of tuberculosis – soon collapsed and had to be taken to hospital. 'Disordered action of the heart' rapidly became a recognized diagnosis. These patients suffered severe breathlessness, debilitation and heart palpitations. In addition to being anxious about their conditions they were also ashamed at their 'failure' to fight.

On 17 January, Australian 'Bluebirds' Hilda Loxton and Minnie Hough left their infectious diseases hospital in Palvas on the Mediterranean, and travelled north to a bitterly cold Paris. Here, it took a week of visiting various government offices and police departments before they could get their papers

in order for a journey to the *zone interdit* – the forbidden zone close to the
front lines in Belgium. Arriving in Dunkirk at 3.30 a.m. on the 27th, they
found themselves 'stranded at the station, no vehicles, didn't know where to
go, pitch black'. The terseness of Hilda's diary gives a sense of the desolation
she and Minnie felt as they stood on the deserted and blacked-out platform.
Eventually, they found a hotel but there were no beds, and they had to sit
in the smoke room overnight. 'Chilled to the bone' and with no food, Hilda
was relieved to find that her companion had taken the precaution of buying
a spirit lamp and a bottle of brandy before setting out from Palvas.

At 2 p.m., twelve hours after their arrival in Dunkirk, the nurses were picked
up by Agnes Warner and an Australian colleague, Sister Wallace, and were taken
by ambulance the twenty miles to Mobile Surgical No. 1. Beveren was lying
under a blanket of snow, beneath slate-grey clouds and Hilda felt 'very cold and
hungry, but very glad to be with friends and kind people'. She declared Agnes
Warner to be 'very sweet, most kind and thoughtful', adding that her *directrice*
had said that she 'looked very sick and very unhappy and depressed'.[1]

Life at Mobile Surgical was one of contrasts. The cold was 'intense';
'everything [was] frozen, flowers in vase, ink in fountain pen' – the Ijzer canal
itself was a solid channel of ice. When the nurses went to bed they took off
their clothes, only to put on 'a good many more'. But they had two Belgian
maids, who brought them hot water twice a day and kept the stove in their
tiny cubicle alight. The snow was falling hard, the Belgian countryside was
a 'perfect picture' and the hospital seemed alive and welcoming. Madeleine
Jaffray – one of the Canadian nurses at Mobile Surgical No. 1, was later to
write of conditions in French field hospitals:

> When we went to France, everything connected with war hospitals
> and nursing was quite different from what it is at present. We were
> pioneers in the field … Sometimes at night we were almost frozen
> to the marrow. The patients in the wards were kept fairly warm
> by the use of every available sheet and blanket, but the nurses on
> duty lived and worked through the coldest of weather, unprotected
> except for what shelter was afforded by the room. I have seen nurses
> come to the breakfast table actually blue with the cold, their fingers
> stiff and aching. Some of them wore their mittens while eating. My
> own feet became so cold at times I could hardly stand.[2]

At Mobile Surgical No. 1, nurses were relieved to discover that their
sleeping huts had small stoves – although they soon also discovered that fuel

was scarce. The unit's 'Directress', Mary Borden Turner, had her own 'villa' – a rather grand name for a square wooden hut close to the centre of the compound. Hilda Loxton declared Mary to be 'rather fascinating and a very clever little woman, had written books and done many other clever things, and seemed to be able to do anything she wanted with ease'. She was no longer running the hospital, but when the Australian nurses had been staying in Paris, she had invited them to a 'very French' lunch, and she made frequent visits to the hospital in her 'little grey motor car with red cross on it'. Agnes Warner was now in charge of the nursing services at the hospital, but its administration was in the hands of society lady Elizabeth Craven, one of Mary Borden's friends.

A month later the entire hospital was dismantled, piece by piece and transferred by train to Oost-hoek, near Adinkerke, well north of Beveren and much closer to the front lines. Hilda commented on how interesting it was 'to see how quickly [the hospital was] taken to pieces'. On 4 March, she and Minnie were taken – as members of a larger group of professional nurses, to stay at the Hôtel Océan, Malo-les-Bains, near Dunkirk, until their new hospital was ready. They were a remarkably international group: Hilda and Minnie, along with Sisters Wallace and Crozier, were from Australia; Sisters Annie Hanning and Mabel Jones, and Sisters Coppice and Robinson, were British; and Sister Madeleine Jaffray was Canadian. While at Malo-les-Bains, they visited La Panne, the residence of the Belgian king and queen and the location of the largest and most significant Belgian base hospital: L'Hôpital de l'Océan.

On 13 March, they were taken to their new hospital, where they found 'everything in hopeless muddle, rain, cold, and mud inches deep … We lived in gumboots, sou-westers, short skirts and blue aprons,' commented Hilda. Her diary entry for the next day summarized the conditions in their compound: 'mud, mud, mud'.[3] But she added that she and Minnie were sharing a cubicle and had 'good and comfy' beds. The hospital was in flat countryside, about six miles behind the Belgian reserve trenches; it was only fifteen kilometres from Nieuwpoort, with Furnes and La Panne close by and Diksmuide on the horizon. The nearest village was Adinkerke, and the nurses were 'as near if not nearer than any other womenfolk' to the front lines of the war. There was a railhead behind them, an aerodrome nearby and anti-aircraft gun emplacements on all sides. For the first few days, they were frequently scolded by their *directrice* for running out into their compound to gaze as aeroplanes of all nations – British, French and German – passed overhead.

Hilda was in charge of 'Salle Larry'. After so much experience of indifferent orderlies, she was delighted to find that she was working with an excellent sergeant: 'Claude' - and 'two good infirmiers'. Claude had been a priest in civilian life; he was a 'fine, big, strong young man'. Hilda took two pictures of him with her new 'Brownie No. 2 camera', one in his sergeant's uniform and one in his priest's cassock. Claude was not unusual: many of the senior orderlies at Mobile Surgical No. 1 were priests. When they were caring for patients, their aim was to preserve life; but when it became clear that a man was close to death, they hastily pulled on their cassocks over their military uniforms, and gave the holy sacrament. The majority of the hospital's patients were Catholics, and priest-orderlies saw it as part of their duty to offer both nursing care and religious solace. Hilda regarded herself as very lucky: Claude was one of the best orderlies in the hospital: he was able to lift men to wash and care for them, and could move them easily from side to side to prevent pressure sores. He was devoted not only to his patients but also to Hilda – never going away on leave without sending her a postcard.

Working alongside nurses and orderlies were several experienced surgeons, among them 'Monsieur Ranvier' (probably the well-known Parisian anatomy professor Louis-Antoine Ranvier), who was quite elderly and was known to be 'devotion and kindness itself', and Monsieur de Parthenay, who was younger, 'very good looking and … much liked by the Sisters'.

The sisters soon became acquainted with many of the ambulance drivers who brought convoys of wounded to the hospital. Among them were members of Hector Munro's Flying Ambulance Corps which was still operating around the Furnes area; one of its drivers, Lady Dorothie Fielding, became a close friend of the Australian nurses. The Quaker Ambulance Unit also brought many casualties to the hospital. Hilda commented that many of the ambulance drivers were young women, while others were 'delicate men', many of them too old for active service; one was an amputee.

By 16 March, Hilda's ward was 'ship shape' and the weather was brighter. But the ominous noise of German aircraft flying over the hospital seemed a portent of trouble to come. Hilda and Minnie had become close friends, but Hilda was chagrined to discover that their hospital colleages seemed to see them very differently:

Everyone here thinks Minnie is very young, and that I am pretty old, due to my grey hair and sedate manner; they never for one moment suspect that there are so few years between our ages; these are some of the names given to Minnie by patients and Sisters:

'Girlie', 'Kiddie', 'Babyface', 'Petite Soeur' and 'Angel Face'. They
call me 'Madame'.[4]

On 25 March, Hilda received her first *'grand blessé'* – or 'dangerously injured'
patient. His name was Picaret, and he was brought into the hospital with a
serious head injury, a shattered left arm and extensive flesh wounds of the
shoulder, neck and chest. He was taken almost immediately to the operating
theatre, where his arm was amputated just above the elbow, and his skull was
trephined – a process involving the drilling of two small holes in the bone to
release clots of blood that were creating swelling and pressure. Several hours
later, he was brought to 'Salle Larry' still unconscious from the anaesthetic.
He had 'a tiny fragment of éclat [shell fragment] in his brain', and his doctor
was warning Hilda that he would not survive. She wrote later in her diary of
the struggle to save Picaret:

> The second night after he was [brought in] he nearly died from
> shock although unconscious; [the night staff] had great difficulty in
> keeping him in bed. The German bombing planes were over, as they
> came every night, and the noise of the guns, machines and bombs
> nearly drove him frantic; they thought he would die that night, but
> he survived … Sergeant Claude [and I] were both very interested
> in Picaret and gave him both our attention. He was the most serious
> case we had at that time. When doing well after he had been with
> us a short time he suddenly developed 'Pleurisy' and because very
> depressed was sure he was going to die, but ultimately he recovered
> completely. In peacetime he was by trade a baker; he often worried
> a great deal about his wife and little girl (the latter he had never
> seen) who were both shut up in 'Lille' [behind enemy lines]. He
> finally left us to go to a hospital in Paris to be fitted with an artificial
> arm. I gave him the £5 [my Aunt] had given me to help buy him a
> better limb and he was very grateful. He wrote to me several times
> after he was made overseer in an Ammunition Factory.[5]

Minnie too received her first *grand blessé* in late March – a man named
Menar with enormous abdominal and back wounds, who was given saline
injections and stimulants for ten days to keep him alive. Because of damage
to his gut, he was not allowed to eat or drink. As he regained consciousness
it became apparent that, even with such terrible and painful wounds, he
was able to find humour in life. He called his saline injections 'beefsteak'

and accepted his treatments – ranging from painful injections to frequent reparative operations and the use of vomit-inducing chloroform as an anaesthetic – with great fortitude. He soon became the 'pet of the hospital'. When he was discharged, Agnes Warner bought him a gold-headed walking stick.

From March onwards, the hospital received large numbers of *grands blessés*. Some haemorrhaged uncontrollably and died on the operating table; others, tragically, lived for weeks suffering great pain before dying eventually. One of Minnie's patients had multiple wounds:

> Shrapnel entered his chest and lodged in abdominal cavity; a heavy piece good inch square. His condition was very grave; young boy only 20 years old, only child. He did not want to live; both parents dead. He eventually developed a large faecal fistula; shocking dressing. Poor lad lived 3 weeks and then died of double pneumonia.

Hilda added that 'Minnie carried a great reputation from Mr Ranvier and the Medecin Chef over this case; it was the first time either of them had seen a trained nurse's work'.[6] She was placed in charge of the 'Salle Edith Cavell' for the most seriously ill cases. One of her patients, Briène, a 'dear little French boy, 19 years of age' lived for ten days in 'absolute agony'. A shell had blown away all of the flesh from one side of his lower back and from one thigh. His dressing had to be changed several times a day, a procedure which he accepted with patience and endurance. But he could not be saved.

At L'Hôpital de l'Ocean, just behind the beach at La Panne, the role of matron had been taken up by British nurse, Violetta Thurstan. For Violetta, the first three years of the war had been a catalogue of adventures, and her memoir, *Field Hospital and Flying Column*, reads almost like a novel.[7] After having been taken prisoner in Belgium and deported by her German captors to neutral Denmark, Violetta had offered her services as a highly qualified nurse to the Russian Red Cross, and had travelled from Denmark to Petrograd in Tsarist Russia. Serving on the Eastern Front, first at a base hospital in Warsaw and then with a so-called *letuchka* or 'flying column' moving rapidly ahead of the Russian retreat, she had experienced several brushes with danger before her luck finally ran out. In January 1915 she was wounded in the leg by shrapnel while working in an advanced dressing station. After recovering from her injury, she experienced another close shave when a high-explosive shell landed close to her at a railhead; fortunately, the bomb buried itself in the ground and exploded upwards, leaving her physically unscathed but severely shell-shocked. She then contracted pleurisy and was, in April 1915, forced to return home.

Following several months in Britain, during which she returned to her pre-war employment as the Organizing and General Secretary of the National Union of Trained Nurses, Violetta returned to Russia, to investigate the possibility of supporting the creation of hospitals for refugees in Petrograd and Moscow. She wrote another book, *The People Who Run*, about the plight of Russia's millions of refugees,[8] before returning, once more, to Britain. In November 1916, she was invited by the Joint Committee of the Red Cross and Order of St John of Jerusalem – working in close cooperation with the Belgian Red Cross – to take on the role of matron at L'Hôpital de l'Océan. Here, she somehow managed to combine the administration of a large base hospital with the writing of yet another book – the highly technical *Text Book of War Nursing*.[9]

From the spring of 1917 onwards, L'Hôpital de l'Océan was bombarded from the air. In an entry dated 24 March in her pocket diary, Violetta noted that shrapnel had penetrated the roof of one of her wards, damaging an empty bed and wounding a stretcher-bearer. By the beginning of May, staff were being ordered to keep their gas masks with them at all times; there were several gas alarms that month, as cloud gases drifted from the front lines towards the hospital. Around this time, Antoine Depage recognized that 1917 was going to be a challenging year on the Belgian front, and he opened a new unit in Vinkem, about eight miles to the south. The Vinkem hospital remained a sub-section of L'Hôpital de l'Océan.

At another large Belgian field hospital, L'Hôpital Elizabeth, near Proven, several nurses were becoming worn down by long periods of relentless work. They had served continuously for most of 1916 and were still on duty in the spring of 1917. Their matron wrote to Violetta Thurstan for help, and she sent Alison and Dorothea Macfie, two cousins from Chester who had been serving as VADs at L'Hôpital de l'Océan, to relieve the nurses. Alison was to write later of how 'tremendously thrilled' she and her cousin were to be working close to the British rest areas and hospital units. Their hospital, in a field behind the Château de Couthove, was right next to a military laundry and de-lousing station.

As Easter Sunday – 8 April – approached, Alison and Dorothea asked their matron for permission to attend an English service. The wards were quiet and she was able to agree. They were taken by ambulance to Rue de l'Hôpital in Poperinge. Here, they discovered Talbot House, the 'Everyman's Club', founded by senior British army chaplain Neville Talbot and run by another chaplain, Philip Clayton, affectionately known as 'Tubby'.[10] The house was unique. Radically egalitarian for its time, it welcomed officers, non-commissioned officers and privates on an equal basis, providing a homely environment in which men could obtain food and drink, browse the library shelves and attend small evening concerts and 'sing-alongs'. Tubby had erected a sign above the door, which read: 'Abandon Rank All Ye Who Enter Here'. Now, for the first time, the Everyman's Club welcomed women too. High in the rafters at the top of the house, the loft had been converted into a small chapel which became widely known as the 'Upper Room'. It could only be reached by climbing several flights of stairs, the last one so steep that it was virtually a ladder – not easy to negotiate in long skirts. Alison wrote:

> I do remember very distinctly ... climbing up the steep stair to the Upper Room and on reaching the level of the floor with my head, I looked around and saw nothing but a sea of very muddy boots and khaki puttees, all much the same in colour. There had been services going on continuously since dawn and still the Chapel was crowded. Room was made for us, and we knelt before that sacred Bench beside men for whom this was a rare and deeply valued opportunity in the dark and dangerous life of the trenches round Ypres. Often, on revisiting Talbot House now, and sitting quietly in a corner of the Upper Room, I can still feel that atmosphere of tense attention.[11]

Kate Luard, sister-in-charge of No. 32 British Casualty Clearing Station, also climbed the stairs to the Upper Room to take communion. Her name and those of the Macfie cousins are among only eight women's names in the communion roll at Talbot House. Kate had befriended Tubby Clayton when she had been in charge of the isolation wards at No. 16 General Hospital, Le Treport in the summer of 1915. In a letter home to his mother, Tubby had described her wards as 'the most wonderful part of the hospital'.[12] Now, renewing his friendship with Kate, he was able to welcome her to his chapel. Years later, he was to write of his admiration for her:

> She had charge of Advanced Casualty Clearing Stations, set up before each Battle area in turn; and for the next three years worked nearer to the line than many men, and saved more lives thereby than anyone can reckon. Her hospitals in the Salient were at Brandhoek and at Elverdinghe; and both were shelled and bombed ... Yet the

risk was worth the running; for the presence of her unit with its marvellous equipment and magnificent team-spirit meant that men who would have died of their wounds on a longer journey, were succoured and saved by immediate operations, conducted on the fringe of the battle itself. Miss Luard is the only woman who came *down* the line to reach Talbot House. Very few surviving men served in more constant danger.[13]

Services at Talbot House became so popular that Tubby was forced to move them from the upstairs chapel into an adjacent hop store. He soon realized that the opportunity to socialize with nurses provided powerful comfort to men resting 'behind the lines'. He wrote to his mother on Tuesday 1 May:

> This afternoon, I have a garden party – tea for two nurses, who turned up in Church last Sunday night, creating a furore in the hearts of those who haven't seen an English lady for a year and more. So I'm having a select party to meet them, two from each unit in the neighbourhood, a Colonel, a Major, Captain, and all the rest N.C.O.s and men. Also 23 of Higgon's gunners, who have just finished a long job, and are having a day off.[14]

So great was the affection for Talbot House that, after the war, the 'Toc H' movement was created to keep its memory – and its activities – alive. Alison Macfie was to become a member of the first Toc H executive committee, formed in 1919. Three years later she was among those elected to serve on the first committee of the Toc H League of Women Helpers.[15]

Talbot House was not the only place nurses and soldiers could socialize. Strict rules governed 'fraternization' at base hospitals. But in the dangerous and stressful environment of the 'zone of the armies' where improvisation was often the rule, these regulations seemed draconian, and were often relaxed – especially in volunteer field hospitals. On 12 May five of the nurses from Mary Borden's Mobile Surgical No. 1 were given leave to attend a large concert for French troops at Coxyde; they were accompanied by three of the doctors. A huge marquee had been erected among the sand dunes. The nurses found themselves sitting with numerous 'notables' ranging from ace pilot Charles Nungesser, whose chest was 'covered with medals', to Lady Dorothie Fielding and the 'Heroines of Pervyse', Elsie Knocker and Mairi Chisholm. By this time, Elsie had married the Baron Harold de T'Serclaes de Rattendael, and was known by all as the 'Baroness de T'Serclaes'.

Of Nungesser, Hilda was to learn more: an eccentric and extremely popular character, he had the skull and crossbones and a coffin with two candles painted onto the side of his aeroplane. During the course of the war, he flew fifty-three successful missions, only to die years later, in May 1927, attempting the first ever trans-Atlantic flight.

Hilda described the Allied aeroplanes as 'beautiful and wonderful things', and the flyers themselves as 'the bravest of the brave'. The nurses of Mobile Surgical No. 1 formed close friendships with pilots based at a nearby aerodrome. On 20 May, when Agnes Warner and British nurses Sisters Coppice and Robinson were decorated with the 'Médaille des Epidemies', two planes flew very low over the compound, their pilots leaning out of their cockpits to wave at the assembled staff.

From early April onwards the nurses noticed an increase in aerial activity from both sides of the lines. Hilda commented that the Allied aeroplanes seemed to 'fly over us so gracefully, like large birds'. German observation planes, by contrast, flew very high and were, at first, difficult to see. One could pick them out by the puffs of smoke created by the shells fired from anti-aircraft guns, which seemed to mushroom all around them. Later, German fighter aircraft flew across the lines, remaining much closer to the ground. During quiet times in the hospital, the nurses would stand and watch dogfights, sometimes involving large numbers of aircraft. But soon things took an ominous turn. Many more German planes seemed to be flying over the hospital – often at night – laden with bombs to be dropped on Furnes or Dunkirk, or even, sometimes, the nearby village of Adinkerke. As the bombers approached, the church bells of surrounding communities could be heard ringing the alarm, warning civilians to seek safety in their cellars. It soon became clear that the hospital was being used as a landmark for German bombers en route to the channel ports.

Madeleine Jaffray was later to write of how awe-inspiring it could be to be so close to the front lines:

> At night we could see the commencement of attacks; the star shells and lights, then the awful noise of heavy artillery and the flash of the big guns lighting the skies. It is dreadful. How those men, after days, weeks and months in the trenches, stand it as they lie there on their sick beds is more than I can tell. How wonderful they are and how much we owe these men who have gone through this for us. They are fighting our fight. We cannot do enough for them, and nothing is too good for them. Many a time when on night duty

we nurses watched those awesome sights beyond us. They seemed only a few fields away. Sick at heart we would turn on our heels finally and make preparations to receive the wounded and dying who would soon come to us.[16]

But it was not only the noise from the bombardment taking place 'fields away' that frightened the hospital's inhabitants. Bombing raids affected a wide region behind the lines; and gas attacks taking place several miles away could mean that drifting toxic fumes affected the areas around field hospitals. Later, after her evacuation from Belgium, Madeleine was to speak to a journalist of her feelings one night when gas reached Mobile Surgical No. 1. She had been on duty that evening, and had helped her patients into their protective masks. Later the same night, as she was getting into bed, the alarm sounded for a second time, and she ran back to her ward, pulling on her own mask as she went: 'When I opened the door I found them all sitting up in bed, panting and struggling to adjust their masks to meet this second attack; and as I stood there looking at them, I felt like a lioness with her cubs. I wanted to fight and kill those who dared to do this fiendish thing!'[17]

Hilda Loxton wrote in her diary that 'Most of the [patients] were very nervous when the planes were bombing around us, almost all were very badly wounded; they were so helpless and there was no protection except the thin wooden roofs. We had no sandbags or dugouts at that time; many remarked they felt safer in the trenches.' On 28 May, as she was sitting at the window of the nurses' barrack, cutting dressings for the next day's work, a shell landed a few feet from a barrack window. It failed to detonate, and was, instead, driven several feet into the earth. She commented in her diary that, had it exploded, 'things would have gone pretty hard for me'.[18]

Just over a week later things did 'go hard'. On 4 June, a clear, moonlit night, German planes flew over at 10 p.m. en route to Furnes and Adinkerke. Annie Hanning, walking between wards, noticed that they were so low that the black crosses on the undersides of their wings could be clearly seen. Just over two hours later one returned, made several passes above the hospital, and then dropped ten bombs. Six of these fell harmlessly in a nearby field, three just a few yards from the nurses' barrack and one in the central compound of the hospital. Twelve sisters in the barrack woke suddenly to hear shell fragments and debris falling on their roof 'like hail stones'. Shrapnel balls and fragments of shell casing flew in all directions. Some, travelling with great velocity, punched right through the thin wooden walls of 'Lister' and 'Edith Cavell' wards, shredding pillows and scattering feathers, smashing bed screens and destroying glass vases. It seemed miraculous that only one occupant of the ward – an orderly sitting at the desk – sustained an injury; his leg was fractured.

Just outside the ward in the hospital compound Madeleine Jaffray, who was on night duty, had no protection. Hilda Loxton later recounted how, 'A large piece of red hot shrapnel flew along the "trottoir" and struck her foot, completely blowing away the heel and under-part of foot – her screams very soon brought everyone out, the whole atmosphere being smoky and smelling of gun powder'.[19]

Madeleine and the injured *infermièr* were both taken directly to the operating theatre, where their wounds were cleaned to prevent infection, packed with antiseptic dressings and securely bandaged. The remainder of the hospital staff went to the wards to reassure the patients. Hilda was later to recount, with some amusement, the story of her attempt to comfort one particularly stoical man:

> The ward which got it worst had 22 gas patients in it who were not very bad. When I went into the ward I patted the first man I came to on the back, and said, "N'avez pas peur", he looked up and smiled and said, "Je n'ai pas peur, mademoiselle". He happened to be the biggest man in the ward and was almost well again. They were more used to this sort of thing than we were, and not ill enough to have lost their nerve. The girls thought this a great joke on me and laughed over it many times.[20]

Although they used humour as a means of coping with the awfulness of their situation, the nurses of Mobile Surgical No. 1 were now seriously frightened. Sister Coppice 'completely collapsed from the shock of the bombing', and was taken to a base hospital.

The next night, the Germans launched a gas attack at Nieuwpoort. Staff at Mobile Surgical No. 1 saw the red warning flares go up in the distance, and their *médecin chef* received a message by phone to say that the gas was being carried towards the hospital. Hilda described how fumes entered the nurses' sleeping barrack through a knot hole, making her and Annie Hanning vomit. All the nurses put on their gas masks, but soon found these so uncomfortable that they resorted to wrapping 'turkish bath towels' around their faces instead. Within three hours, large numbers of gassed patients were being brought into the hospital. Being poisoned by gas was one of the nurses' greatest fears. Hilda commented: 'our hospital had 2 high flag poles in front, on one flew the French flag, on the other a Red Cross one. How eagerly every night we watched these to see if the wind was in our direction for gas.'[21]

On 6 June Agnes Warner was able to find time to sit down and write a letter to Madeleine Jaffray's parents. The emotions evoked by the responsibility of running a large field hospital so close to the front lines resonate through her writing:

> I am so grieved to have to send you such bad news today, but hope your daughter's cable reassured you a little … She has been so brave and patient we are all proud of her and the doctors are full of admiration for her courage. All of the generals of the division came to see her today and she is to get the Croix de Guerre … Everything possible is being done for her, and she herself feels that she could not have better care. One of the orderlies was also wounded and one of the patients. We all feel so dreadfully about it and I have sent in a protest to the Red Cross of Geneva. But it is war in one of its worst forms and we are in the war zone.[22]

The early summer of 1917 was a tense time. Sir Douglas Haig had been planning an assault in the Ypres Sector for over six months, and the time seemed to be drawing near for him to carry out his plans. Everyone knew this, including the German high command, which was bringing additional units to this part of the Western Front. Alongside their focus on the mobilization of troops, both sides were beginning to sense that the side with the greatest airpower might win the war. Gotha raids on areas behind the lines were becoming a regular occurrence and nurses were coming to realize that CCSs and field hospitals in the 'zone of the armies' really were part of the 'front lines' of the war.

*Chapter Six*

# Moving 'Up the Line'

O n 6 April the United States Congress declared war on Imperial Germany. The U.S. base hospitals that had been so carefully planned the previous year were now scrambled into action. George Crile mobilized Base Hospital No. 4 (the Lakeside Unit from Cleveland, Ohio) at the end of April. Soon afterwards, on Sunday 2 May, Richard Harte asked Margaret Dunlop to have fifty nurses ready to embark for France with Base Hospital No. 10 (the Pennsylvania Hospital Unit) the following Friday. She struggled to contact women who had signed up for the U.S. Army Nurse Corps Reserve the year before: many were working in senior positions in hospitals far from their home city. Reinforcements had to be found – but by Wednesday 16 May, the newly formed Nursing Corps of Base Hospital No. 10 was ready to leave for France.

Helen Fairchild had just – weeks previously – accepted a new position as a visiting nurse at Great Neck on Long Island. She was suffering from gastric symptoms and was keen to take work that was 'less confining' than hospital nursing. She had said what she thought was a final farewell to her colleagues at the Pennsylvania Hospital in early May, and had been much moved by a gift given to her by the pupil nurses:

> Went kind of hard to leave all my friends at the hospital, but it had to be done sometime, but must confess I swallowed salt water enough to drown a whale the morning I left. The pupil nurses gave me a dandy case of instruments when I left, had in it a hypo-syringe, a pair of bandage scissors and a pair of dressing scissors, forceps, folding scalpel, a little instrument for taking out foreign bodies, 2 probes, a pen knife and a glass catheter, and a thermometer, and I surely appreciated that, for they had all contributed to it and it was the spirit of the thing that touched me so much.[1]

Helen had been watching as her country moved closer and closer to war. By the time she travelled to Long Island, the USA had already been at war for several weeks, and she was only mildly surprised to find herself recalled to

Philadelphia. She resigned her position and, though a little dismayed to be giving up the new life she had chosen, went willingly to join her country's war effort as part of Base Hospital No. 10. On Sunday 14 May, she wrote to her brother, Ned:

> I am glad to be one of the ones to go, but feel sorry for mother. If she would only not worry so much … I'll be a long way from home so write me often and tell me all you are doing. And don't feel uneasy about me ever, for the folks at home will be notified immediately if anything should happen and will let you know, so even tho' you may not hear from me for a long time you'll know I'm all right. And try and write mother often, for she worries when she doesn't hear from you often.[2]

Helen's mother had good reason to worry. Helen had been suffering from gastric symptoms and was not in the best of health.

On the evening of 16 May, just before her unit left Philadelphia, Helen wrote to soothe her mother's fears, advising her that the censorship of letters written by members of the base hospital would be strict. To prevent any information on the movements of the unit's transport ship from falling into enemy hands, staff would not be allowed to write any letters until they were safely in Europe. Relatives might not receive any word for four or six weeks, but would be sent a telegram once the unit reached its destination safely. At the end of her letter, Helen wrote: 'my appetite is coming up and I have only had indigestion twice since I came down, and my legs don't ache as much as they did. Hope it lasts. I am going to stop the rheumatic medicine soon, but am going to keep up the blood tonic for a while.'[3] Whatever condition was causing Helen's gastritis (inflammation of the stomach), she does not appear to have been given a definitive diagnosis. Had she lived a hundred years later, she would almost certainly have been tested to see if her stomach was infected by the spiral bacterium, Helicobater pylori, the most common cause of stomach ulcers and other peptic conditions. But the discovery of the malign influence of H. pylori was still many decades away. Helen would continue to take her 'blood tonic' in an attempt to counter the damaging results of the failure of her gastrointestinal system to absorb the vitamins her body needed, without realizing the cause of her debility.

On 18 May, the unit assembled at the railway station and then boarded the train for New York, where the nurses received their plain dark-blue uniforms – earning themselves the soubriquet 'the Pennsylvania Hospital orphans'. Then they boarded the steamer *St Paul*. As their transport moved out into the Atlantic Ocean, it was joined by a protective convoy of two American destroyers, which 'ran along with us, crossing our bows and dashing back around our stern, like porpoises'.[4] The danger from submarine attack was very real, and staff were ordered to carry their life jackets with them at all times.

From the moment the *St Paul* moved out into the swell of the Atlantic until the day it docked, Helen suffered from seasickness. She vomited frequently, and her condition was worsened by the after-effects of a series of typhoid vaccinations. She wrote to her mother:

> We were on the water just eight days, went on the boat at noon Sat., and by 6 o'clock p.m. I felt as if the floors were coming up to meet me, and the whole universe was whirling so you see I didn't waste much time getting sea sick, and like to die all day Sunday and Monday, but Tues. morn had to have para-typhoid vaccine, everybody had to take it, and everybody had quite a severe reaction, but it sure made me sick until Fri. eve I began to feel a little better. I could sit up in my chair and by Sat., was on my feet again, and yesterday felt fine, and do today although pesky tired.[5]

As they neared the British Isles, their protective convoy was replaced by two British destroyers, and Matron Margaret Dunlop was later to comment on the discomfort of their last night at sea 'spent sitting on the deck with life belts on, and small valuables handy'. To their relief, the *St Paul* docked safely at Liverpool on 27 May. The nurses were accommodated at the Adelphi Hotel and, for the next month, they enjoyed celebrity status, as some of the earliest Americans to arrive in England on active service. They were taken by train to London, where they were housed at the Waldorf Hotel. For several weeks they enjoyed visits to historic houses, cathedrals and theatrical performances. They were special guests at the home of the American ambassador, treated to a reception at Claridges, invited to the home of Lady Astor and taken to an investiture by the king at Hyde Park. At first, it seemed to Margaret Dunlop that this was nothing but a 'wonderful joy-ride', but she soon recognized its purpose: the nurses were the perfect guests, and their very visible presence in London helped cement the bonds of friendship and loyalty between British and American allies.

By 8 June, Helen Fairchild was already 'tired of sight seeing'. But it was not until Saturday 28 June, that the staff members of Base Hospital No.

10 embarked at Southampton and were escorted by destroyers across the English Channel, reaching Le Havre the next morning at 4 a.m. Here, the celebrity treatment ended abruptly, when they were told that they must disembark immediately to make way for a convoy of severely wounded patients. They were moved by train to Le Treport, where they were to take over No. 16 British General Hospital. The journey lasted for over twelve hours and no arrangements had been made for food or drink. At one station, Captain Krumbhaar, their escort, went off in search of food, returning just as the train was pulling away, 'flying down the road followed by two French women lugging baskets'. The nurses' arrival at No. 16 General Hospital was unexpected – 'an overwhelming avalanche, the descent of sixty-eight women', but their British hosts gave up their own beds until additional accommodation could be found.[6]

Le Treport was a small fishing town and modest seaside resort. Its magnificent cliffs – or *falaises* – towered above a pebbly beach. The British military medical services had taken over a large tract of land close to the edge of these cliffs, and staff could visit the town by walking down a winding road or taking a series of cement steps cut into the hillside. As an adventurous alternative, they could use the funicular, which, in happier times, had been one of the town's touristic assets, but which was now – it was laughingly agreed – 'one of the risks of the war'. When the tide was out, nurses could take walks across the shingle, but at high tide – particularly on stormy days – the crashing of waves against the bases of the *falaises* could be clearly heard in the hospitals above. Helen Fairchild wrote to her family that she did not 'mind the cold', though the wind 'makes me cross'.[7] On Sunday 15 July, she wrote that the 'rather cold damp climate brings out all the rheumatic tendency that anyone has, as I am finding out'. She added that 'It is nearing sunset now and almost everyone takes a walk along the cliffs about that time to watch the sun go down, the sunsets are beautiful. I haven't been out for a walk for several evenings, so think I will go tonight. I guess I'll put my heavy dress on, for it gets very cool in the evening'.[8]

No. 16 General Hospital was composed of huts and tents, radiating out in a semicircle from a central point, and backing onto No. 47 Canadian. Close by, the Trianon Hotel had been converted into No. 3 British General Hospital. No. 16 had a large 'isolation division', which was set apart from the rest of the complex. The nurses' quarters consisted of huts connected by corridors, the largest of which was partitioned into a dining room and sitting room. The long sleeping huts were partitioned into smaller rooms, each of which was shared by two nurses. Their most prized possessions were a small canvas basin, in which they washed, and a stove with its ration of ten pieces of coal per week.

The open ground next to the hospital provided adequate space for tennis courts and a cricket pitch. Soon after their arrival, the American staff added a baseball diamond. The British were said to be 'chagrined' at having their hospital taken from them, but the newly arrived American staff agreed that their welcome was, nevertheless 'courteous and kindly'. The British moved out within a few weeks, leaving a problem for the commanding officer, Matthew Delaney, and the matron, Margaret Dunlop. Their unit had been designed to care for a total patient population of 500, but the hospital had well over 2,000 beds. Realizing that 'sixty-four nurses could not adequately take care of 2,000 patients covering an area equal to about five or six city squares' Margaret called for 'reinforcements', which were hastily sent out from Philadelphia.[9]

From the first, the American Base Hospital had two nurse-anaesthetists, Miss Burkey and Miss Murphy. Paul Hoeber, editor of a history of the Pennsylvania unit observed that,

> throughout the British Army anaesthetics had hitherto only been administered by doctors and when shortly after our arrival our women began their work they were greatly astonished. The skill and care which was displayed soon caused their amazement to yield to admiration. The idea was soon adopted by the British authorities and in the early spring of 1918 classes were formed of British nurses who received instruction at our hospital and at several others.[10]

The arrival of American base hospitals was creating a general 'shake-up' of clinical practice. Three years of war had, in many ways, been a creative force in Allied surgical practice, as new crises drove ever-more inventive innovations. But the military medical and nursing services were also worn out by active service; by 1917, they were drained of both energy and resources. The entry of the USA into the war brought a welcome injection of both commodities – although it also caused some resentment among 'veteran' practitioners, who viewed the up-beat confidence of the newcomers with scepticism. George Crile was in command of U.S. Base Hospital No. 4, which had taken over the site of No. 9 British General Hospital at Rouen. One of his earliest actions was to order the design and manufacture of cannulae for blood transfusion – extending the practice throughout the hospital. He also initiated a programme of clinical trials. His team experimented with a variety of wound-care practices, ranging from the Carrel-Dakin treatment to the use of salt-packs, an antiseptic paste known as 'BIP' (consisting of bismuth, iodoform and paraffin) and the use of electric light treatment. Beyond this, the hospital also conducted trials to test the hypothesis that the use of nitrous oxide as an anaesthetic caused fewer side effects than either chloroform or ether.

Nurses were fascinated by these developments, and were forming their own opinions about the efficacy of new approaches. Australian nurse Nellie Morrice, who had served in Egypt, Lemnos and England, was posted to the Western Front in April 1917. In June, her matron took her to Compiègne to attend a course of instruction in the proper use of the Carrel-Dakin technique. Nellie was impressed by what she saw. Some of the most severe, infected compound fracture wounds could be freed from infection in just nine days if the treatment was used conscientiously. Cleanliness and asepsis were everything: it was essential that the skin surrounding the wound be washed with liquid soap before the treatment was applied. It was also vital that tubes should be removed from the wound every two to three days to be cleaned and then thoroughly sterilized. During the treatment, the nurse must carefully swab the wound to check for infection; only after a completely 'clear' swab had been obtained could its margins be stitched. Some nurses told Nellie that the treatment carried a risk of haemorrhage. As the Dakins solution scoured the wound and removed infection, it could also corrode normal tissue, sometimes damaging quite large arteries or veins. She considered herself lucky that she never witnessed such haemorrhage – she had seen 'only the best results'.[11]

Thirty miles behind the lines, Catherine Black was in charge of a ward for shell-shocked officers at No. 7 British General Hospital, Saint-Omer. The hospital was a converted monastery: 'a beautiful old Gothic building whose shady cloisters, barred cells, and high-walled garden still seemed to hold the atmosphere of peace in spite of the German warplanes that buzzed over our heads every few days and the dull roar of the big guns at Poperinghe'.[12] Catherine found work with shell-shocked men fascinating yet challenging. All had experienced terrible trauma, but each had unique problems and symptoms, and they had to be treated as individuals. A treatment that worked for one could be 'disastrous' for another. Catherine seems to have been well-suited to the work, recognizing that only rest and care could heal these damaged men. She gave them opiates at night to enable them to rest, built their physical strength by giving the most nourishing food possible, and spent hours with them, re-training those who had lost the power of speech to talk again, and those who were paralyzed to walk.

Sir Douglas Haig was continuing to plan for his new series of offensives at the northern end of the Western Front. He believed that the war could be won in the north. If the Allies could push back the Germans at Ypres they would not only protect their own vital ports of Calais and Dunkirk, they could also threaten the Central Powers' only outlet to the sea at Ostend and Zeebrugge, loosening the German U-boat stranglehold on North Sea merchant shipping that threatened to push the British people towards starvation. If the Allies could achieve an overwhelming breakthrough at this point, they might push eastwards and take control of the vital railhead at Roulers (modern-day Roeselare), cutting-off German communications and opening up a route into the heart of Belgium. Haig's focus was on Ypres, and his attitude was becoming increasingly accepting of the logistics of attrition. Even if his army could not take Roulers, the effort of defending this part of the line would 'bleed his enemy dry', as they were forced to commit more and more men to the region. A major assault at Ypres, followed by an amphibious landing on the coast of Belgium, would permit the Allies to take the northern sector of the Western Front.

Convinced that the war would be won by the most technologically advanced army, Haig had persuaded the British government to invest heavily in tanks, machine guns, aircraft and high-explosive shells. Allied commanders had learned much from the failure of the Somme campaign. They now knew that aerial reconnaissance was vital to determine the nature of the enemy's defences, that an artillery barrage would not necessarily destroy the enemy's barbed-wire, and that 'no man's land' had acquired its name for a reason: infantry regiments could not attack without covering fire. Nurses in CCSs found themselves working, eating and attempting to sleep in an environment of almost constant noise from the artillery emplacements located beside and behind their positions. For days prior to an attack, the barrage would build to a fever pitch until nurses became almost accustomed to it.

Closer to the battlefield, commanders were working to perfect the strategy of the 'creeping barrage'. Range-finders were trained to ensure that shells landed approximately fifty yards ahead of the advancing troops. The protective barrage was then 'lifted' incrementally, usually by about a hundred yards every few minutes, permitting troops to advance behind it. Of course, a serious drawback of this otherwise brilliant tactic was that men were sometimes hit by shellfire from their own artillery. Another was that the 'creeping barrage' sometimes lifted too rapidly, leaving the troops exposed to enemy counter-barrage. The problems were exacerbated by poor, or non-existent, battlefield communications.

The Germans, too, had planned carefully for the anticipated Allied offensives of 1917. Their trench systems were becoming even more complex, designed to provide in-depth protection. Their front line trenches were relatively shallow and thinly defended, but behind these were increasingly deep and solidly constructed fortifications, protected by machine-gun emplacements in thickly walled concrete bunkers which only a direct hit by a high-explosive shell could destroy. If Allied forces threatened the front line, this could easily be abandoned in favour of the stronger defences further back, leaving the attackers in exposed positions. By June 1917, the Germans had no fewer than six distinct lines of defence: a thinly defended front line along the Pilckem Ridge and Gheluvelt Plateau; a second line on the eastern slope of the ridge; a third line behind this, 'Flanders I' along the front of the Passchendaele Ridge and the eastern slope of the Gheluvelt Plateau and 'Flanders II' and 'III' behind these. On the Gheluvelt Plateau and in the Houlthurst Forest they had two massively defended positions consisting of ruined farm buildings among which were built large numbers of small concrete emplacements or 'pillboxes'.

Behind the Allied lines, medical science had been struggling to keep pace with advances in industrial weaponry. The experiences of the previous two and a half years had taught senior medical officers and nurses that speed was a key element in the treatment of traumatized casualties. If wounded men could be stabilized quickly they were less likely to be overwhelmed by wound-shock. Haemorrhage must be stemmed, fluid must be pumped through wide-bore needles into the soft tissues beneath the skin of the axillae and groins and morphine, anti-tetanus serum and stimulants must be injected into the muscles. Some of this work could be done in a regimental aid post, but most of it had to wait until the patient reached a CCS. The work was intricate, demanding immediate one-to-one attention, yet everyone knew that during the assault, patients would arrive in rushes several hundred at a time – unloaded from convoys of ambulances until the floors of reception huts were thickly covered with narrow stretchers.

In June, three British CCSs – the 4th, 47th and 61st – were brought together in a large area of land which was given the name 'Dozinghem'. No. 4 was just beside 'Lavender Bend', in a field belonging to farmer Kamel Inion. Just beyond this was 'Dodo Wood', its Belgian name denoting a place for sleep; a decade later, it would be the location of part of the Dozinghem Commonwealth War Graves Cemetery.

The 'processing' of casualties was becoming more highly organized. Since the earliest months of the war, 'field medical cards' – which looked very much like luggage labels – had been used to convey information about patients' wounds and treatment. When a man was first assessed at a regimental aid post, one of these cards was pinned to his lapel, detailing the nature of his wound and any immediate treatment offered. When he arrived at the casualty clearing station, he was re-assessed, often by nurses, to determine his next course of treatment. Staff members in CCSs were now being given strict instructions that field medical cards must always be carefully completed and signed at every stage in the treatment process. Senior medical officers were particularly anxious that the term 'Not Yet Diagnosed' (or 'NYD'), which saved time, and was a useful means of moving patients rapidly to the next part of the line, must not be used. A clear diagnosis must be given, along with an indication of what treatment had been implemented. The letters 'CD' must be added to the card if Carrel-Dakin treatment had been commenced. Information about anti-tetanic serum was considered particularly vital. If the field medical card left the CCS staff in any doubt if this had been given at the regimental aid post, then it must be given again at the reception hut or dressing room, and the letters 'AT' marked on the back of both the patient's wrists before he was loaded onto an ambulance train. Particular cases must be given priority and taken to specialist CCSs. These included any men with head injuries where a fractured skull was suspected, those with severe chest wounds, particularly where the missile was still lodged in the body, abdominal wounds, particularly where the projectile had entered through the lower chest or through the buttock or back, and wounds of the knee-joint, which were very prone to infection.

In preparation for the planned assault, the bed capacities of CCSs close to the Salient – particularly those to the east of Messines – were increased. New CCSs were established and patients not requiring immediate surgery were evacuated to base hospitals in France. It was already quite common for individual CCSs to specialize in particular types of wounds: abdominal or chest wounds, limb fractures or head injuries. There were even special units for cases of shell-shock and for patients with self-inflicted wounds. At Remy Siding, Nos. 10 and 17 British CCSs were already working closely with Nos. 2 and 3 Canadian.

The Salient had been one of the quieter parts of the Western Front that spring. Many British troops had been relocated to the Arras region to launch an assault in support of the Nivelle Offensive. Now they were returned to the Ypres sector. No. 32 British CCS, where Kate Luard was sister-in-charge, was moved to Brandhock, about three miles from the front lines. No. 44 was also moved forward; one of its sisters, Yorkshire nurse Minnie Wood, had just been promoted to sister-in-charge. Minnie had joined the Queen Alexandra's Imperial Military Nursing Service in 1912 and had been in France since 17 August 1914. She was mentioned in despatches in January 1916, and in May 1917 was awarded the Royal Red Cross (Second Class). Following a brief period of duty at No. 6 Stationary Hospital in Frevent, she had been posted to No. 44 on 18 May. She had clearly impressed Maud McCarthy, the Matron-in-Chief in France and Flanders, by both her skill and her coolness under pressure.

Nellie Spindler, who had enlisted with the QA Reserve in October 1915, was accepted for overseas service in 1917, and embarked at Ramsgate on 23 May. She was posted to No. 2 British General Hospital, Le Havre, but was transferred up the line after only three days – first to No, 42 Stationary Hospital, and then to No. 44 Casualty Clearing Station at Brandhoek, under the command of Minnie Wood. Nellie had written a will on 18 May, shortly before departing for France, bequeathing all her money and personal effects to her mother.

Nos. 32 and 44 British CCSs were to be joined in late July by No. 3 Australian CCS to form an enormous 'Advanced Abdominal Centre'. During large rushes, each unit would admit patients until full, when it would close its doors, and concentrate on the care and treatment of existing patients, handing over to one of its 'partners'. By admitting patients in rotation, CCSs were much less likely to be overwhelmed by rushes of casualties than they had been during the early years of the war.

By 1917, professional cooperation was becoming more sophisticated. So-called 'surgical teams', each consisting of a surgeon, a nurse, an anaesthetist and an orderly were formed at base hospitals, and were then moved as a group to or between CCSs. American base hospitals soon began to supply teams to the CCSs, which were becoming international centres for the treatment of the wounded. On 7 June, George Crile moved up to No. 17 CCS at Remy Siding with a surgical team. Here, he recorded in his diary how he had conducted a number of medical experiments – particularly into the use of 'oxygen, passed through brandy and inhaled through a nasal tube', for gassed patients. He found that some patients 'became quite jolly under the treatment'. He wrote of the moribund – or, in his words, the 'moratorium' – ward, where 'one Briton was gurgling on toward dissolution with the respiratory tract full of blood from a penetrating wound', and 'a German in a dark corner was repeating two words over and over. He was shading into mild delirium, with fading pulse and cold hand from gas gangrene. The two words he spoke were *Mutter! Schwester!*" ["Mother! Sister!"]'. Crile decided that 'moratorium wards' should be renamed 'resuscitation wards' and that specialist resuscitation teams should work with patients to see if any of them could be saved. One of the more extraordinary experimental treatments he attempted was the infusion of seawater into patients' bodies to reverse shock.[13]

Australian nurse Violet Minnie Payne arrived in France in March 1917, and served at No. 1 British General Hospital at Rouen for three months, before being moved up the line to No. 17 British CCS, at around the same time as the teams from the No 4 American Base Hospital. She was later to write a narrative of her experiences, which were both 'fascinating' and 'terrifying':

> The boom of those terrible guns I shall never forget – for a week I scarcely closed an eye and my head ached. They fairly shook the earth continuously day and night. I volunteered for night work. It was all so weird and awful. It fascinated me so much I asked to remain for two months instead of only one. At times the sky was lit up like gorgeous firework displays. Here we felt we were really needed. The comfort those poor boys felt at a woman's presence when they became conscious.[14]

May Tilton, another Australian nurse, had already amassed a range of trauma-care experiences by the time she arrived on the Continent. After serving with the No. 1 and No. 3 Australian General Hospitals in Cairo and Suez, caring for severely ill, shell-shocked and wounded patients from the Gallipoli campaign, she had been posted to the hospital ship, *Essequibo*, bringing damaged patients back to Britain for convalescence. In England, she served at military hospitals in Rubery, Dartford and Brighton, before being transferred to France, to the No. 4 British General Hospital at Camiers, where she arrived in May 1917. The base at Camiers was like a 'huge city of canvas', and No. 4 alone had 2,000 beds. It was 'deplorably understaffed': May was in charge of an acute surgical ward of sixty beds, full of patients labelled 'dangerously ill', with only one VAD and two orderlies to assist her. She later wrote in her memoir:

> One hesitates to write of the havoc the war played among these precious human lives, or to give an insight into the work of the wards. A load of responsibility rested on the shoulders of every sister. The days were never long enough. No matter how hard

we worked, we were compelled to go off duty with a hopeless feeling of how little had been accomplished. There was no time to sponge the fevered bodies. The imperative work was attending to the dressings of ghastly wounds. Almost daily, new patients filled beds where previous occupants had died.[15]

She commented that, without the help of British VADs, she dared 'not think how we should have managed'. She found herself deeply moved by the 'willing service and unselfish devotion' of these volunteer nurses with minimal training and almost no prior experience of nursing work. Most of her patients were suffering from trench nephritis and pneumonia – desperate cases of men debilitated by trench life to the point where their bodies had been unable to stave off life-threatening infections. She and her staff spent much of their time improvising 'vapour baths' to assist the breathing of the chest cases. Frequently, she would be awoken in the early hours of the morning to assist the night staff to admit a convoy of acute cases. Soon, she herself was placed on night duty, in charge of 220 patients in five wards.

The early summer of 1917 was hot and sunny. The Arras campaign had ground to a halt and May's workload had eased. She revelled in the beauty of the French countryside, spending most of her leave time walking in the woods close to Camiers. Australian soldiers in camps nearby brought 'great bunches of lovely flowers – lily of the valley, forget-me-not, daisies, iris, buttercups, pansies, violets' to the hospitals. On 15 July, she and all the Australian nurses in the area were brought together at the No. 3 Australian General Hospital, Abbeville. Here, they were surrounded by fields of ripening corn liberally scattered with poppies, cornflowers and marguerites.

Closer to the front, in the villages surrounding Poperinge, Belgian civilians and military personnel felt the peace and loveliness of the surrounding countryside acutely. They knew that, just beyond the horizon, the land was a devastated sea of mud, concrete bunkers and barbed wire, and that men were dying daily. They could hear the bombardment – but, here, even though they might be in the 'zone of the armies' they were beyond the 'devastated zone'. They were, for the time being, safe but they knew that safety could not last. Uncertainty bred a zest for life that was muted by enforced discipline. Most nurses spent their leave days exploring the surrounding countryside, enjoying picnics and teas with officers in neighbouring rest camps, and visiting Poperinge – affectionately known to all as 'Pop'.

In the early summer, Australian nurse Effie Garden, was told that she could, if she wished, accept a posting to a CCS near the Ypres front. She agreed with alacrity, knowing that preparations were being made for the 'big push'. Before travelling to Belgium, Effie was ordered to attend a training session at a nearby engineering camp. Having learned how to put on her cumbersome, suffocating gas mask in six carefully timed seconds, she was told to walk through a gas-filled trench wearing it. Realizing that this was as much a test of composure as of skill, she managed to remain calm and achieved her goal: she was assigned to a surgical team that was due to travel to 12 CCS at Needinghem, near Proven. On arriving at their destination, the dangers of their front-line posting were brought home to Effie and her surgical-team colleagues when they were issued with grimy, blood-stained helmets that had been taken from men so badly wounded that they no longer had need of them. These they cleaned in carbolic solution. They soon learned the value of a good steel helmet, as shells began to land close to their hospital compound.[16]

Preparations for the assault on the Ypres front continued throughout the early summer of 1917. And the German army responded by bombing areas behind the lines, using both long-range artillery and aerial bombardment. From their vantage point on the ridges east of Ypres, German officers could view the accumulation of men and weaponry behind the Salient. One thing was certain: the element of surprise would not be a feature of the assault that was to be named the 'Third Battle of Ypres'.

*Chapter Seven*

# Edge of Hell

As June 1917 opened, the Allies were finalizing plans for the Ypres Campaign. The opening battle would capture the Messines Ridge, a long rim of raised land to the south-east of the city. Standing only 260 feet above sea level, it hardly deserved the name 'ridge' – yet, from it the Germans could gain a clear view of the movement of troops and artillery batteries in the southern part of the Salient. In 1917, the German front line was on its crest, and soldiers in deep bunkers were well aware that Allied engineers were digging beneath their feet. The Germans had, in fact, made extensive excavations of their own, and had succeeded in finding and destroying some of the Allied tunnels. In spite of these setbacks, the Allies had, by the early summer of 1917, succeeded in placing over twenty explosive mines in chambers directly beneath the German defences. Lloyd George was still unwilling to give the go-ahead for an Allied assault at Ypres, but the failure of Nivelle's offensive at the Chemin des Dames meant that Haig believed he had the right to pursue the campaign. He was convinced that the German Army was close to collapse and that he could count on French support in the Salient. His intelligence was fatally flawed. The Germans were far from defeat, while the French, convinced that their commanders had acted both recklessly and callously at the Chemin des Dames, were on the verge of an all-out mutiny. Many believed that Nivelle had sent men to almost certain destruction without making adequate plans for evacuation of the wounded.

Allied forces nevertheless continued to prepare for the attack on Messines Ridge that was to preface the 'big push' throughout the Ypres Salient. Between 21 May and 7 June 1917, Allied artillery fired a preliminary bombardment of well over three million shells. Then, just before 3 a.m. on 7 June, the ammonal-packed devices beneath the Messines Ridge and nearby lower-lying hills were detonated, creating a series of explosions so immense that they were felt and heard in London. In their bell tents in CCSs within ten miles of the lines, sleeping nurses woke in shock as the ground shook beneath them and the air boomed. They knew they could soon expect to receive enormous numbers of casualties. As far away as Camiers, May Tilton heard the guns 'pounding away incessantly'. The distant rumble of the bombardment was accompanied by a series of terrifying summer storms, in which several men in the camps were killed by lightning strikes and the thunder sounded like an 'eighteen-pounder barrage'.[1]

Even as the debris of earth, rocks and bomb casings from the explosions was settling, British infantry divisions were attacking, protected by a creeping barrage and supported by tanks and machine-gun units. Incendiary bombs were dropped just ahead of the advance, inflicting horrific burns on many of the defending Germans who had survived the explosion of the mines. The Messines' assault was, from the Allied point of view, a complete success. The front-line German defences on the Messines and Wytschaete ridges were captured, and the Germans were no longer able to look down on the Ypres Salient from these southern high points. German casualties from the Battle of the Messines Ridge were enormous, but those suffered by the Allies were also significant. The exploding of the Messines Ridge was one of the most destructive moments in one of the most devastating wars of modern times. Few of those on the ridge emerged unscathed. CCSs were overwhelmed with casualties, including large numbers of wounded prisoners of war.

In reception huts and resuscitation wards, fully trained nurses moved from patient to patient prioritizing the work, stabilizing waiting men by warming them with blankets and gas heaters, and pushing fluid into their bodies. Patients were rehydrated as rapidly as possible, using sterile saline solution or colloid preparations made from 'gum Arabic', a natural compound produced from the sap of the acacia tree. The priority was to bulk-out the fluid circulating in their bodies in order to prevent their collapse into irreversible shock. From the earliest years of the war, surgeons had experimented with techniques for blood transfusion, but these involved highly risky procedures, such as suturing a donor's brachial artery to that of his recipient. Typically, blood donors were 'up patients' – those with relatively minor wounds, and those who were close to recovery. They were treated as heroes, given bacon and eggs to eat, champagne to drink, and a 'Blighty ticket' to permit their transfer to England rather than to a rest camp in France.

Lawrence Bruce Robertson, an experienced Canadian surgeon and medical scientist, was working at Remy Siding with No. 2 Canadian CCS in 1917. Robertson had begun to take an interest in developing new methods for transfusing blood while practising in New York and Toronto before the war. In 1914, he had volunteered for active service, and, in 1915, had been posted overseas. While serving at No. 14 Canadian General Hospital that autumn, he had conducted a number of trials, publishing his findings in the *British Medical Journal* towards the end of 1916. Large numbers of Allied surgeons had taken an interest, and many had adopted his techniques. At Remy, with the support of careful, observant nurses, he performed further experimental trials on patients, developing safer methods, using rubber tubing and paraffin-coated syringes to draw blood from the donor's artery to that of the patient, and using sodium citrate to prevent clotting. He continued to publish his findings in the *British Medical Journal*, winning recognition for his work. Blood transfusion, nevertheless, remained a cumbersome and time-consuming method of reviving shocked patients until, later that year, American surgeon and scientist Oswald Hope Robertson began work on devising methods for storing blood in large, glass bottles using both sodium citrate and glucose to permit longer-term storage. So-called 'blood banks' began to be available in 1918, during the final months of the war.

It was not only physical wounding that was destroying lives. Emotional trauma was a widespread and serious problem. On 17 June, American surgeon George Crile had visited the special shell-shock unit at Saint-Omer. He was told that five per cent of those wounded at the Battle of the Messines Ridge were 'shell-shock cases'. The men were suffering a wide range of symptoms: 'some were only weak, some stammering, some mute, many deaf, some with hands and feet sweating, some with blue nails, others with diarrhoea or constipation, many with tremors'.[2] Most were sweating profusely and had a rapid pulse. Crile attributed the condition to the body's failure to recover after the natural stress reaction of war. It was as if these men's bodies had become 'stuck' in a constant state of fear.

At the northernmost point in the 'zone of the armies', Violetta Thurstan was running L'Hôpital de l'Océan, just behind the beach and sand dunes at La Panne. For several days in early July, there was a tremendous bombardment in the neighbourhood of the hospital. On 6 June, Violetta had received news that a young Canadian sister at nearby Adinkerke had been wounded. The next day, she travelled the two miles to Mobile Surgical No. 1 to visit Madeleine Jaffray. By the middle of the month, it was clear that the British Second Army was moving into the northernmost section of the Western Front – into areas previously held by the Belgians. 'Excitement seethes among the Sisters,' she commented in her diary. On the 13th she heard that L'Hôpital de l'Océan was to be used by the British services, and on the 26th she was advised that the new colonel in charge was considering posting nurses to advanced dressing stations. On the 28th she was writing of 'heavy fighting at Nieuwport' and the arrival of 'English wounded' at the hospital. By mid-July, she had left L'Hôpital de l'Océan and, soon afterwards, she was posted to a British dressing station serving XV Corps at Coxyde.[3]

On 17 June, at Mobile Surgical No 1 in Adinkerke, Madeleine Jaffray and colleague, Hilda Gill, who had come to her aid during the bombing of the hospital, were awarded the Croix de Guerre. The same day, Madeleine was moved to the American Ambulance in Paris, where New York surgeon Dr. Joseph Blake, would amputate part of her foot, and fit her with a prosthetic device to enable her to walk. After her departure from Mobile Surgical, Sister Helen McMurrich wrote an encouraging letter to her parents:

> Her courage and patience is the admiration of all, and we felt that nothing would or could be too good for her, for she certainly stuck to the post like a soldier … Sister McIntyre is looking after her and M. Rouviere [sic] is an A1 surgeon and more than kind … Yesterday she was decorated with the Croix de Guerre. Her room was filled with officers and sisters, all there to see it presented. I told her I was going to write to you and asked her if she had any message. Her reply was, 'Tell my father not to worry and that I am going to get the Croix de Guerre. He will be so pleased.'[4]

Madeleine's recovery was painfully slow, and when her colleagues from Mobile Surgical visited her while on leave in June they found her struggling with boredom, pain and deep frustration.

On 20 June, the high command of the French Service de Santé des Armées decided that Adinkerke was too dangerous a location, and the hospital was moved once more – this time to the small village of Rousbrugge, just a few miles from its original home in Beveren. As she left the hospital compound at 8 a.m. that day, Hilda Loxton noticed how beautiful the surrounding landscape was: the clover was two or three feet high, and it was difficult to believe that this place had been shelled and gassed only weeks earlier. She and the other Australians – Lynette Crozier, Minnie Hough and (Sister) Wallace – were sent on leave while their hospital was being prepared; they spent a month touring the Alps, the French Riviera and Brittany.

They returned to Belgium at the end of July, to find that their new hospital at Rousbrugge was composed of Nissen huts, curved like tunnels, with windows only at the ends. Patients would be much better protected from flying shrapnel here. Gassed patients – in four large tents – would be more vulnerable, yet the airiness of tented wards would assist their breathing. The nurses arrived on 21 July, as preparations for the Third Ypres Campaign were building. The road beside the hospital – which led from the French border to the city of Ypres – was 'one continuous stream of traffic – troops and cannons of every description'. Thirty-two observation balloons could be seen from the hospital compound. Hilda's ward was 'No. 18' and Minnie's was 'No. 17' next door. Minnie's first patient was an American aviator, whose plane had been shot down nearby; he had had what was considered a 'marvellous escape'. He took a great liking to Minnie, writing frequently, and even sending her a piece of German plane as a souvenir following his discharge.

Sir Douglas Haig had wanted to follow up the success of the Battle of the Messines Ridge with an almost immediate full assault across the whole of the Ypres Salient. But the plan was impractical. It was to take three days just to move the required artillery from Messines to the region of the Salient, over uneven and boggy ground. As the heavy artillery of Sir Hubert Gough's Fifth Army was lumbering slowly into place, the French First Army was moving forward into supporting positions on its left flank just west of the Houlthurst Forest. The German high command was able to view the preparations for the assault from its vantage points beyond Ypres. It intensified its campaign of aerial bombardment of railheads west of the ruined city, in order to disrupt the Allied supply chain; many of its bombs landed perilously close to the CCSs which were also located close to railheads to permit the more efficient evacuation of the wounded, and which were now being expanded in preparation for the anticipated casualties of the assault.

The preliminary bombardment, intended to supress the German artillery ahead of the planned Allied advance, began on 16 July. Gough's original intention had been to attack the first line of German trenches nine days later on the 25th, but his plans were delayed because neither the British artillery nor the French army was in place. The streams and ditches that had made the Flanders farmland so fertile for centuries had been transformed by almost three years' shelling into a quagmire. Even the moderate rainfall experienced in mid-July turned the ground into a morass and the task of moving heavy artillery guns into a herculean effort. A new date was set for the assault: 31 July. In the meantime, the divisions that were being brought forward were rehearsing the planned breakthrough on scale models of the Ypres Salient situated in a rest area near Poperinge. The benefits of such meticulous rehearsal were clear; but one of its main disadvantages was the fact that by late July no one could be in any doubt that a huge assault was being planned, and many of the details of Haig's plans had been leaked to the Germans.

The Allied bombardment was fierce. It succeeded in destroying many of the German batteries for a distance of over 2,000 yards. It nevertheless failed to touch large concentrations of heavy artillery situated further back within the six lines of the German defence-in-depth that constituted the impenetrable barrier facing the Allied armies. Many batteries located behind the Passchendaele Ridge and Gheluvelt Plateau could not be seen by Allied spotters in observation balloons and aeroplanes. The low cloud and poor visibility meant that many strongpoints – even some of those just behind the German first line defences – remained undetected.

Surgical teams were moving forwards to staff the multiple operating tables that were being set up in each CCS. George Crile travelled up the line with three surgical teams from American Base Hospital No. 4 at Rouen. Among them were three nursing sisters and one nurse-anaesthetist, 'Miss Roche', who worked closely with Ed Lower, and assisted in implementing experimental oxygen treatments for phosgene gas poisoning.

British Casualty Clearing Station No. 32, which was already specializing in abdominal injuries, was moved from Warlencourt to Brandhoek towards the end of July. It was to join No. 44 CCS, whose nurses were under the command of head sister Minnie Wood. These small, but rapidly expanding, units were located just over three miles from the reserve trenches. Kate Luard, head sister at No. 32, arrived on 25 July with a small contingent of nurses, anticipating that her complement of staff would rise to thirty before the commencement of the 'big push'. 'We are for abdomens and chests,' she wrote in her journal – with evident satisfaction, knowing that theirs would be among the most vital work of the war. Nos. 32 and 44 were soon to be joined by No. 3 Australian CCS, creating a formidable unit of three hospitals which could rotate their 'take-in' – each admitting in turn, permitting the other two to focus on resuscitation, treatment and recovery of existing casualties.

Kate soon found that one of the problems associated with her new posting was the almost incessant noise from the bombardment. The commanding officer was quick to explain to the nurses 'which noise means a burst beyond you, which means a burst on your right or left, and that the one that does you in you don't hear!'[5] The entire hospital was under canvas, apart from the operating theatre, which was a long wooden hut. Wide duckboards ran between the tents.

On Sunday 29 July May Tilton and eleven other Australian nurses began the slow journey from Abbeville to Brandhoek to help establish and staff the No. 3 Australian CCS that was to work in tandem with Nos. 32 and 44. From the safety of a base almost eighty miles behind the front, the Australian nurses were to find themselves within a few miles of the reserve trenches. After much confusion, caused by the secrecy of their orders and the shelling of various points on their route, they began the last leg of their journey – a 'thrilling drive' to Brandhoek. 'Fritz was shelling Poperinghe' and the guns were 'pounding away at a terrific rate'.[6] Unable to reach their destination that night, they retreated to No. 62 British CCS near Proven, where they met their matron, Miss O'Dwyer. The thunder of the nearby bombardment and the constant, unwanted attentions of the local mosquitoes made sleep impossible, and they were anxious to reach their posting. Finally, on 31 July, the day of the attack, they arrived at No. 3 Australian CCS. Here, along with British CCSs Nos. 44 and 32, they were to be part of the enormous 'Advanced Abdominal Centre' already being created and which would deal with all of the most urgent cases coming from the Third Battle of Ypres – not just abdominal cases, but 'chests' and 'fractured femurs' as well. Such cases were the most urgent of the war, requiring treatment within two or three hours to prevent the galloping infections that were now known to kill with such rapidity. Most CCSs could be reached within six hours (provided all went smoothly with the transport of wounded to regimental aid posts and advanced dressing stations, and then their transfer by motor ambulance), but this cluster of forward field hospitals – so close to the lines that they were right up against the local field ambulances – could be reached in half that time: surgeons could begin operating within just three hours. Proximity to the battlefield saved lives. As long as patients could be found and removed from no man's land by stretcher-bearers, treated rapidly in regimental aid posts, and transferred almost immediately by motor ambulance, they had a good chance of survival. Kate Luard had included a wry comment in a letter to her family. On 26 July, soon after her own unit's arrival at Brandhoek, Sir Anthony Bowlby, consulting surgeon to the BEF, had called to see her, declaring: 'How d'you like the site this time? Front pew what? Front row dress circle.' 'It is his pet scheme,' she remarked, 'getting the operations done up here within an hour or two of getting hit.'[7] Soon after Bowlby's visit, Kate and her staff were dismayed to be ordered to two Canadian CCSs about six miles further west. Their commanding officer had become nervous and sent an order at 10 p.m. that the women must retreat. The next morning, after one of the quietest nights for weeks, they were permitted to return, and continued the job of getting their hospital ready.

On 30 July, George Crile, based at Remy Siding, wrote in his diary that

Surgical teams are arriving daily; every bed is cleared; hospital trains are mobilized; new tentage for emergencies is on hand. Guns boom louder and louder. General Jacob told me that tonight his sector, six thousand yards of the Front will be given eight thousand gas shells; that there is a gun for each seven yards of Front; that the bombardment will be the heaviest in history. The evening is clear; the moon dim; the roll of the guns majestic.[8]

Crile later commented that the hospitals behind the Ypres Salient were located in 'a gateway between the main highway and the main railway'. A vast area of territory stretching from Ypres to Hazebrouck, Cassel and Saint-Omer was 'bombardable', and many hospital units were located within this corridor. He described how, night after night, hospital staff heard 'the heavy German bombing machines come groaning along with a rhythmic whirr, like a flat tire'.[9]

Nurses arriving at CCSs found their first experiences of being under shellfire both fascinating and terrifying. Shell after shell flew overhead towards Allied artillery emplacements. The bombardment seemed to form a peculiar pattern: first came the faint boom, and the suspense of waiting, knowing that a shell had been fired; this was followed by a distant whine as it began to approach; then the whine became a scream which amplified and intensified as the shell drew nearer; next came the deafening crash and the shaking of the earth beneath one's feet, as it landed; finally, the zip and whizz of splinters, as shrapnel and shell fragments of many sizes tore through the air in all directions.

May Tilton described her first night at Brandhoek, watching the bombardment that preceded the Third Battle of Ypres:

The flashes from the guns and the marvellous illuminations in the sky [were] more dazzling than any lightning. A continuous rumble and roar, as of an immense factory of vibrating machinery, filled the night. The pulsings and vibration worked into our bodies and brains; the screech of big shells, and the awful crash when they burst at no great distance, kept our nerves on edge; but even to this terrific noise we became accustomed.[10]

Close to the hospital was an emplacement of 'Big Bobs (15-inch guns)', which 'split the air with terrific force and made the earth rock and tremble'. In the sky almost directly above them were eighteen observation balloons. May and her companions felt they were almost on the battlefield.

On 30 July, Kate Luard recorded in her journal that her hospital – No. 32 CCS - was nearly ready for the 'big push'. 'By the time you get this,' she commented to her family, 'it will be history for better or worse.' The hospital was ready to perform huge numbers of operations, with fifteen theatre sisters, and a complement of thirty-three fully trained nurses in all. They had experienced their first gas drill that evening, finding that most of them were unable to get their masks on within the required six seconds. With her usual sense of dry humour, Kate commented: 'We take about six minutes!' The 'roar' from the bombardment that night was 'stupefying'.[11]

The first infantry assault of the Ypres Campaign opened on 31 July with the battle for Pilckem Ridge. Assaults on Hill 70, Langemarck and a number of smaller objectives would follow in August. Preparations had been disrupted by the French mutiny, which meant that the movement of French artillery to the sector was delayed. British aerial reconnaissance had also had to be curtailed, because flyers had been relocated to Britain following a devastating bombing of London, which had destroyed an infant school, killing eighteen children. The result was that the Allies were not fully aware of the massing defenders on the German side of the lines.

On the night of 30 July the front-line trenches were crowded with men, waiting for the command to go 'over the top' and take Pilckem Ridge. Their objectives were the so-called 'black line' (the ridge itself) and the blue, green and red lines behind it which corresponded with what the Allies understood to be the German defensive positions. Zero hour had been set for 3.50 a.m. Some men had crept out into no man's land and were lying on their stomachs, waiting to form the first line of the assault. The Germans – knowing that an attack was due – kept up a steady bombardment, and many of the waiting Allied troops were hit. No stretcher-bearers could get through the crowded trenches, so the casualties had to wait for rescue until after the attack had been launched. At dawn it began to drizzle, and any emerging light was blocked out by the complete cloud cover. As the whistles blew, signalling the order to attack, it was raining steadily. Men climbed their trench walls, or hoisted themselves up makeshift ladders into no man's land and began to advance. At the same time, an enormous artillery barrage began. Huge flashes of light showed where high-explosive shells and were bombarding enemy lines. Fifty yards behind the creeping barrage the noise was almost deafening.

The advance in the north, including the forward push by the French army on the left flank of Gough's XIV Corps, was highly successful. The black line on Pilckem Ridge was taken relatively easily, but further south, around villages such as St Julien and Zonnebeke, the advance faltered as the Germans withdrew behind their much stronger defences beyond the

Portrait of Kate Luard as a young woman.
(Image appears by kind courtesy of Caroline Stevens)

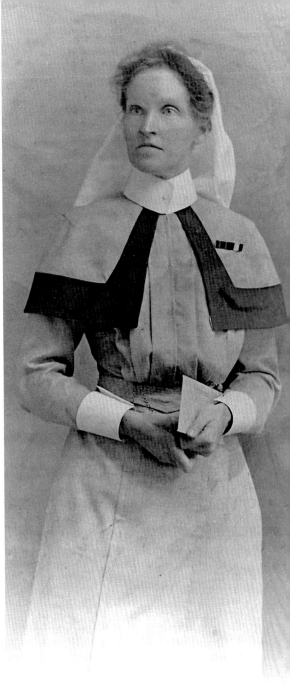

Portrait of Sister Kate Luard.
(Image appears by kind courtesy of Caroline Stevens)

Portrait of Sister Kate Luard seated outside her home, Birch Rectory, Essex, while on leave during the war.
(Image appears by kind courtesy of Caroline Stevens)

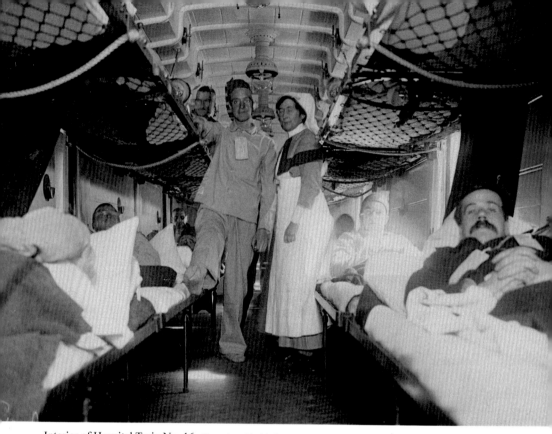

Interior of Hospital Train No. 16. (Reproduced by kind courtesy of the Wills family and with the assistance of the National Railway Museum)

Photograph taken in a treatment area at L'Hôpital de l'Océan's Vinkem site.
(© The Belgian Red Cross Archives, Brussels; reproduced with their permission)

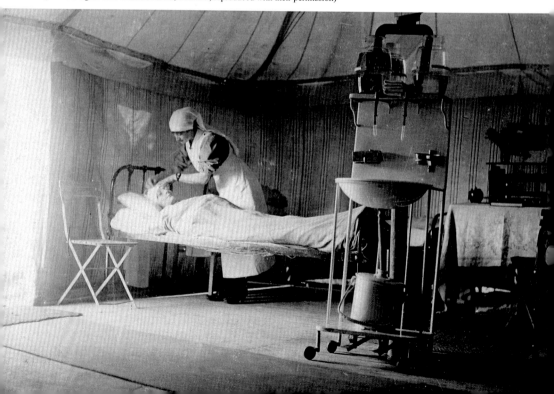

Exterior view of No. 8 British General Hospital at Rouen.
(From the collection of Kate Maxey; reproduced by kind permission of the Defty and Varley families)

Interior of a ward at No. 1 British General Hospital, Étretat.
(From the collection of Kate Maxey; reproduced by kind permission of the Defty and Varley families)

A nursing sister with a group of 'walking wounded' patients.
(From the collection of Kate Maxey; reproduced by kind permission of the Defty and Varley families)

Wound irrigation being performed by surgeon and nurses at L'Hôpital de l'Océan, La Panne.
(© The Belgian Red Cross Archives, Brussels; reproduced with their permission)

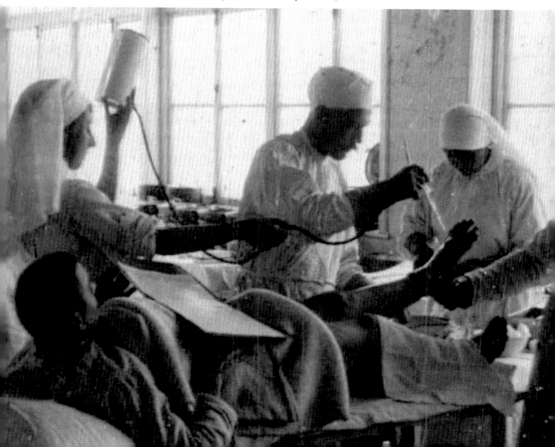

Portrait of Dorothea McFie, British volunteer
nurse at L'Hôpital de l'Océan.
(Reproduced by kind permission of Talbot House, Poperinge)

Portrait of Alison McFie, British volunteer
nurse at L'Hôpital de l'Océan.
(Reproduced by kind permission of Talbot House, Poperinge)

Château Couthove, Proven, as it appeared in 1917.
(Reproduced by kind permission of Talbot House, Poperinge)

Portrait of Nellie Morrice.
(Reproduced with the permission of the
Australian War Memorial, Canberra, Australia (H16062_2))

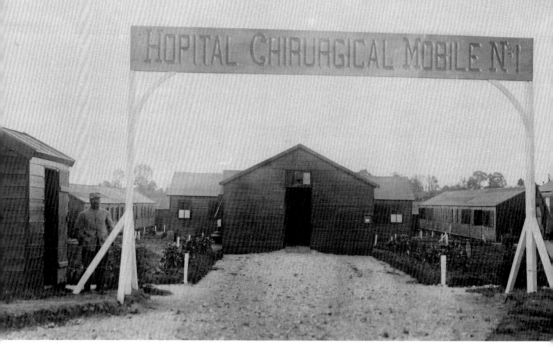

Mobile Surgical No. 1: sentry box and gateway, with reception hut beyond.
(Reproduced with the permission of the Australian War Memorial, Canberra, Australia (PO1908_030))

Mobile Surgical No. 1: on the far right is Agnes Warner, second from the right is Mary Borden.
(From the Collection of Madeleine Morrison; reproduced by kind permission of the Provincial Archives of Alberta
(PR1986.0054.0012.0001))

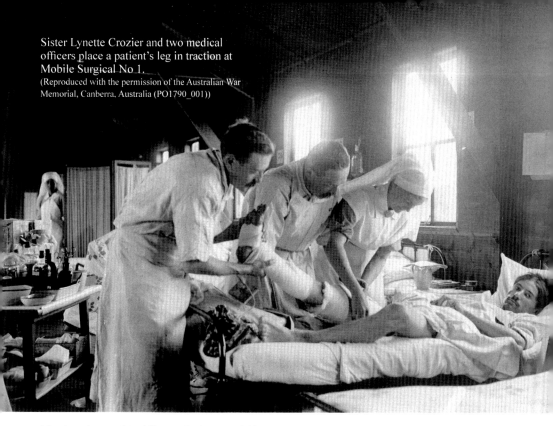

Sister Lynette Crozier and two medical officers place a patient's leg in traction at Mobile Surgical No 1.
(Reproduced with the permission of the Australian War Memorial, Canberra, Australia (PO1790_001))

Nursing sisters of Mobile Surgical No. 1 visiting a slit trench. At the front, facing camera, from left: Annie Hanning, Agnes Warner, Hilda Loxton, Minnie Hough.
(Reproduced with the permission of the Australian War Memorial, Canberra, Australia (PO1790_002))

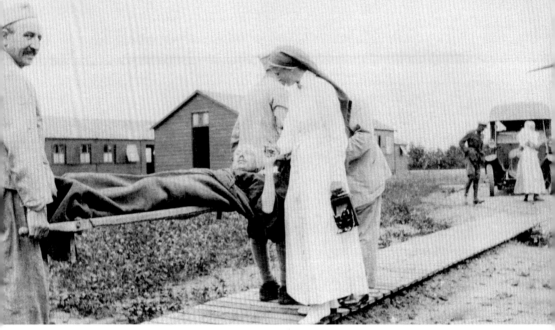

Hilda Loxton bidding a patient goodbye at Mobile Surgical No. 1.
(Reproduced with the permission of the Australian War Memorial, Canberra, Australia (PO1790_003))

Minnie Hough wearing
her gas mask at Mobile
Surgical No. 1.
(Reproduced with the permission
of the Australian War Memorial,
Canberra, Australia (PO1790_019))

The grave of Adrien Le Roux at Roeselare.
(Reproduced by kind courtesy of Dirk Claerhout)

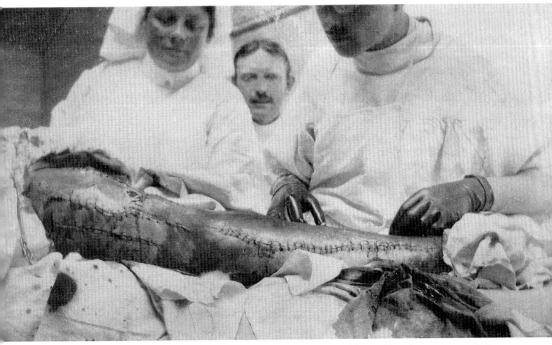

Annie Hanning working in the theatre of Mobile Surgical No. 1, with two French surgeons, suturing a series of leg wounds. (Reproduced with the permission of the Australian War Memorial, Canberra, Australia (PO1790_026))

The Maxey family; Kate Maxey seated on the ground, far right.
(Reproduced by kind courtesy of the Defty and Varley families)

Portrait of Kate Maxey in her Leeds General Infirmary uniform.
(Reproduced by kind courtesy of the Defty and Varley families)

Image of a hutted hospital. (From the Collection of Kate Maxey; reproduced by kind courtesy of the Defty and Varley families)

Sister Kate Maxey (TFNS) with a group of patients.
(Reproduced by kind courtesy of the Defty and Varley families)

Sister Kate Maxey with an unnamed orderly.
(Reproduced by kind courtesy of the Defty and Varley families)

Image of a tented hospital, possibly British Casualty Clearing Station No. 58. (From the Collection of Kate Maxey; reproduced by kind courtesy of the Defty and Varley families)

Mobile Surgical No. 1. Two nurses and a medical officer with a group of departing patients.
(From the Collection of Madeleine Morrison; reproduced by kind permission of the Provincial Archives of Alberta (PR.1986.0054.00d12.0002))

Madeleine Jaffray with a group of patients at Mobile Surgical No. 1
(Reproduced with the permission of the Australian War Memorial, Canberra, Australia (P01908_008))

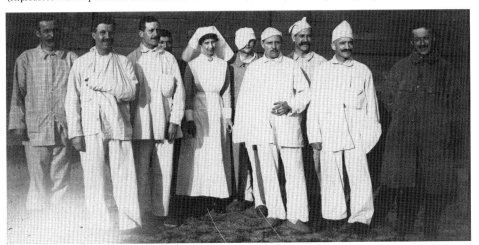

Madeleine Jaffray with a group of 'up patients' at the door to her ward at Mobile Surgical No. 1
(From the Collection of Madeleine Morrison; reproduced by kind permission of the Provincial Archives of Alberta (PR.1986.0054.0012.0003))

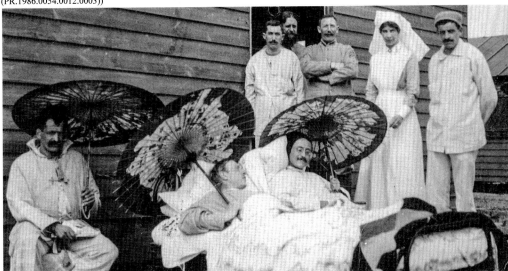

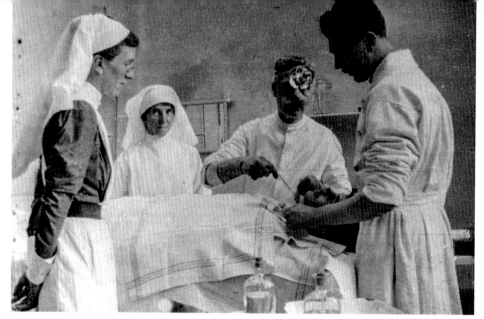

In the operating theatre. (From the Collection of Madeleine Morrison; reproduced by kind permission of the Provincial Archives of Alberta (PR.1986.0054.0012.0004))

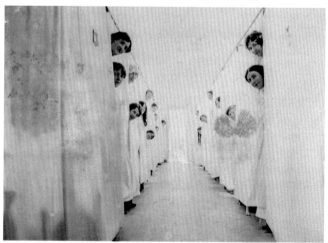

Nurses' sleeping quarters (From the Collection of Madeleine Morrison; reproduced by kind permission of the Provincial Archives of Alberta (PR.1986.0054.0012.0005))

Photograph of shell hole in the hospital compound of Mobile Surgical No. 1. (From the Collection of Madeleine Morrison; reproduced by kind permission of the Provincial Archives of Alberta (PR.1986.0054.0012.0006))

Madeleine Jaffray departing Mobile Surgical No. 1 by ambulance following her injury.
(Reproduced by kind permission of the Provincial Archives of Alberta (PR.1986.0054.0013. 0001))

Madeleine Morrison (née Jaffray) with her husband, Byron Morrison. (Reproduced by kind permission of the Provincial Archives of Alberta)

Portrait of Madeleine Jaffray wearing her service medals and badges, including the Croix de Guerre.
(Reproduced by kind permission of the Provincial Archives of Alberta (A14050))

Portrait of Nellie Spindler.
(Reproduced by permission and with the kind assistance
of the Lijssenthoek Cemetery Visitor Centre)

Nellie Spindler's grave at Lijssenthoek Cemetery, 2016.
(Author's collection)

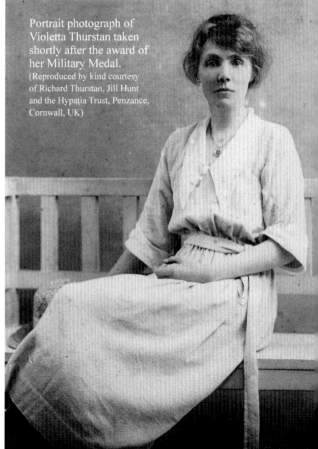

Portrait photograph of
Violetta Thurstan taken
shortly after the award of
her Military Medal.
(Reproduced by kind courtesy
of Richard Thurstan, Jill Hunt
and the Hypatia Trust, Penzance,
Cornwall, UK)

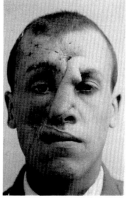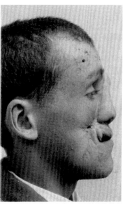

The Gillies British patient file of Sidney Beldam, MS0513/1/1/ID133.
(Reproduced by kind courtesy of Marilyn McInnes and with the permission of The Archives at the Royal College of Surgeons of England)

Portrait of Sidney Beldam in his
Machine Gun Corps uniform.
(Reproduced by kind courtesy of Marilyn
McInnes)

Portrait of Winifred Winkworth,
who later married Sidney Beldam.
(Reproduced by kind courtesy of Marilyn
McInnes)

Portrait of Helen Fairchild in her
Pennsylvania Hospital uniform.
(Reproduced by kind courtesy of Nelle Rote)

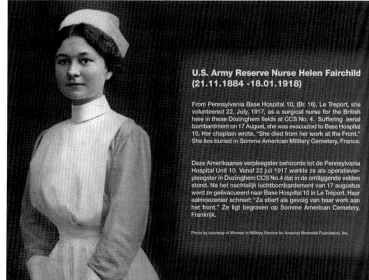

Memorial Plaque to Helen
Fairchild at Dozinghem.
(Reproduced by kind permission of Luc
Inion, Nelle Rote and the Women in
Military Service for America Memorial
Foundation, Inc)

**U.S. Army Reserve Nurse Helen Fairchild**
**(21.11.1884 -18.01.1918)**

From Pennsylvania Base Hospital 10, (Br. 16), Le Treport, she
volunteered 22, July, 1917, as a surgical nurse for the British
here in these Dozinghem fields at CCS No. 4. Suffering aerial
bombardment on 17 August, she was evacuated to Base Hospital
10, Her chaplain wrote, "She died from her work at the Front."
She lies buried in Somme American Military Cemetery, France.

Deze Amerikaanse verpleegster behoorde tot de Pennsylvania
Hospital Unit 10. Vanaf 22 juli 1917 werkte ze als operatiever-
pleegster in Dozinghem CCS No.4 dat in de omliggende velden
stond. Na het nachtelijk luchtbombardement van 17 augustus
werd ze geëvacueerd naar Base Hospital 10 in Le Tréport. Haar
aalmoezenier schreef: "Ze stierf als gevolg van haar werk aan
het front." Ze ligt begraven op Somme American Cemetery,
Frankrijk.

Photo by courtesy of Women in Military Service for America Memorial Foundation, Inc.

Portrait photograph of
**Minnie Wood.** (Reproduced
by permission of the Imperial War
Museum, London, UK (WWC_
D4_1_2_1(1))

Portrait of May Tilton
(From: May Tilton, The Grey
Battalion (Sydney, Angus &
Robertson Ltd., 1933))

Steenbeek River (which was now an extended morass). The Allied advance was literally bogged down. Men were struggling through the thick, black, sucking mud of no man's land, sheltering from enemy machine-gun fire in deep shell holes, sometimes up to their armpits in filthy, soupy water. The southernmost part of the advance was the slowest. German resistance on the Gheluvelt Plateau was fierce; the preliminary bombardment had failed to touch strongpoints in places such as Nonne Boschen, Glencourse Wood and Sanctuary Wood. Here, men pulled each other out of the mud and somehow forced themselves forward towards heavily fortified positions, only to find that the German barbed wire was completely intact. They were forced to retreat under continued heavy shelling and machine-gun fire.

Progress in most areas was so slow that they were unable to keep up with the 'creeping barrage' that was supposed to be protecting them. Lieutenant M. Walkinton of the 24th Machine Gun Company described how:

> As we crossed the German support line their barrage fell on us. Shells screamed down and burst all around. I felt as if I had been kicked hard in the backside by an elephant. I was lifted high in the air and fell with a crash, unable to move my left leg. I felt no pain but my leg was completely numb. A little blood came through the trouser leg. Sergeant Carter shouted, 'You alright, Sir?' 'Yes', I said, 'keep going.' On he went into the smoke, flame and dust taking the men with him.[12]

Walkinton was able to drag himself into a shell hole where he waited until rescued by stretcher-bearers. At the regimental aid post, he was given morphine and anti-tetanus serum and loaded, with other stretcher-cases, into a motor ambulance. At the CCS, he was given fluids and stimulants and moved as quickly as possible into the operating theatre, where a surgeon scraped the shell splinters, mud, fragments of uniform and other debris from the wound in his buttock with a sterile curette, before packing the wound with antiseptic-soaked gauze. Walkinton was one of the lucky ones. He survived to tell his story.

Even in the northern sector of the assault, the advance was slowing to a near-halt. As the infantry moved down the east side of the Pilckem Ridge, their supporting artillery were losing sight of them and getting stuck in the cloying mud. The creeping barrage was beginning to fail badly. Rowland Luther, a driver with the 92nd Brigade Royal Field Artillery, described the desperation he felt as he and the rest of his team tried to move their guns forward to within range of the advance. They knew that delay would leave their infantry exposed to shelling and machine-gun fire from the fortified farmhouses and heavy concrete pillboxes between the German first and second lines. Their comrades could only survive if they could move forward towards the protective second-line trenches, and this could only happen if the German strongpoints were destroyed – or, at least, suppressed. He described how, finding an area of dry ground, he and comrades drove their horse teams forward, not seeing a cluster of men lying on the ground. As the horse team jumped over the inert bodies, dragging the heavy guns behind them, 'the wheels went over the bodies, wounded or dead. It made no difference – it was advance. The Germany artillery was peppering us with shells of all calibres.' Later in the advance, he described how he tried to save a comrade with a head wound: 'One of our men was hit with a large piece of shrapnel, it had scalped him and as we laid him down his brains were spewing over his forehead. I tried to smooth it back again and put the top of his scalp back again, thinking he might live – those are some of the things one tries to do in our state.'[13] It was not surprising that, as survivors began to return from the assault, many were suffering from acute shell-shock. Most were dazed and confused, some were unable to speak or walk, others were hallucinating and a few were in a state of complete physical and mental collapse.

Nurses were becoming adept at the work of triage: assessing their patient's needs. Those most in need of life-saving surgery – including those with smashed limbs from which large vessels were still leaking blood, torn abdominal and chest walls, and heads in need of trepanning to relieve pressure on damaged brains – were sent straight to theatre, until the floors outside operating rooms became as crowded as those of reception huts. Surgeons worked steadily through multiple operations, supported by theatre nurses, anaesthetists and orderlies. U.S. surgeon George Crile, based at No. 17 British CCS at Remy Siding, described the scenes at the 'Siding' on the opening day of the Third Ypres Campaign:

The stream of wounded began to increase in volume slowly at first, then rapidly, until the entire Remy Siding was swamped. By the night of August first, every bed, every aisle, every tent, every inch of floor space was occupied by stretchers – then the rows of stretchers spread out over the lawn, around the huts, flowing out toward the railway ... Whether stretcher cases, or walking cases all showed the usual grave demeanour – the mud-coloured, gray, shrunken face, the careworn, war-exhausted countenance ... The operating rooms ran day and night without ceasing. Teams worked steadily for twelve hours on, then twelve hours off, relieving each other like night-day-night shifts … There passed through the Remy Siding group of CCSs over ten thousand wounded in the first forty-eight hours. I had two hundred deaths in one night, in my own service. The seriously wounded piled up so fast that nothing could be done with them, so I told the Sister to administer as near an overdose of morphine as was possible to keep them alive but free of suffering.[14]

Australian nurse Violet Payne was one of those caring for the thousands of casualties:

At one time so many wounded came in that every available space held a stretcher. Then the stretchers had to be placed outside everywhere imaginable, and to add to their misery a drizzly rain fell. The only shelter was a ground sheet placed over them, but how gratefully and cheerfully the poor fellows accepted even this poor effort. They were so thankful to be out of that inferno. The first words invariably uttered: "Sister, do you think it might be a Blighty?" even though you knew often they were fatal.[15]

CCSs were almost overwhelmed by rushes of casualties. Effie Garden later wrote of how nurses began to take on work that would normally have been performed by surgeons:

Each team had two tables; while one patient was being bandaged the next one was being given his anaesthetic, the men still in their uniforms. Our team worked from 1am to 5pm, when necessary and shorter hours between battles. Our CCS was supposed to take head cases but it was seldom that there were not other wounds as well and I was often given a scalpel to take out small pieces of shell etc., and clean up minor wounds which saved time for the more serious cases.

May Tilton described the desolation of No. 32 British CCS, as the first rush of casualties arrived. Men were carried in completely covered with mud from head to foot, and the CCS itself was like a swamp of mud. Her own unit, No. 3 Australian, was still not ready to open, but ten of its nurses had been loaned to No. 32. Kate Luard commented that they were 'a handsome crowd and very nice'. The staff of No. 44 were also working hard to get their hospital ready to re-open.

Soon after her arrival at Brandhoek, May Tilton received the news that her cousin, Norman, had been killed in the assault. She and a friend, Elsie Grant, spent a leave-day walking to Dickebusch, 'ploughing through mud and slush'. They found Norman's newly covered grave among three short rows of mounds. By the end of the campaign, the burial ground in which his body was lying would have been expanded many times. Today, the Old and New Dickebusch Military Cemeteries and the New Cemetery Extension collectively contain 1,228 war graves.

One of the most horrifying elements of the Third Battle of Ypres was the use, for the first time, of mustard gas, or dichlorethyl sulphide – the 'new gas' that was to become so familiar to staff throughout the lines of evacuation. Stealthy in its action and terrifying in its effects, mustard gas burned any piece of skin or mucous membrane it touched – including the tissues of the airways and lungs, and the walls of the gut. Soldiers sheltering in shell holes on the battlefield beyond the Salient saw and heard strange shells, which landed close by but did not burst. They seemed to 'plop' into the ground, half burying themselves in the mud, and then they opened to release a substance that was half-oily, half-liquid – which mushroomed into a gaseous cloud as it touched the atmosphere. Its action was delayed, and even as the man was wondering what was happening, the sulphur mustard was burning his skin and lungs. After a short time, he would begin to sneeze, then choke and retch. Then burns would begin to appear on the vesicular parts of the body – areas where there was a concentration of lymph glands, such as the armpits, groin and neck. His eyes would sting, then swell and close as the gas burned their delicate tissues. The blindness that followed would last at least ten days.

In CCSs near Proven and Westvleteren, nurses were battling to save the lives of these dreadfully damaged men. British CCS No. 47 had several wards devoted to acute gassed cases, where staff moved rapidly from patient to patient. Men were given morphine to relieve their agony, and oxygen was administered through masks to ease their laboured breathing – but many pushed the masks away in desperate attempts to gain more fresh air. Persuading them to take the oxygen required a skill and tact that was difficult to muster after a sleepless night, when one was so exhausted that it was difficult to talk at all. Many patients were on the edge of collapse; they were prescribed stimulants, which nurses injected into their muscles through carefully sterilized and sharpened needles. All gas-damaged eyes were protected by pads soaked in bicarbonate of soda; nurses circled the wards constantly, removing these and bathing the gluey and inflamed eyes beneath. They tried to reach each patient every two hours – but found themselves racing against time. May Tilton described how dangerous this work could be for nurses themselves: 'We were unable to work for any length of time in these gassed wards. Stooping over the patients, we soon became affected by inhaling the gas. Our throats became sore and set us coughing, while our eyes smarted and became weak and watery. The odour of the ward was in our nostrils for weeks.'[16] Nurses were also living with the fear that they could be seriously poisoned. There was a risk that gas from attacks in the front lines might reach personnel in rest areas – as had already happened at Adinkerke – or that gas shells might be fired beyond the second-line trenches. All medical workers in the zone of the armies were given new gas masks with extensions containing 'lime permanganate' to neutralize the mustard gas.

At No. 17 British CCS, Australian nurse Violet Payne was working with the most up-to-date equipment:

> The tents for the gassed patients were most interesting. Cylinders and pipes for the oxygen were placed down the centre of the tent, then the stretchers on either side with the patients' heads almost touching. Attached to the main tube were nasal tubes. These were inserted in each man's nostril and a gentle pressure of oxygen kept on almost continuously, as it relieved the chest considerably. Every two hours the eyes had to be bathed with a sod-bicarb lotion, and the mouth cleaned regularly … the eyes were so swollen and red that for days they were as helpless as infants … The sides of the tents were rolled up day and night to allow all the air possible.[17]

Work with mustard-gas-poisoned patients had been a 'baptism of horror' for the nurses of American Base Hospital No. 10 at Le Treport. Soon after their arrival, the hospital had received a huge convoy of patients, all poisoned by the gas. Matron Margaret Dunlop described the scene:

> These patients were horribly gassed and were pictures of misery and intense suffering. They poured upon us in great numbers – 600 in less than forty-eight hours – and their sufferings were pitiful to see, but their bravery, unselfishness and fortitude were impressed upon us very fully. The nurses worked hard and faithfully during

this short period, but the awfulness and immensity of suffering and cruel barbarity of war upon the individual were a soul-harrowing experience to them all.[18]

Mobile Surgical No. 1 was now located well north and west of Poperinge. It had been strategically placed to receive wounded men from the French First Army advance on the left flank of Gough's Fifth Army. It was further away from the front lines than the CCSs at Brandhoek; yet its new location did not seem to be any safer than its previous one at Adinkerke. The headquarters of the French First Army was at Rousbrugge, and an anti-aircraft gun had been placed in the tower of the village church. It seemed to fire right over the nurses' huts. But the unit had a dugout in which nurses could take shelter during bombing raids. On the opening day of the Ypres Campaign wounded 'poured in' to the hospital and the theatres were operational for three days and three nights without a break. In the overcrowded wards, sisters and *infermièrs* were overwhelmed, and the hospital's elderly ambulance drivers, Mr de Malyns and Mr Phillips came in to help them, taking drinks to patients and keeping delirious men in their beds. Many patients were severely shocked, and all were dehydrated. Hilda Loxton could never forget their 'pathetic' cries, '*J'ai soif; J'ai soif; veux boire.*'[19]

From early August onwards, the hospital endured frequent bombing raids and, when the alarm sounded, nurses who were not on duty were ordered to take shelter in the dugout. Hilda commented in her diary that 'these night parades in wrapper, helmet and torch take much out of the Sisters'. The entire district was being severely bombarded and Hilda was later to paste an undated newspaper clipping into her journal. It reported that 'Dunkirk held the record for the number of times a French town has been bombarded'.

On 1 August all three of the CCSs at Brandhoek became one enormous flooded morass. 'Everything is a swamp and a pond,' commented Kate Luard. In all three hospitals tents were leaking and floors were saturated. In some wards, the water reached halfway up the legs of the beds and nurses found themselves wading from patient to patient. The Australian nurses had an added problem: their luggage had been lost somewhere on the journey between Abbeville, Proven and Brandhoek. Their clothes soon became sodden with rain and mud, and the only coats they had were lent to them by their orderlies. They were instructed to wear 'heavy and headachey' steel helmets at all times,[20] and were given gas masks, but they had to wait several days before any changes of uniform arrived.

Kate Luard was beginning to feel anxious about her own staff at No. 32, commenting that

> the work thickens as the wards fill up and new wards have to be opened ... The staffing of the wards for Night Duty both of Sisters and Orderlies is the problem, even with my 33. Some of these are first-class. It is getting very ghastly; the men all look so appalling when they are brought in and so many die. I don't see how the 'break-the-news' letters are going to be written because the moment for sitting down literally never comes.[21]

A day later, she was writing of how men were being brought in 'with mud over their eyes and mouths, and 126 have died in three and a half days'.[22] On 3 August, a 'special order was issued by the Director of Medical Services'. He wished 'to place on record his high appreciation of the work done by [No. 32] Casualty Clearing Station, and [to thank] all Ranks for excellent work done under very trying circumstances'. Kate Luard commented wryly that by 'trying circumstances' he must have meant 'the simultaneous inundation of hundreds of abdominals, mud, floods, and bursting shells'.[23]

*Chapter Eight*

# August Raids

B y the end of 31 July approximately eighteen square miles of territory had been captured by the Allies. Publicly, Haig and Gough declared that the day had been a success, but, privately, they were forced to recognize that many of the initial gains around St Julien had been relinquished to German counter-attacks, while objectives on the high ground of the Gheluvelt Plateau had never been captured. Gough decided to launch a series of further operations to take these objectives. As men were brought forward for the assault, the rain began to fall. It would not stop for seven days. An unsuccessful attack on 10 August yielded well over 2,200 casualties, and CCSs south of Poperinge were flooded with casualties. Six days later, Gough and Haig decided to attempt a further attack on a wide front. This time, the British forces sustained over 15,000 casualties.

From a strategic point of view, the so-called Third Battle of Ypres was descending into farce. For the men who called themselves the 'poor bloody infantry', it was becoming a hellish nightmare. Lessons that had been learned at the Somme and Arras were, apparently, being ignored. The awful weather meant that the ground was drenched and the mud was becoming ever more impenetrable. Low cloud and poor visibility made it impossible for observers in balloons or aeroplanes to spot enemy artillery batteries; hence, counter-bombardment could not be directed with any precision and it became impossible to protect the advancing foot soldiers. In spite of these disadvantages, forces in the north were moderately successful, taking a significant amount of territory including the village of Langemarck. But, in the south, the Gheluvelt Plateau remained in German hands.

One of the ways in which the German high command chose to respond to the terrible battle of attrition taking place east of Ypres, was to find ways to fight and destroy its enemies behind their own lines. In the so-called rest areas there was an intensification of aerial bombardment. As bombing raids increased, CCSs became more vulnerable. Nurses arriving at their postings found that they were closer to the 'fighting front' than they had anticipated; the bombing was terrifying. In diaries and memoirs, they wrote of raids by 'Taubes', but the Taube – ironically, named using the German word for a 'dove' – was an out-dated and unstable aircraft. By 1917, it had largely been replaced by new and more manoeuvrable types, built to permit accurate aerial bombardment and fitted with machine guns, the actions of which were synchronized with the rotation of the propellers. The design of aeroplanes had advanced rapidly in just three years: both sides had invested heavily in aircraft engineering, recognizing that such technology could offer a distinct advantage in a war of entrenchment. From the use of unstable monoplanes designed purely for aerial reconnaissance and artillery spotting, through fighter aircraft armed with hand grenades and primitive machine guns, both sides were now building sophisticated and highly destructive flying machines that could perform a range of functions. Aeronautical engineers on opposing sides were engaged in an ever-more-sophisticated arms race. By 1917, bombing raids employed specially designed 'Gothas', each of which could carry over 500 kilograms of bombs.

They came over singly, in pairs, or, sometimes, in squadrons. On a clear night, the light humming of their engines could be heard in the distance, carried on the still summer air, becoming gradually louder. At times, aircraft flew so low that during daytime raids, watching nurses joked that they could see the pilots' moustaches. Hospital staff were fascinated by the flying machines. Aeroplanes of any kind were a novelty to them, and they often found themselves standing in the compounds of their units, watching dogfights between fighter planes. It was not wise to watch for too long, though; one could be hit by flying debris from fragmenting aircraft or from one's own 'archies' – the anti-aircraft guns that were situated so close to CCSs. During a bombing raid, the unwary observer might even get caught in the sights of a cockpit's machine gun.

Perhaps one of the reasons that bombs were being dropped so close to the CCSs at Brandhoek was the light railway that carried ammunition, and ran directly through the compound of No. 32 CCS. Kate Luard commented on the apparent 'cheeriness' of the 'baby trains' carrying their deadly loads, and on how one often had to wait until they had passed before it was possible to cross from one side of the hospital to the other. On 5 August, German Gothas flew over Brandhoek in larger numbers, bombing the railhead and narrowly missing the CCSs. May commented that the experience was

> more terrifying than anything we had yet known. The explosion was terrific in its unexpectedness, like a frightful peal of thunder, and was followed by a rain of shots from our archies [anti-aircraft guns]. Hardly had we recovered from the shock, than there was

another ear-splitting explosion nearer. They came again at 10pm, and all through the night peppered us with bombs, though none fell directly on our camp … It was terrifying lying in bed, expecting every minute to be blown to pieces … I could not control the violent trembling of my legs. My knees positively knocked together. I could laugh at myself, but I could not stop the trembling.[1]

The commanding officer of the CCS wanted to send the nurses westwards to safety, and ordered them to pack. But the road back towards Proven and Vlamertinghe was being steadily bombed, and was, in fact, the most dangerous place in the zone around Poperinge that night. It was not until the following day that the nurses were driven back to No. 63 British CCS, where they slept for ten hours. Even this far behind the lines, the entire district had been severely bombarded.

No. 32 British CCS remained at Brandhoek, all that was left of the 'Advanced Abdominal Centre' for the time being. It may have been that the British commanding officer was less anxious about the safety of his staff than the Australian, but it is more likely that No. 32 remained where it was because it was fully operational and completely full of patients. The cost in soldiers' lives of evacuating the nurses seemed too great. Kate Luard was beginning to worry; she was experiencing 'brain-fag' brought on by sixteen-hour shifts, and constant wakefulness, and was beginning to feel that she was losing her decision-making abilities. It was around this time that Captain Noel Chavasse, a medical officer who had already been awarded the Victoria Cross, was brought into No. 32. He was nursed at the CCS for forty-eight hours, but died in the early hours of the morning of 4 August. His night nurse, Ida Leedam, later wrote to his fiancée, recounting how he had asked her to say: "give her my love. Tell her Duty called and called me to obey.' For the action that led to his wounding in early August, Noel Chavasse was awarded a second Victoria Cross.

On 7 August, Matron O'Dwyer, the sister-in-charge of No. 3 Australian CCS – who was still waiting for her own unit to open, but who had remained in Brandhoek – wrote 209 of Kate's 'break-the-news' letters to the relatives of those who had died in No. 32. Kate herself was remarking in her journal how 'the ones that recover are tremendously proud of having done it, as they are always being told what marvels they are!'

No. 44 re-opened on 9 August, and the work of No. 32 began to ease. Nurses, orderlies and doctors were able to work more normal shifts – and one might have expected the sisters to take advantage of their off-duty time to sleep and recuperate. Yet one of the most astonishing features of the work done by Kate and her team of nurses was their morale-boosting 'social' work. Every Sunday they held 'At Home' parties in the sisters' mess. Off-duty sisters served tea and cake, as if they were at a garden party in the Hampshire Hills rather than at a CCS close the front lines of a destructive military campaign. Kate commented on the amazement of visiting officers:

> The tea-tables and the party-tea, our uniforms, our work, our hospitality, our tin-hats, roaring guns and our other noises moved [one officer] to such soulful speeches I nearly laughed. 'And to think of all the beastly women at home selling flags,' he said in a pained voice.[2]

On 14 August No. 3 Australian CCS reopened at Brandhoek amid a thunderstorm. At first the hospital had four surgical teams, but the number of staff was gradually increased as other teams were transferred in from base hospitals. Eventually, the matron-in-chief for France and Flanders, Maud McCarthy, was to comment that the site on which the three CCSs were operating was more like an enormous stationary hospital than a forward field hospital. Kate Luard – the most experienced nurse on the site – wrote in her journal that it was more 'like a battlefield'. Indeed, by mid-August, she was beginning to suspect that German aviators were deliberately targeting CCSs. Although she recognized that her own unit and those next to it might inadvertently be hit because of their close proximity to railheads and ammunition dumps, she felt certain that hospitals behind the line were likely to be clearly marked on German maps, and considered the bombing of their compounds to be a 'dirty trick'.

As soon as she arrived back at Brandhoek, May Tilton volunteered for night duty. The three CCSs were now admitting fifty patients each in rotation. May was put in charge of the resuscitation ward, with two orderlies. She described later how terrifying it was to hold such a responsible role with so few resources. Although her orderlies were 'splendid', it was impossible for them to save every patient, many of whom were slipping away even as they were brought into the ward:

> Torrents of rain were falling, and poor fellows were carried in, saturated and covered with mud, stone cold and pulseless. Three primus stoves provided our hot water supply. Many of our patients died as we lifted them from the stretchers. By midnight, the

ward was full of moaning, groaning wrecks. I was appalled by the immensity and hopelessness of the task before us. At the faintest sign of a pulse beat, we were injecting salines, and working like mad to restore life sufficiently to get the patient to the operating table.[3]

On 16 August, a day when as many as twenty aircraft could be seen in the sky above Brandhoek, the site was inspected by two of the most senior matrons on the Western Front: Evelyn Conyers, matron-in-chief of the Australian Army Nursing Service, and Maud McCarthy, matron-in-chief of the British Expeditionary Force in France and Flanders. They were horrified that nurses had been posted so close to the front line, and to an area that was clearly a target for both long-range artillery and aerial bombardment. Reluctantly, they permitted their staff to remain, knowing that the CCSs could not operate without expert nurses. That night a bombing raid by German Gothas killed a medical officer and two orderlies. The sisters' bell tents were protected by high external walls of sandbags, but their canvas was still riddled with holes. May Tilton began to feel permanently dazed – vaguely aware that emotional and physical tension were draining her body of its vitality. It was only her will that kept her working. She knew that the men on the battlefield were fighting their way through 'big shells, bombs, rifle shot, grenades, mine explosions … liquid fire and poison gas'. How, she asked herself, could she give in while they were still forced to go on?

> We worked night after night, in the din of raging battles; dressed and bandaged the wounded; comforted them; praised their courage, their grit and strength of will. The atmosphere reeked with the mingled odours of blood and humanity, antiseptic and gas … 'I don't want to die, sister,' said one nice-looking Englishman. 'I've got a wife and two little girls.' He had a tourniquet above a frightfully smashed up leg that fell to bits as we lifted him from the stretcher. He never saw daylight again … A big shell came over at 3am and killed fourteen gunners alongside us.[4]

The military cemetery next to the CCSs was rapidly filling, as bodies were buried 'twenty deep in one large pit'. Kate Luard commented that 'dreaming in those cornfields and woods at St Pol in June, I used to think a lot about this offensive, but I didn't think it would be as stiff as this'.[5] Casualties were returning from the Salient with stories of how the bodies of dead and wounded were piling up on parts of the battlefield, of how stretcher-bearers were unable to reach them through the flooded quagmire, and how, even if one could drag oneself to safety, it was difficult to see any landmarks in the wasteland of the Salient. Many simply died slowly of haemorrhage or infection, lost in that wilderness; countless others lay helpless in shell holes as the rain-water rose slowly until it drowned them.

Some managed to reach the safety of a regimental aid post and were taken to a CCS where they died of wounds. Nurses were glad that they had at least eased the final hours of these men they saw as heroes.

Kate Luard recounted the story of a 'corpse-like child' who had been taken to the moribund ward:

> We got to work on resuscitation, with some success. He had been bleeding from his subclavian artery and heard them leave him for dead in a shell hole. But he crawled out and was eventually tended in a dug out by 'a lad what said prayers with me', and later the hole in his chest was plugged and he reached us – what was left of him. When, after two days, he belonged to this world again, I got Capt. B to see him, and he got Major C. to operate and tied the twisted artery which I had re-plugged – he couldn't be touched before – and covered with muscle the hole through which he was breathing, and he is now a great hero known as 'the Prince of Wales'. 'There's only me and Mother,' he says, so she will be pleased. But he is not out of the wood yet.[6]

Patients often expressed their surprise that nurses were stationed so close to the battlefield. Many were indignant that women should be put in such danger, seeing it as 'man's job' to go off to war – to protect the women and children who, naturally, should remain at home. But nurses were proud to be in the 'zone of the armies'. Even those who were not overt campaigners for women's suffrage saw that their work was making an important political point. They recognized that 'active service' of the type that took them within range of enemy fire robbed patriarchal male politicians of their primary argument for denying women the vote: that it was only men who made the supreme sacrifice, by dying for their country.

General John Joseph Pershing arrived in France in early June, 1917, and, although U.S. recruits would not be ready to fight alongside the Allies for several months, American doctors and nurses were already caring for Allied soldiers. In July, some of these were sent to support the work of CCSs near the front lines. Among the numerous surgical teams at Dozinghem, near

Westvleteren were two that had left No. 10 Base Hospital at Le Treport on 22 July. The first consisted of surgeon Major Richard Harte, anaesthetist Captain Norris Vaux, highly experienced nurse Helen Fairchild and orderly Private John Marren. They travelled to No. 4 British CCS. The second was led by Captain Charles Mitchell, with Captain Francis Packard as his anaesthetist, Helen Grace McClelland as the nursing sister and Private Seward Jabaut as their orderly. They were posted to No. 61. Margaret Dunlop had chosen Helen McClelland and Helen Fairchild for CCS duty because of their 'ability, long tried and known'. Neither could have anticipated the ordeals they would face. Margaret Dunlop was later to comment that 'the living conditions were rather trying'.[7] She was, perhaps, being euphemistic. Staff at the CCSs were, by now, working twelve- to sixteen-hour shifts, living in tents, and spending a large part of every night sheltering from raids in shallow underground dugouts.

It seems surprising that a member of staff who was already known to be ill was sent into the strenuous environment of the 'zone of the armies'. It may be that Helen was making light of the gastric symptoms that had been troubling her since before her departure from Philadelphia. It is also possible that her senior colleagues had no idea how awful conditions were at Westvleteren. On 13 August, Helen wrote a letter to her mother, concealing the ghastly realities of life at No 4 CCS:

> I am out with an operating team. We are about 100 miles away from our own hospital, close to the fighting lines, and I surely will have lots to tell you about this experience when I get home. We have been up here three weeks and see no signs of going back yet, although when we came we only expected to be here a few days; so, of course, we didn't bring much with us. I had two white dresses and two aprons and two combinations. Now can you imagine trying to keep decent looking for three weeks with that much clothing, in a place where it rains nearly every day, and we live in tents, and wade through mud to and from the operating room. It was some task, but finally dear old Major Harte, who I am up here with, got a car and a man to go down to our own hospital and get us some things ... This has been a very novel experience, but I will be glad when we get orders to go back ... Oh, I shall have books to tell you all when I get home ... Heaps and heaps of love to you one and all, Your very own Helen.[8]

One of the horrors faced by staff in forward CCSs was the likelihood that gas shells containing the new and deadly mustard gas would burst in rest areas west of Ypres, close enough for their contents to be carried into CCS compounds. Influential surgeon Harvey Cushing, serving at No. 46 British CCS at Mendinghem, commented that 'the Boches are using an entirely new gas which gives bad gastrointestinal symptoms'.[9] Helen Fairchild, with her pre-existing gastric condition, would clearly be highly vulnerable to the poisons contained in the mustard gas that were exhaled from these shells.

CCSs 4, 47 and 61 were on a site close to St Sixtus Monastery, a Cistercian community of monks dating back to the Middle Ages. It was only four miles from the small town of Poperinge which, the Americans were amazed to discover, retained its lively social atmosphere, in spite of the constant threat from Gothas. The site was bombed on five occasions in early-to-mid-August. Major Charles Biddell, an American serving with the French Air Force, wrote an eyewitness account of a raid that took place on 17 August. Biddell was staying with doctor friends at No. 61. He had been told that the bombing of CCSs had, at first, been considered a mistake; but when it happened repeatedly, staff began to suspect that it might be deliberate. He agreed that it probably was:

> This is a big field hospital in white tents and lots of red crosses plainly visible. I have myself seen it from the air and you can see it more distinctly than anything else in the neighbourhood. A couple of days before, a bomb had landed on a cook shack about twenty yards from Dr. P-'s tent. The cook's leg came through the roof of the tent next door and the guy ropes of Dr. P-'s tent were decorated with his entrails. Nice party don't you think? … It was a dark night but very clear, with millions of stars. On every side were the muzzle flashes of the anti-aircraft guns, the sky was filled with the flashes of the bursting shells, and the two seemingly joined by streams of tracer bullets from machine guns. These latter look much like Roman candles except they go much faster and keep on going up for thousands of feet … Add to this the roar of the guns and bursting shells and you can imagine what a quiet evening in a field hospital back of the front is like.[10]

The official war diaries of No. 61 British CCS at Dozinghem and No. 2 Canadian CCS at Remy Siding both state that the officers commanding these hospitals believed that the bombing raids were deliberately targeting hospitals.[11]

During the raid on No. 61 at Dozinghem, one of the nurses' tents was hit by flying shrapnel. Helen McClelland and Beatrice McDonald had just gone to bed and were lying in their camp beds talking, when they heard the Gothas approaching. Helen lay down and placed her steel helmet over her face, but Beatrice was still lying propped on one elbow when a number of shell fragments ripped through the tent at high velocity. Several went into her face – more than one hitting her eye. A terrified Helen leaped from her bed and rapidly applied dressings to the wounds to stem the bleeding. The two friends then lay on the ground in their tent until the bombing was over. The shrapnel that had hit Beatrice was said to have been from a so-called 'daisy-cutter bomb', of a type that exploded so close to the ground that it would hit even a low object. For her courage in remaining with her wounded colleague Helen was awarded the Distinguished Service Cross. When interviewed later by a newspaper reporter, she is said to have declared that she was 'too scared to run'.

The same night – 17 August – British CCS No. 17 at Remy Siding was also bombed. US surgeon George Crile described how:

> As they struck the earth, the huge bombs made a flash and crash. Two! Three! Each came nearer, the fourth being just outside our grounds! Before the fifth crashed, I managed to reach my hut followed by my striker Gillet, who struck a match and handed me my steel helmet. We ran for safety, Gillet straight ahead, but I threw myself on the ground, face down. Another crash! Moans! Gillet was fragmented ... The tents throughout the camp were wrecked. Flashlights revealed contortions, anatomical confusion, mangled dead and wounded.[12]

The next day Dr Davey, the officer commanding No. 2 Canadian CCS at Remy Siding, wrote to headquarters asking for permission to build a protective dugout for his nurses. Permission was not granted, but Davey had the dugout built anyway, convinced that the site was being deliberately targeted.[13] By 14 September, George Crile could comment in his diary that

> the orderlies have dug trenches. The Sisters have an utterly inadequate dugout. The medical personnel have divers ways; some have small burrows at the brink of a deep, banked brook; others have burrows surrounded by high mounds of earth; a few have private dugouts in their tent ... some merely put on their helmets, lie on their sides and trust to luck.[14]

In mid-August, Major Richard Harte and Helen Fairchild travelled back down the line to Le Treport. There are conflicting reports as to exactly when they left No. 4 CCS, but their departure took place at a time of nightly bombing raids, when the units were under intense pressure – probably on 17 August, the night of the worst raids.

Following Helen's return, her close friend Florence Wagner was sent out to No. 4 British CCS as a replacement. Surgical Team No. 1 performed a total of 302 operations between 22 July and 18 September. Many of these involved multiple surgical procedures on individual patients – the extraction of bullets and shrapnel from various different parts of the body. Many were amputations, some involving the removal of more than one limb. Team No. 2 remained for much longer and performed 666 operations.

Helen McClelland remained at Dozinghem until 6 October, when her surgical team was relieved by another from Le Treport, which included Eva Gerhard, who remained until 5 December. Dr John Gibbon was later to write of his experiences as part of this team. He found war-torn Belgium 'depressing' and completely devoid of 'creature comforts'. During the later weeks of the Third Ypres Campaign, the operating theatre was constantly at work, its floor 'covered with wounded men on stretchers' waiting their turn for one of the five operating tables. Gibbon found that the work varied enormously. On some days, the team could be working for sixteen hours at a time, with only brief breaks for food; on others time 'hung heavy on [their] hands'. He found his time at No. 61 distressing, because of the 'horrible wounds, the suffering, the high mortality [and] the disturbing visits of Hun planes'. Added to this was 'the most distressing sight which human eye can witnesss, that is the re-wounding and killing of already wounded men by an enemy's bomb dropped suddenly in the dead of night'.[15]

John Gibbon and his colleague 'Newlin' shared a tent. In late November, they had holes which they referred to as 'funk holes', and – using even darker humour - as 'shallow graves', dug into the ground inside their tents. These were six feet long and eighteen inches deep. When the bombing began, they lay in these holes and pulled sheets of iron over themselves. The nurses had to leave their tents and shelter in a large dugout, in which they sat crowded together, waiting for the Gothas to pass over. Gibbon was deeply impressed by the courage of his nurse colleagues:

> Night bombing is a terrifying thing and those who are not disturbed by it possess unusual qualities. It was terrifying to Tommies and officers alike, but I believe that the women nurses showed less fear

than any one. Our own nurse, Miss Gerhart, really seemed to enjoy her experience and I think was the only one who had any regret at leaving No. 61. She was always cheerful and always working. She was liked by the British, both men and women, who at first called her the 'American Sister', but later spoke of her less respectfully, but more affectionately as 'Cat-Gut-Katie'.[16]

By the summer of 1917, the British Army Medical Services had put in place a system for the handling of cases of so-called 'shell-shock'. The army high command were anxious that individuals with emotional trauma should not be labelled as 'ill' or 'injured' and the term 'shell-shock' had been banned. The label 'Not Yet Diagnosed Nervous' was being used instead, and patients with this tentative label were being sent to specialist wards in casualty clearing stations within easy reach of the rest areas, with a view to returning them to active service as quickly as possible. Only the severest cases were being sent down the line to base hospitals. One specialist 'shell-shock' CCS was British CCS No. 62 at Bandaghem. During the bombing raids, many of the unit's patients were said to have run from their wards to look for safer shelter.

On the battlefield, several corps of Sir Hubert Gough's Fifth Army were struggling to gain strategic territory along the Gheluvelt–Langemarck line. In the absence of adequate protection from heavy artillery, they were using a combination of light machine-gun fire, the lobbing of hand grenades and, ultimately, bitter hand-to-hand fighting, to clear a series of fortified farms and pillboxes. This was war of attrition at its darkest: some of those who survived admitted later that prisoners had been killed for fear that they would turn on their captors.

Close to Proven, the bombing was becoming even more intense. At 9.15 p.m. on 20 August, Ellen Byrne was on duty in the theatre at No. 47 British CCS, at Dozinghem. A raid on the hospital caused sixty-eight casualties, of which fourteen were deaths. Ellen, who had already been on duty for thirteen hours, hurried to help the wounded then returned to her operating table to work all night repairing their injuries. She was awarded the Military Medal, her citation declaring that she had 'showed remarkable coolness and gallantry under the most trying circumstances'.[17]

On the morning of Tuesday 21 August the outdated claim that only men could die for their country, was decisively overturned when the random destructiveness of industrial warfare took the life of Nellie Spindler, the young staff nurse from Wakefield, who had been posted to No. 44 British

CCS under the command of her fellow Yorkshirewoman, Minnie Wood. The overnight raids had been particularly bad. It seemed as though the CCSs really were being targeted. At No. 3 Australian CCS, a shell had landed on the quartermaster stores, completely destroying it. That morning the night staff came off duty exhausted by the heavy work of caring for acutely ill men in the middle of almost constant bombing raids. They had been severely short-staffed. The three CCS head sisters were unwilling to put more than a skeleton staff on night duty, knowing that the wards were much more likely to be bombed at night than during the day, and wanting to keep as many of their staff safe as was possible. One sister had already been sent to the base the day before, apparently suffering from nervous exhaustion and shell-shock. Nellie had been sharing a bell tent with her – but on this morning she walked the short distance from her ward to her tent alone, and settled down for a much-needed sleep. Another nurse, whose tent was next to Nellie's, had decided to spend some time 'unwinding' to relieve the stress of the night. Kate Luard's journal recorded that she had gone out 'for a walk', but May Tilton knew better: the sister had been

> 'lorry hopping', a form of recreation we took to help us forget the horrors of the wards. It was forbidden us to leave the camp [but] the boys, ever ready to accommodate the sisters, would invite us to 'hop up' and would take us as far as they could before branching away towards the line. Then we would hop down and on to another lorry travelling in the opposite direction, thus working back to the camp. It gave us something besides the wards to think about before trying to induce sleep.[18]

May herself, and her friend, Emma Slater, came off night duty 'almost dropping with fatigue'.

Around 10 a.m. a squadron of Gothas came over Brandhoek. Two bombs exploded close to the hospital compound; the third landed within it, exploding between the sisters' quarters at No. 44 and an acute surgical ward at No. 32, where staff nurse Elizabeth Jane Eckett, who was in charge of the ward, was doing her morning round. An empty ward next to Elizabeth's was 'blown to bits'; so was the absent sister's sleeping tent. Shrapnel balls and pieces of shell casing flew in all directions, some landing at the feet of head sisters Kate Luard and Minnie Wood as they ran to the scene. A piece of shrapnel just missed a night sister getting into bed, and several shards ripped through the canvas walls of Elizabeth Eckett's ward. Fearing the worst, Kate rushed into the tent to see

Elizabeth 'as white as paper but smiling happily and comforting the terrified patients'. For her courage that day Elizabeth Eckett was awarded the Military Medal. Her citation described how: 'although the ward was twice riddled by enemy aircraft, she continued attending the patients, and by her example prevented many of them from injuring themselves'.[19] In No. 3 Australian CCS Alice Kelly ran to her ward sluice, grabbed a supply of enamel washbasins, placed one over the head of each patient to protect them from flying shrapnel and then stood in the middle of the ward encouraging and reassuring them. She, too, was awarded the Military Medal, along with the Royal Red Cross.

Minnie Wood ran to her own sisters' bell tents, to find Nellie Spindler still lying where she had fallen asleep an hour earlier, now awake, shocked and bleeding profusely. Several medical officers arrived, but even as matron and doctors struggled to stem Nellie's bleeding, they knew she had no chance of survival. A piece of shell casing had ripped through her body from back to front, just below the level of her heart, tearing at least one major blood vessel, and releasing a catastrophic haemorrhage. All Minnie could do was hold Nellie in her arms as the young nurse lost consciousness. Twenty minutes later the twenty-six-year-old staff nurse, who had struggled all night to save the lives of her patients only to become, herself, a target for enemy shellfire, was dead. Her body was taken to Lijssenthoek, near Remy Siding, where it was later interred.

May Tilton and Emma Slater woke suddenly in their bell tent as the first shell exploded. May described what happened next:

A very agitated M.O. pushed his head into our tent and said: 'Come on, you girls. Put on your coats and slippers. The C.O. says you have to get into a dugout at once. They are shelling us.' We were incensed because he would not allow us to wait long enough to get into our clothes. We wanted to go to the wards, not into a burrow in the ground. 'Good God! That first shell killed a night sister in 44 in bed asleep. Come on!' he said… we scuttled across no man's land to some trenches occupied by Scotch Canadians who were out of the line resting. Before I reached them, another long-drawn-out crescendo followed me closely. 'I'm gone,' flashed through my mind. The men shouted, 'Run!' Others called, 'Drop quickly!' My slipper tripped me, and I fell just as the shell fell in the cemetery behind. I looked back to see a huge mass of black smoke and debris flying in all directions; felt myself lifted and dragged into a huge dugout where all the day staff had gathered. Every one of them was upset at the C.O.'s orders and distressed to leave the patients.[20]

Kate Luard offered accommodation in her own sisters' bell tents to the night staff of No. 44. Noticing that three of them were severely shell-shocked, she had them taken immediately by ambulance to a base hospital in Boulogne. The bombing continued until the cemetery, the church hut and a nearby field ambulance had all been destroyed. Arriving to assess the situation, the Director of Medical Services and the Quarter Master General met with the matrons and commanding officers of Nos. 32 and 44. At first they wanted to close No. 44 British and No. 3 Australian CCSs, but keep No. 32 open. Kate was later to describe, in her usual sardonic way, how, just as the decision had been taken, 'Fritz tactfully landed one of his best long-drawn crescendoing scream and crash, just on the railway.' There was now nothing for it but to close all three hospitals. The evacuation was achieved with a speed born out of desperation. All three were packed up and on the road for Saint-Omer within a few hours. The 'Prince of Wales', the patient who had been 'one of the pets' of No. 32, died en route.

Minnie Wood achieved the evacuation of her nurses with great rapidity. She was later awarded the Military Medal, her citation describing how 'this lady never lost her nerve for a moment and during the whole of a most trying day, carried out her duties with the greatest steadiness and coolness. By her work and example she greatly assisted in the speedy evacuation of the patients and the transfer of the sisters.'[21] Just after the nurses had been driven away, a shell landed in a partially evacuated ward tent, injuring two orderlies, one of whom lost an arm and a leg.

No. 3 Australian CCS was similarly evacuated by a calm and apparently unruffled Ida O'Dwyer. Once all patients had been moved out, the nurses sheltered behind a brick wall, waiting for the ambulance that was to take them west, to safety. Just as their transport pulled away, the wall was 'blown to atoms' by a shell. As they moved across the devastated zone, the nurses were shocked by what they saw. The war had truly overtaken them. The railway station at Abeele, at which they had arrived only weeks previously, had completely disappeared and Hazebrouck was a ruin. 'We were nearly dropping with weariness, want of sleep and hunger,' wrote May later. 'Some of the girls were vomiting all the way down.'

Minnie Wood wrote later to Nellie Spindler's parents:

> Before you receive this letter I expect you have heard of your great loss. I don't know what to say to you, for I cannot express my feelings in writing, and no words of mind can soften the blow. There is one consolation for you; your daughter became unconscious

immediately after she was hit, and she passed away perfectly peacefully at 11.20am – just twenty minutes afterwards. I was with her at the time, but [after] the first minute or two she did not know me. It was a great mercy she was oblivious to her surroundings, for the shells continued to fall in for the rest of the day.[22]

On the night of 21 August, American neurosurgeon Harvey Cushing, who was based at the specialist head injuries centre at No. 46 British CCS, commented in his diary that:

They have really had a shocking time. At No. 61 five bombs had been dropped, four with so horizontal a spread – 'daisy cutters' – that lying down did not suffice to escape fragments … There were three killed and twenty wounded, all among the personnel … It's ugly business. Evidently the Hun is laying for the 5th Army CCSs – Brandhoek, Remy, Dosinghem [sic] – only Bandagehem and Mendinghem have escaped so far from actual losses. They were all much upset at Dosinghem [sic] because General Skinner had ordered an electric Red Cross to be shown at night – a good mark to shoot at.[23]

Cushing was convinced that German bombers were deliberately targeting British CCSs. He had even heard a rumour that these bombings were reprisals for the destruction of a German hospital in Roulers by a long-range bombardment from a naval vessel located in the North Sea. Australian nurse, Minnie Payne, who was based at Remy Siding, was to write later that staff had received warning of the intended raids: leaflets had been dropped from aeroplanes on 16 August, warning that hospitals were to be bombed for the next six nights.

On 21 August, about a hundred personnel were evacuated from the Brandhoek and other sites. They had to be accommodated in CCSs and billets around Saint-Omer. Australian nurse Ellen McClelland commented that the drive to Saint-Omer was a 'most exciting trip with shells falling dangerously near. Fortunately, we escaped without casualties, and on arrival at St Omer, we found that several other clearing stations had taken refuge there.'[24] It took half the night for senior staff to find sufficient sleeping space in the small town, but, eventually, by about 1 p.m., all had collapsed into some form of makeshift bed – many on the floors of empty houses. The next day, ten of Kate Luard's nurses were moved back up the line to help at

No. 10 CCS, while the other 17 were accommodated on the top floor of an old convent, only to be moved down to a lower floor that night during a raid. The nurses of No. 3 Australian were accommodated at No. 4 Canadian CCS. May Tilton's fiancé, an Australian soldier who was out of the line in a rest area, had heard of the bombing at Brandhoek. He travelled to Saint-Omer in search of May, and was relieved to find her safe and well. When her matron gave her a day's leave, the two were able to spend several precious hours together. The next day, his unit was moved into the front line trenches for the late August assaults near Langemark. May never saw him again.

Saint-Omer was no safe haven. One night in late August, the sleeping tents of the Australian nurses were, again, riddled with shrapnel holes. One in the wall of May's tent was big enough to push a fist through; she found a large, jagged piece of shrapnel on the floor next to her stretcher and took it home as a souvenir. After that the nurses were ordered to sleep in the château overlooking the CCS. Although the feather beds seemed luxurious after hard stretchers, it took time – and a long period of backache – before they got used to them.

On 23 August, Kate Luard was able to write with some satisfaction that 'Westhoek Ridge is ours … we've done well.' The less seriously wounded men being brought back to CCS No. 32 were relating how the new tanks had knocked out the concrete German pillboxes that had been holding up the advance. In reality, tanks had been of little use in the quagmire of the Salient, with one exception: on 19 August, just before the heaviest bombardments of hospitals behind the Allied lines, tanks had been driven up a few remaining solid roads in the middle of the battlefield towards a series of fortified farms and pillboxes, under cover of a smoke barrage. They had been able to move round the back of these strongpoints and open fire on the occupants.

On Saturday 25 August, just four days after their evacuation, the sisters of No. 32 British CCS returned to their site at Brandhoek. Significant improvements had been made to their accommodation. Their bell tents were lined to waist height with sandbags, and they had been provided with low mattress-covered stretchers to ensure that their bodies would be close to the ground – well below the protective barricade – while they slept. A concrete dugout, known as the 'Elephant' had been built for shelter during the worst raids – and this, too, was to be covered with sandbags. The work in late August was 'slack', and staff were able to work normal shifts and sleep well, in spite of continuing raids. A piano had been salvaged from the deserted No. 44 and Kate allowed nurses to stay up until 10.30 – way beyond their normal hours – for sing-songs with medical officers. 'One mustn't be too much of a Dragon,' she wrote in her letter-journal. The singing provided 'good and cheery cover for some rather nasty shelling'. On 27 August, she wrote again:

> I am writing this in my extraordinarily cosy stretcher-and-mattress bed at 9.30 p.m., with the comfortable knowledge of two feet of sandbags between me and anything that may burst outside. Anything that may burst on top of you, whether armour-piercing 9.2's like Tuesday's or bombs from above – you would know nothing about, as you'd merely wake to a better and more peaceful world.[25]

Even as she was settling into her newly sandbagged bell tent, the rain was falling once more, and men waiting to go 'over the top' for a series of subsidiary assaults to support the gains of the battles for Pilckem Ridge, Westhoek Ridge and Langemarck, were unable to lie down for fear of drowning. The work began to increase again, as these debilitated men were brought back to Brandhoek in collapsed states, many with fatal injuries.

That summer, Mary Borden had returned to Mobile Surgical No. 1 for several weeks. She had spent much of the autumn of 1916 establishing a new hospital – L'Hôpital d'Évacuation – at Bray, on the Somme front. Then, at the beginning of 1917, she had created a third unit at Villers-sur-Condon to support the Nivelle Offensive. Now with the largest campaign of the year taking place on the Ypres front, she had returned to Belgium. A small villa of three rooms had been constructed for her within the compound of Mobile Surgical, and she was living there with her French maid, Emilie, and her dog, Bray. While she had been in the Somme region, she had met Captain Edward Louis Spears, a liaison officer with the British Expeditionary Force. The two had begun to write to each other and, soon afterwards, had embarked on a passionate and secret love affair. When off duty Mary sat in the privacy of her villa, and wrote many letters and poems to Edward, confiding to him how deeply she was disturbed by the horror of war's injuries.

Nurses at the hospital received occasional visits from relatives and friends. These were always a source of great joy. On 10 August, Minnie Hough's cousin, Eric Gaston, walked to Rousbrugge from the shell-shock unit at British CCS No. 63, ten miles away. He had just heard of his mother's death and was in a 'very depressed state of health'. Five days later, Minnie's brother, Reg, cycled from an Australian rest camp at Dickebusch to see her. It was, Hilda recounted, 'very sad to hear him speak of the terrible conditions of war which they were facing day after day – they most often feel desperate and think war will never end.' Yet, she added, 'he took such a fine, brave, sensible outlook on life at the front.'[26]

Five days later, a much more prestigious visitor arrived: Elisabeth, Queen of the Belgians, accompanied by various French and Belgian dignitaries, toured the wards, handing cigarettes and chocolate to patients, and shaking hands with the nurses. Her visit was filmed, resulting in one of the most evocative – though brief – 'silent movies' of the time. Mobile Surgical No. 1 was, by now, taking on the status of a 'celebrity hospital'. On 22 August General Sir Hubert Gough, the commander of the British Fifth Army arrived, accompanied by Edward Spears, but Hilda was disappointed when the two officers were 'rushed away' by Mary Borden, before they could chat.

On 14 August, General Pétain had decorated Mary with a second palm for her Croix de Guerre. The staff of Mobile Surgical No. 1 now had quite a collection of medals between them. Agnes Warner had been awarded the Médaille des Epidemies for distinguished service; and Hilda Gill had the Croix de Guerre, not only for the assistance she had given Madeleine Jaffray on the night of the bombing at Oost-hoek, but also for assisting wounded men to shelter during a bombing raid at her previous posting in Bergues. Mary Borden was, however, without doubt, the most decorated woman in the 'zone of the armies', having been awarded the Médaille des Epidemies and the Croix de Guerre, with two palms.

That August Mary sent the full manuscript of her book, *The Forbidden Zone*, to Collins, the London-based publisher. The British censor instructed her that she must cut material from the book before it could be released, and she decided to withhold publication for the time being. A few days later, she was rushed to hospital in Paris. It has been suggested that her illness was due to a miscarriage, though it is clear that she had also contracted pneumonia.

On 23 August, Mobile Surgical was enlarged and divided into two sections. The wards on one side were run entirely by French nurses. Here, in one of the huts, German prisoners were cared for. The other side of the hospital was supervised by the international team of Australian, Canadian and British nurses, who had the 'officers' ward' as one of their huts. On 27 August, Hilda commented that it was a 'lovely dark night and rain!!!', adding, 'only those who have experienced bombs and Gothas have the joy of a dark or wet night in the War zone'. Several days later, the nurses heard that Mary Borden had been decorated in Paris with the Legion d'Honneur, the highest possible French decoration. Hilda observed in her diary that Mary now had 'all the medals that can be given to her', adding that the doctors of the unit were indignant when they heard the news, believing that 'the Sisters who do the work' and who had remained at the hospital throughout the recent bombardments should also have been decorated. 'The French doctors are very loyal to the British Nurses,' she noted. Her own opinion was that Mary Borden was 'a wonderful little woman, only looks 17, has been under shellfire many times, has equipped [the] hospital and given thousands of francs to French wounded. She deserves all she gets.'

About fifteen miles north of Rousbrugge, at the XV Corps Main Dressing Station at Coxyde, Violetta Thurstan was one of the nurses closest to the front lines. Here, right on the coast of Flanders, a secret operation had commenced. The plan was to synchronize an attack on this part of the line with an Allied breakthrough east of Ypres. British troops would overrun the German lines and link with an amphibious landing on the Belgian coast. Since July, when British troops had taken over the sector, casualties had been heavy due to the bombardment of the lines and the frequent use of mustard gas. The routine at the dressing station was relentless and conditions were dreadful, as poor weather turned the fields around Coxyde to mud. On Monday 27 August, Violetta wrote in her diary:

> Our dressing station was shelled and the padre killed, 3 wounded –
> the huts hit, the farm and two tents set on fire. I got knocked on the
> head. We all had to evacuate, Mardie and I to the Canadian CCS
> where the matron gave me her own bedroom.[27]

This somewhat prosaic account effectively obscures the full details of Violetta's wounding. A later report described how

> she dragged a wounded man into a shelter at great personal risk
> and afterwards she assisted at an operation and in dressing the
> wounded though at the time the shelling was very heavy and part
> of the hut in which the dressings were being performed was struck
> by a shell. She was herself hit on the head and dazed by a piece of
> falling timber. Nevertheless, she continued to work and assist in the
> evacuation of the helpless wounded – a most stimulating example to
> all. When removed to the Casualty Clearing Station she protested
> at being detained there and expressed an urgent desire to return to
> the Corps Main Dressing Station.[28]

About a week later, Violetta went back to her pocket diary and composed a brief entry with a note 'written afterwards'. She realized how dazed and shocked she had been; the injury to her head had caused a severe concussion and, on being put into a bed at the CCS, she had lapsed into unconsciousness. For about a week afterwards she could neither think nor see clearly. In fact, she felt like a 'worm of the earth'. Eventually, on 3 September, she was moved to Boulogne. Ten days later, she got out of bed and sat in an armchair for a few hours, but commented in her diary that being out of bed 'wasn't a wild success'.[29]

Throughout the Ypres Salient, gas raids were continuing. Work with gas-poisoned casualties continued through the summer months in CCSs and base hospitals, although by late August familiarity with the new weapon meant that soldiers were now better protected by more effective gas masks. Helen Fairchild, who had experienced one of the earliest mustard gas incidents while at Dozinghem, was now back at No. 10. She was still writing cheerful letters home to her mother. On 29 August, she wrote:

> Once again I am having my half day off and spent it downtown shopping, ordered some pretty things for myself and Christine, each one of us a beautiful hand-embroidered night gown and envelope chemise ... This week has been terribly cold and rainy and I have never seen such wind, almost sweeps you off your feet, and this weather brings out rheumatic aches fine. I've been mighty stiff and sore the last two days, just will have to take some of my medicine.[30]

At the end of August, fine weather returned. On the 31st, at Mobile Surgical No. 1, Hilda Loxton and Annie Hanning endured a 'wretched night' as Gothas bombed nearby. For the next five nights the bombings continued. 'To the end of time', wrote Hilda in her diary, 'moonlight nights will always remind us of Taubes, Gothas, Belgium and France.' On the night of the 5th, she noted, the church bells of Rousbrugge had tolled their warnings on three separate occasions. She added that 'some [patients] very nervous. Say they prefer trenches where they felt safe in dugouts. Here, have only tin roof over them ... We sometimes wonder if we will ever get home again ... I hope we will always have sufficient strength and courage for whatever may come. Often feel we are in very great danger'.[31] Early September was a time of sadness. News came to the hospital of the deaths of twelve pregnant women and a one-day-old baby during the bombing of a maternity hospital in Dunkirk; and when a front-line *poste de secours* (dressing station) was bombed, patients were brought into the hospital with gangrene already taking rapid hold. Third Ypres was descending rapidly into a campaign of pure attrition.

## Chapter Nine

# Battle for Lives

Augusthad been a terrible month. The Third Ypres Campaign was truly bogged down; no real gains had been made, yet casualties had been enormous. At the end of the month, Sir Douglas Haig removed Sir Hubert Gough from overall command, replacing him with Herbert Plumer, whose Second Army was now moved to the central and southern sections of the line. Gough's forces were moved north and were given the ultimate objective of gaining control of the Passchendaele Ridge. French forces were still on the left flank of the campaign, close to the Houlthurst Forest.

Plumer's campaign strategy was – at least to begin with – very different from Gough's. All-out assaults on distant objectives were replaced by 'bite-and-hold' tactics, in which short-range objectives would be pin-pointed, won and then strengthened, allowing time for artillery to be moved forward before other limited objectives were targeted. The September assaults – the Battles of the Menin Road (20 September) and Polygon Wood (26 September) – were successful in gaining their limited objectives. But casualties were no fewer than those sustained during the disastrous earlier phase of the campaign. On 20 September, the British forces took control of about five and a half square miles of ground, and sustained approximately 21,000 casualties. Historians Robin Prior and Trevor Wilson have calculated that this represents approximately 3,800 casualties per square mile; they refer to the Battle of the Menin Road as a 'triumph over adversity'.[1] German strongpoints on the Gheluvelt Plateau: Glencorse Wood, Inverness Copse and Tower Hamlets – place names redolent of the soldiers' longing for home – were captured with the help of an artillery bombardment that was three times as concentrated as that of 31 July. The creeping barrage was carefully planned, and was sustained throughout the assaults, preventing counter-attacks and allowing Allied troops to fortify their freshly taken positions. In spite of this, the German artillery was able to bombard the battlefield with high-explosive and shrapnel shells; Allied soldiers later described how crossing no man's land felt like moving between 'curtains of steel'. Those who survived somehow narrowly avoided both their own and the enemy's bombardment.

On 13 September twenty-two-year-old Second Lieutenant Glynne Morris, of the Sherwood Foresters, had been hit by shrapnel in a trench at Shrewsbury Forest and severely wounded. He was taken by stretcher-bearers to an Advanced Operating Centre belonging to No. 140 Field Ambulance. Sister Annie Wright wrote to his mother:

> Dear Mrs Morris, I do hope you will have this note before learning from the War Office. Your son Lieutenant J. G. Morris was admitted to our Ambulance about 9 o/c this morning suffering from abdominal wounds, and is very dangerously ill. He was operated on shortly after admission [and] is just as well as we can expect. He is young and strong and we hope with God's help to pull him round for you. I will write again tomorrow and tell you how he is. Need I say how deeply we sympathise with you in your anxiety for your brave lad.[2]

A day later, Annie wrote again to say that Glynne had had a 'fair night' and was 'holding his own'. She added that he was 'very bright and very hopeful and [making] a good fight for recovery'. But two days later it was becoming clear that Glynne's condition had worsened. A deep wound infection was probably taking hold. He had suffered a restless night and was 'tired out'. Annie assured Mrs Morris that the staff would 'do all in our power to send him back well again to you'.

On the 19th, the day before the Menin Road assault, Annie was writing to Glynn's father:

> Dear Mr Morris, I promised to write again telling you of your son's condition. He is still alive but his condition is not as satisfactory as we could wish. He slept well last night and if anything this morning he is a little stronger. He has every attention and comfort possible and we pray we may yet be able to send him down to you ... I will write again in a day or two. You have our deepest sympathy in your anxiety and rest assured no one will spare themselves if it is to save his life.

Two days later, Glynne's condition was clearly hopeless. Annie tried to soften the blow, writing to his father that Glynne had had a restless night and took 'no interest in life', adding 'we give him all possible care'. The next day she wrote again, preparing Glynne's parents for the worst: 'I regret to tell you that the surgeon holds out very little hope of his recovery. He has no pain, lies today as if asleep taking no interest in anything.' Finally, on 23 September, ten days after Glynne's wounding, Annie wrote:

Dear Mr Morris, Your wire came this morning just an hour too late, your dear boy having passed peacefully away at 9 o/c. Sister Rickard was with him and took this little piece of hair for you. She also put some white flowers in his hands in your name, she was very, very good to him and he seemed to prefer her looking after him. It may be of some comfort to you to know he didn't suffer, only from the very first seemed tired out. His wound which was an abdominal one did very well indeed. I cannot tell you how sorry we are not to have been able to save him for you, but really if you had only seen how wearied he looked you would not grudge him to rest. With deepest sympathy with all his friends, Yours Sincerely, Annie Wright

By the time Annie wrote her last letter to Mr Morris, the Battle of the Menin Road had been raging for three days and 140 Field Ambulance must have been inundated with casualties. The fact that she took the time – probably after every shift, as she came off duty – to write such carefully personal letters is a testament to her commitment not only to her patients but also to their relatives. John Glynne Morris is buried in Reninghelst New Military Cemetery; he was 'one of 99,100 Third and Fifth Army casualties recorded between 31 July and 14 September 1917'.[3]

The assaults of late September were successful in achieving their objectives. With much of the Gheluvelt Plateau under Allied control, Plumer now issued instructions for Polygon Wood, Zonnebeke and Broodseinde to be captured. Haig still anticipated that Allied forces would, within a few days, break out of the Salient, capture the railhead at Roulers, and then advance across thirty miles of enemy-held territory to take the Belgian ports. With the benefit of hindsight, his aspirations seem astonishing now. Still, the 'bite-and-hold' strategy was continuing to meet its limited objectives. And now all eyes seemed to be directed towards what had once been a small nondescript rural village at the top of a low ridge in the gently rolling Flanders countryside. Passchendaele was now a devastated ruin; it was also an increasingly significant military objective. The Polygon Wood assault allowed the Allies to press forwards towards the ridge, and the village was now just over 4,500 yards away from their 'front line' trenches; but Polygon Wood had claimed 15,375 British and Dominion casualties.

A further 'push' – the battle for Broodseinde – began at 6 a.m. on 4 October. ANZAC troops successfully took territory on the Broodseinde Ridge and around Poelcappelle, at a cost of approximately 20,000 casualties – but Allied forces were being drawn north-east into a new salient, with enemy machine-gun fire on three sides. On 9 October, exhausted soldiers made a further assault across the devastated terrain that had once been Poelcappelle.

In the minds of Haig, Plumer and Gough, Passchendaele had become the one objective that *must* be gained before winter conditions forced an end to their campaign – but the weather was already so hostile that guns could not be brought into position to support the infantry, and stretcher-bearers were unable to transport the wounded to safety. Soldiers moving up the line into position for attacks had to walk along precarious duckboards across more than three miles of bog. They knew that, for many of them, this would be a place of 'no return'.

As plans for the assaults on the Menin Road and Polygon Wood were taking shape, British and Dominion nurses across the Western Front were being mobilized for service in Flanders. Many were being sent there to replace worn-out or shell-shocked nurses who had been caring for the wounded of the disastrous August assaults. In the middle of August, Catherine Black was moved up the line to No. 17 British CCS at Remy Siding. Many years later she would write of the feelings evoked by her experiences in the lines of evacuation behind the Ypres Salient:

> You could not go through the things we went through, see the things we saw, and remain the same. You went into it young and light-hearted. You came out older than any span of years could make you. But at the time you did not reflect on it much, or on anything else. You did not dare to. Instead you filled your mind with concrete facts – pulses and temperatures, dressings and treatments – because you soon learned that if you concentrated hard enough on them it stopped you remembering other things.[4]

Among Catherine's most traumatic experiences were watching as two German airmen burned alive after their aeroplane crashed in a field near the CCS, and caring for a 'young Highlander' who had lain for five days and nights in no man's land before being brought to the hospital. He died in a state of delirium, endlessly repeating the words, 'Oh, God, don't let the others be like me!'[5]

At the end of August, the nurses of Australian CCS No. 3 had been relocated to the area just north of Westvleteren. For the time being, they were to support the work of British CCS No. 47 at St Sixtus, the site of the old Cistercian Monastery. 'The whole world seemed to be in this area,' commented May Tilton. No. 47 itself, situated alongside Nos. 4 and 61, was a huge encampment. Here, the bombardment preceding the battles for Polygon Wood, Broodseinde and Poelcapelle was experienced as a 'constant thunder', and casualties poured in, threatening to completely overwhelm the hospitals. May commented in her diary that,

> There was only time to attend to urgent dressings and make them as comfortable as possible. How we longed to give them the extra attentions which they needed.
> One day, after I had finished dressing extensive wounds of a plucky little Tommy, I brought him a glass of champagne.
> He exclaimed: 'Oh, sister! You are too kind to me.'
> Then he wept.
> 'Kind!' I replied. 'But see what has happened to you, fighting for me.'
> 'Oh, is that how you look at it? Well, I'm glad I came then.' And he smiled as I dried his tears.[6]

The gratitude and concern of patients was one of the most rewarding things about working in a CCS. On one occasion, during a particularly fierce aerial bombardment, a patient 'whose two arms were spread-eagled in splints and who was minus a leg' tried to persuade May Tilton to climb under his bed for safety.

In the CCSs near Proven, quartermasters were scouring local farms for supplies of nutritious food for severely debilitated patients. Nurses were given a free hand in deciding what their patients should eat, and were able to give chicken, eggs and milk, as well as alcoholic stimulants ranging from champagne to stout. They were also free to determine dosages of drugs such as morphine and atropine. During bombing raids, patients sometimes begged for morphine to calm their fears and induce sleep, and the exhausted nurses had to exercise careful discretion to ensure they did not overdose these patients. Aerial bombardment of rest areas continued, and the noise – particularly at night – from enemy shells and one's own anti-aircraft guns could be terrifying. May described an incident in which she went to reassure a colleague newly posted to the 'zone of the armies', who had never experienced bombardment before:

I rushed across with some coffee, and to assure her there was no need to be afraid as long as he was not directly overhead. I could not find her – her bed was empty. I groped about in the dark, and discovered her under the bed, crouched against the sandbags. The coffee, with a dash of cognac, helped a lot, and she crept back to bed, feeling much better.[7]

On 21 September, May Tilton became suddenly depressed and anxious, 'as if something had happened to spoil my life'. She was so ill that her head sister sent her off duty to rest. She later learned that her fiancé had died just before the Battle of Polygon Wood. On the same day Kate Maxey, who had been serving at No. 12 British Stationary Hospital at St Pol throughout the summer, was, once more, moved up the line to Lillers. She reported for duty at No. 58 CCS – this time as sister-in-charge.

That month, staff at Mobile Surgical No. 1 were struggling with almost-overwhelming numbers of casualties. Working closely together for so long under such emotional and physical strain had forged close relationships between team members. The nurses felt particular admiration for two of the most hardworking, gentle and caring of the doctors: the elderly university anatomist, Monsieur Ranvier and the 'fine, big, good looking, healthy' de Parthenay, who was only 28 but looked much older. Hilda commented of the latter: 'we all (Australian sisters) love him, but he loves only one (Crozier).'

A particularly bad convoy reached the hospital on 26 September. One patient – who was taken to Minnie Hough's ward – had severe wounds to the head and jaw, injuries to both arms and legs, and several pieces of shell fragment lodged in his lungs. He was delirious from the moment he entered the ward, believing that he was still on the battlefield, but, in rare, lucid moments, he became gentle and thoughtful. He died the next day.

Hilda described one of the cases in her own ward:

I had one little boy admitted … He had a large back wound, the éclat [shell fragment] entering the lower part of the back passed the diaphragm, a part of the liver, and lodged in one lung. He was very ill from the beginning. The piece of éclat was extracted by Dr de Parthenay, and he was put on Dakins treatment. His back wound was stitched up but had to be reopened again and he had several chest operations, but he steadily became worse, would not eat and was always miserable, developed kidney trouble and infective rheumatism; arms and legs swelled up to twice their size.

Dr said he was dying from septicaemia, so de Parthenay tried a new treatment for him, injections of Peptone intramuscularly. He showed signs of improvement at once and after several injections made steady progress towards recovery, had a splendid appetite and became quite fat. After staying with us for about 3 months he was discharged walking and cured. He was only 19 years and very frightened that if he got better he would be sent back to the trenches again, but the Dr said he would not be fit for a long time for that.[8]

Peptone was a protein treatment, designed to build the patient's muscle mass and restore strength. It was never widely used and it is not clear whether this treatment, the Dakins treatment, or just good nursing care – or a combination of all three – secured his recovery. There is no doubt that he was one of the most heartening case studies of nursing at Mobile Surgical.

At the end of September, the Australian nurses were invited to sign new contracts of service that would expire in July 1918. All signed up despite the return of 'horrible' nights of bombing in the district around Rousbrugge. The nurses found it easier to be on duty during these nights, when they could still their own fears by reassuring their patients. The night nurses did 'rounds' of the hospital wearing dark coats and carrying dimmed lanterns. The windows of the wards were painted dark blue, but staff still maintained a complete blackout during bombing raids, making it almost impossible to assess patients' wounds, check for haemorrhage, or give adequate care and comfort to dying patients. On 1 October, Gothas approaching the hospital could be seen clearly, outlined against a vivid harvest moon:

The Gothas had a different sound to our Handley Page mechanisms. Noise of anti-aircrafts, church bells ringing, searchlights out, it was quite a different world to the old world we knew and the noise was most nerve-wracking. Pieces of shrapnel used to drop on our huts from our aircraft shells and we were always warned to stay indoors, though sometimes large pieces of shrapnel came through a double roof. In one case one of the infirmiers was about to sit down to his meal in their refectory, when a hail [of bullets] from a mitrailleuse [machine gun] came through the roof… and fell on the floor. He kept [one] as souvenir.[9]

One of the worst times for Mobile Surgical No. 1 was following a particularly fierce French assault on Houlthurst Forest. Many very seriously injured men were admitted, and surgeons worked night and day in the operating theatre, leaving their nurse colleagues to assess patients, decide on treatments and medications, perform all complex dressings and supervise other care. Many of their assistants – the *infermièrs* – struggled to give care to vulnerable patients. Some of these nursing orderlies were elderly, others very young; many had disabilities ranging from mild learning disorders to severe deafness and skeletal deformities. Patients with head injuries often tried to get out of bed, and the staff resorted to moving their beds against the wall, and pushing the beds of other, less seriously injured men against them. Hilda Loxton commented that it was

> not unusual to have a bad head seemingly quietly asleep, and to come back to find he had taken off all his bandages and dressings, rolled up everything tidily, even sticking the pins in, and had a bald head with a big wound on it lying on the pillow, and when spoken to knew nothing about it and would promise not to do it again. Even if one was in a darkened ward, and you were there all the time, they would take off their dressings under the bed clothes – apparently they would be asleep ... [They] had to be cared for like young babies. Morphine was our greatest love.[10]

Hilda's commentary illustrates the ethical dilemmas faced by professional nurses caring for very large numbers of critically ill cases with only minimal assistance from unqualified personnel. Doctors depended heavily on them to do much medical and surgical work, while nurses were, in turn, dependent upon *infermièrs* to provide intimate care to frightened and vulnerable patients. In forward field hospitals, during severe rushes of casualties, nurses were operating as front-line responders, focusing only on the preservation of life, and trusting that more detailed plans of care could be put in place once the rush was over, or after patients had been moved further down the line.

Even those nurses who were working many miles from the front lines were enduring a desperate autumn. Australian nurse Emma Cuthbert was at the No. 2 Australian General Hospital, Wimereux, where, in a special ward for 'fractured-femur cases', many patients had 'scaffolding' built around them to permit the more effective traction of limbs. Patients were immobile and the work was heavy. By October, the weather had become colder, and Emma commented on how nurses pulled on coats and gumboots, placed rain hats over their shower caps and tucked towels under their arms, to walk from their hutted accommodation to their shower block. That month, the hospital was subjected to aerial bombardment, and Emma was 'wakened up by the explosion of a bomb quite near and the noise of bursting shrapnel falling on the roofs of our quarters, which were shaking on their foundations'.[11]

Sixty miles away, U.S. Base Hospital No. 10, on top of the Le Treport *falaises* was badly exposed to the elements. Helen Fairchild wrote home to her teenage sister, Christine: 'I do not mind the rain much, but the wind makes me cross, and it blows a perfect gale about half the time even in sunny weather. You should see our clothes now. No fancy things for us. I have two rain hats, two rain coats and a pair of rubber boots.'[12] Later that month, Helen contracted tonsillitis and was confined to bed for several days. As she began to recover, she tried to persuade Margaret Dunlop to allow her to go back on duty, but her matron refused, insisting that she must rest. Helen was beginning to realize that there had always been something in her own personality which had driven her to overwork. Alone in her bed in the nurses' quarters at No. 10, she had plenty of time for reflection. She received a letter from Christine, in which her sister described the pressures she was under at school. Somehow, she recognized an element of herself in her sister's striving for perfection. As she wrote back, she chose a philosophical tone:

Chris, let me give you some good advice. Don't worry yourself sick over those lessons, either you or Don, for you are both very young and if you don't pass this year you will next, and don't kill yourself trying to keep at the head of the class, just plug away and get what you can and if you don't get it all today, just remember there is another day coming, so now just get over the idea that you have to get everything perfect. Do your best and let it go hang, and take it from me, Chris, I sometimes wonder if it really pays to always work too hard, for the older I get, the more I find that the more you do, the more people expect of you, and the more they demand of you ... Being sick this far from home is no fun, but everyone has been fine to me, my room is filled with flowers they bring me, and fruit galore.[13]

In October, May Tilton and her colleagues were reunited with their own unit, No. 3 Australian CCS at Nine Elms, two miles from Poperinge. Here, the hospital was so overwhelmed by casualties from the assaults on

Broodseinde and Poelcapelle that, one night, patients were accidentally put into a tent with no staff. They were discovered by two nurses, who, going off duty just after midnight, heard their groans and alerted the matron to their condition. May was assigned, once more, to the resuscitation ward, where the work was 'indescribable': 'The butchery of those precious lives ... Their frightful condition was appalling: clothes saturated; faces caked with mud; the conscious ones smiling grimly, glad to be wounded and out of it.' Heavy artillery was thundering over the hospital towards Poperinge. May commented in her memoir:

> We hated and dreaded the days that followed this incessant thundering, when the torn, bleeding and pitifully broken human beings were brought in, their eyes filled with horror and pain; those who could walk staggering dumbly, pitifully, in the wrong direction. Days later men were carried in who had been found lying in shell holes, starved, cold, and pulseless, but, by some miracle, still alive. Many died of exposure and the dreaded gas gangrene.[14]

Some were saved, apparently against all odds – like the Scottish soldier, who had a large piece of shell removed from his abdomen and who took hours to 'thaw'. But May's memoir also told many tragic stories, such as one of a 'dear plucky lad', who 'suffered a painful existence: one arm amputated, the other badly wounded, and a hole through his throat'. He spent several days in the CCS, but he died later, of a catastrophic haemorrhage following his transfer to the base.[15]

On 18 October, the commanding officer of No. 3 Australian CCS asked for three extra surgical sisters to support the existing teams. In less than one month, the hospital had experienced 260 deaths, and the matron, Miss O'Dwyer, was struggling to write letters to all of the relatives of the dead. That month, May Tilton was assigned to work as sister to a surgical team. At No. 3 Australian CCS there were twelve teams and six tables were in continuous use. The CCS was becoming quite international: American, Canadian and South African surgical teams had all been added to the complement. Each worked twelve- to sixteen-hour shifts, with only short meal breaks. May described a typical night shift: her team went on duty at 8 p.m., had a ten-minute break at midnight then worked continuously for eight hours, before having breakfast at 8 a.m. During rushes all the theatre teams did was work, eat and sleep. After a long night they would return to their bell tents, collapse into their beds and sleep before going back on duty the next evening. Under such circumstances, food had to be bolted rapidly and rest was anything but restorative. It is unsurprising that any nurse with a pre-existing illness became much worse during her 'stint' at the CCS. May had worked almost continuously since well before the Third Ypres Campaign opened, and was now becoming severely debilitated.

Sisters in surgical teams often performed minor surgery. May described how the surgeon she was working with asked her to 'Get on with the minor wounds, sister, or we won't save this chap.' When she demurred, pointing out that she had never before performed such work, he advised her to 'forget yourself and think only of our patient'. Men who were brought into the theatre often asked whether their wounds were 'Blighty' ones. All – even those from the British Dominions who had no hope of actually reaching their own homes – longed to escape the Western Front and reach the peace and safety of England.

On 12 October, in spite of continuing rain and a failure to bring heavy artillery forward, an assault was launched towards Passchendaele. Troops – many of them ANZACs – ran into a storm of shrapnel and gas shells as they laboured up the slope towards the village. Those who survived the bombardment were halted by swathes of uncut barbed wire, and were forced to retreat under a hail of continuing fire. Many became literally 'bogged down' in the slimy, sucking mud that covered the land to a depth, in places, of several feet, and were cut down by machine-gun fire from pillboxes and other fortified positions as they struggled in the morass. Robin Prior and Trevor Wilson assert that 'The First Battle of Passchendaele' was nothing more than 'the name by which [this] fiasco has since been dignified'.[16] The assault achieved nothing and resulted in approximately 13,000 casualties. Yet, the British high command remained determined to take the Passchendaele Ridge. Bringing in the Canadian Corps under the command of General Sir Aurthur Currie, Haig ordered a further assault. Currie insisted on a two-week delay to permit heavy artillery to be brought forward. He also planned a three-stage advance using the 'bite-and-hold' tactics that had proved effective under Plumer in September. Small advances were achieved on 26 and 30 October. On 6 November, the Canadians finally staggered into what had once been the village of Passchendaele, only to be ordered to take a further swathe of high ground to its north and east. The final assault of the Third Ypres Campaign took place on 10 November. It served only to extend the narrow salient upon which Allied forces were exposed.

Soon after the last action at Passchendaele, Sir Herbert Plumer's Second Army was moved to Italy. Sir Henry Rawlinson took over command of the lines of the now much-extended Ypres Salient. Assessing the defensibility of the Salient, he concluded that, if the Germans were to launch a concerted attack, the Allies would have to fall back and create a straighter and more secure line. Such an attack was becoming increasingly likely: the Russian Revolution had already effectively disabled one of the largest of the Allies, enabling the German army to turn its attention on breaking through the Western Front.

Even after the cessation of operations on the Ypres Front, men were still being wounded in the wasteland of the Salient. Sidney Beldam, a young Cambridge man, aged 18, sustained severe facial injuries in late November. Sidney had been torn from his peaceful life as a commercial traveller in 1916, when the Military Service Acts had enforced the conscription of all men between the ages of 18 and forty-one. He had joined the Army Service Corps and had spent his first weeks as a soldier driving a lorry in southern England. But in April he had been transferred to the Machine Gun Corps and shipped to the continent. During the last actions of the Battle of Passchendaele, Sidney was peppered by shrapnel in a shell hole next to a brick barn; his face was blown apart by flying splinters of metal. He was left for dead, face down. It was a matter of pure luck that the blood from his wounds dripped downward into the mud rather than into his throat. As the blood began to clot, he became conscious, but was unable to move. Three days later, he became aware of stretcher-bearers approaching. He felt himself being rolled over and then heard the words, 'Blimey! This one's still alive!' He was transferred to a CCS, where he received shock therapy and emergency surgery. Several days later, he was taken down the line to a base hospital. Somehow, the surgeons, nurses and orderlies in the lines of evacuation managed to keep him alive until he reached an auxiliary hospital at Rawtenstall in Lancashire, where he underwent further surgery.

In June 1918, Sidney was transferred to the Queen's Hospital in Sidcup, where Harold Gillies, the New Zealand surgeon, whose patients had been nursed by Catherine Black at Aldershot in 1915, performed plastic surgery. Sidney was 'Case Number 598'. He was to have over forty operations – and his treatment would last well into the 1930s.

In Belgium the bombing of rest areas behind the lines was continuing. On 29 November, at No. 63 British CCS, at Bandaghem, Sister Eileen King was on night duty in her tented ward when an air raid began. Moving rapidly from patient to patient, offering comfort and reassurance, Eileen listened as the bombing moved closer. Four shells landed directly outside the tent, blasting large quantities of shrapnel through the canvas. Eileen was badly wounded but continued to supervise the care of her patients. She was later awarded the Military Medal, her citation describing how 'She was severely wounded in both legs and though suffering from shock and loss of blood, continued to give directions etc., as to the care of the wounded. She showed great pluck and presence of mind.'[17]

Nurses might continue to show pluck – but many were becoming increasingly demoralized. In mid–October, May Tilton heard of the death of her fiancé, and immediately began to sink into depression. She felt that 'something had happened to my head, which was all tight inside'. After three months' continuous work and strain in Belgian CCSs, she was clearly suffering from shell-shock. Her bereavement was simply hastening an inevitable collapse, and, in December, her head sister sent her on leave to the Convalescent Nursing Sisters' Home at Hôtel de l'Estrel in Cannes on the French Riviera. She recovered sufficiently to return to active service at the No. 3 Australian General Hospital at Abbeville in January.

The severely concussed Violetta Thurstan was taken by hospital ship back to England on 18 September. Following a short stay in a nursing home, she was able to go home. On Wednesday 14 November, she was awarded the Military Medal for bravery. Her name appears in the *Supplement to the London Gazette* for 19 November 1917, alongside those of 'Baroness Elsie Blackall de T'Serclaes' and 'Marie Lambert Chisholm Gooden Chisholm' [sic], the 'Heroines of Pervyse'.[18]

The Third Battle of Ypres was, undoubtedly, one of the most horrific events in the history of Western Europe. The campaign itself, and the so-called 'Battle of Passchendaele' confound our modern understandings of warfare. The 'known facts' – that British and Dominion forces sustained approximately 275,000 casualties (including over 70,000 dead);[19] that civilized societies knowingly sent young men to their doom in the hell of the Flanders mud; that both sides employed weapons of mass destruction; that governments stood by and watched as the slaughter continued – defy imagination. The British prime minister, David Lloyd George, had already condemned the strategy of 'attrition' that had seemed to characterize Haig's conduct of the Somme Campaign, yet, for some reason, was unable to stop the slaughter of Passchendaele.

Nurses in CCSs and field hospitals close to the front lines were among the few who saw and understood what was happening. They had a sense of Passchendaele's relentless inevitability: to embark on such a campaign was easy; to end it almost impossible. They also understood its true cost: the destruction of tens of thousands of hopeful, young lives. In the face of such despair, they focused on what they could achieve. They could save some men – knowing that these saved lives would once more be returned to the conflict. They could ease the pain and suffering of those who reached the relative safety of a CCS. But for those who died on the battlefield they could do nothing, and the knowledge of those forsaken men – some of whom were their own loved ones – haunted them for the rest of their lives.

## Chapter Ten

# End of Days

The Third Ypres Campaign had not only failed to secure its objectives, it had also severely depleted the strength, will and energy of surviving Allied soldiers. Nurses were demoralized too; many were beginning to wonder just how long this war could go on. In Abbeville, May Tilton was experiencing a recurrence of her 'shell-shock' symptoms. Severe headaches were affecting her ability to work, her head was, once more, feeling 'tight inside', and she 'felt stupid'. Boils appeared on her arms, and she was obliged to take on the lightest work – on the convalescent ward, where her patients and orderlies treated her as if she were the casualty. Still, she refused to take sick leave. In March, she was transferred to the Australian Auxiliary Hospital in London, where she worked in a ward of 'fifteen patients who had three legs between them'.

At Lillers, on 16 January, Kate Maxey had just returned from leave. Her sector, well south of Ypres was quiet, but men – some of whom had been on active service for well over three years – were coming into the CCS with dangerously damaged trench feet, and with illnesses ranging from relatively mild cases of trench fever through to acute meningitis, scarlet fever and influenza. Nurses themselves were at risk of contracting these diseases as they worked closely with their patients, offering personal comfort-care, maintaining cleanliness and reducing fevers by sponging bodies, and building strength by offering sustaining food and fluids.

American Base Hospital No. 10 at Le Treport had a new commanding officer. Matthew Delaney had left to take up a position as liaison officer in London, and his command was taken over by Colonel Richard Harte. Margaret Dunlop continued as matron. The winter of 1917–18 was quiet with, at times, only 800 patients. A band was formed, with brand-new instruments sent out from Boosey and Co. in London. The nurses had their own 'concert company', which toured the wards, performing as both choir and dance troupe. Margaret was amused when an English officer approached her to congratulate her on their talents: 'It was so well done,' he said, 'so dainty and so un-American.'[1]

In December 1917, Helen Fairchild became seriously ill. She had travelled to Europe already suffering from dyspepsia. At the CCS her working conditions undoubtedly worsened the stomach ulcer which had probably been extending and deepening for several months. She had been feeling nauseous and exhausted for some time, but had assumed that her condition was due to the stress of her CCS work and lack of sleep. Just before Christmas, she began to vomit after every meal, yet, on 29 December, she wrote the usual chatty letter to her mother. The only indication that she might have been anything but well and happy came towards its end when she asked her mother to write often, 'for I get a little homesick sometimes'. She was seriously considering returning home, but was terrified of the seasickness that had accompanied her outward journey.

In January Helen was advised to undergo surgery for what was clearly some sort of obstruction in her stomach. She asked Major Charles Mitchell to perform the operation, and he did so on 15 January. At first, things seemed to go well. The surgery, which was performed in Canadian Stationary Hospital No. 3, revealed an enormous ulcer around Helen's pylorus, which was trapping food in her stomach, and preventing it from moving down into her intestines. The obstruction was removed, and Helen was carefully nursed back to the point where she could begin to take small sips of water. Then, suddenly, she seemed to relapse. She became jaundiced, then quickly lapsed into a coma. She died at 11.20 a.m. on 18 January. On 21 January, the *Official Bulletin* of the United States announced that Helen Fairchild had died of 'acute yellow atrophy of the liver'. It was assumed by her medical colleagues that this had been due to a reaction to the chloroform used as an anaesthetic during the surgery, but it is also possible that her liver had already been damaged by the exposure of her gastrointestinal tract to mustard gas at the CCS and then subsequently at base hospital No. 10.

Helen was buried in the Huon Cemetery at Le Treport. Her funeral was conducted with full military honours; it was said that every member of staff who was not on duty attended. Representatives from all of the hospital units in the area and from other military organizations came too, forming a long procession and gathering around her grave, which had been carefully lined with evergreens by staff from Canadian Stationary Hospital No. 3. The simple ceremony ended with the playing of the Last Post. Helen's close friend and roommate, Florence Wagner, was said to be inconsolable.

Helen's parents received a brief letter of condolence from Dora Thompson, the Superintendent of the Army Nurse Corps, and a more heartfelt one from Charles Mitchell, the surgeon who had performed the unsuccessful operation:

My dear Mrs. Fairchild, It is the hardest task to write you the sad news of your daughter. I hardly know how to do it. We all loved her as our own, and feeling as we do toward her we can in but a small way realize what it must mean to you, and if it can comfort any to know that she was the best beloved of our nurses and the most esteemed of the Medical Officers... Miss Fairchild has been to me like a daughter ... We cannot express enough how deeply we all feel with you.[2]

Margaret Dunlop wrote in similarly emotional terms: 'I loved Miss Fairchild as my own, and if it had been possible in any way to have gotten her home I would have done so.'[3]

On 3 March 1918, Russia's Bolshevik government signed the Treaty of Brest-Litovsk with the Central Powers, formalizing an armistice that had been agreed in the December of the previous year. Russian involvement in the First World War was at an end, and the German high command could shut down its operations on the Eastern Front and concentrate on planning for a decisive breakthrough in the West. That breakthrough was not long in coming.

In March the bombardment of Allied positions in Belgium intensified. On the 17th, Elsie, Baroness de T'Serclaes, woke early in her bunk in the Cellar House at Pervyse, filled with a sense of foreboding and anxiety. She roused Mairi and the two orderlies who also slept in the Cellar House, and all four began to climb out of their 'funk holes' and reach for their gas masks. At that moment, gas shells began to fall just outside the building and mustard gas poured in through cracks in the walls. All four were badly poisoned. Elsie later described the experience in her memoir:

I vaguely remember being carried to an ambulance. The driver was saying, 'For Christ's sake hurry' ... We were taken to the hospital at La Panne, but I had no time to speculate about this, since I was coughing and gasping for breath, together with dozens of soldiers all around me, until I thought my lungs must burst or be torn from my body.[4]

Elsie was later taken from La Panne to general hospitals in Boulogne and then London, where she eventually made a full recovery. She never went back to Pervyse.

Four days later, on 21 March, in one of the most dramatic episodes of the war, the German forces launched their so-called 'Spring Offensive', a massive assault that ruptured the Allied lines in several places. At Ypres, in just three days, they overran the Messines Ridge and territory around Passchendaele, Poelcapelle, Broodseinde, Langemarck and St Julien that had taken four months to capture, at a cost of well over 70,000 Allied lives.

As part of the advance, strategically important centres on the Allied rail network were targeted by concerted Gotha raids. One of the fiercest of these focused on the railway station at Lillers. During one raid, a train loaded with ammunition took a direct hit, and exploded, blasting a wide area with shells and debris. CCS No. 58, located close to the station, was badly damaged. Both Kate Maxey and one of her nursing sisters were hit by debris, each sustaining multiple shrapnel wounds. Kate's right side was blasted with shrapnel, wounding her forehead, neck, forearm, thigh and foot. Her left thigh was also injured. Her right radius was fractured; a nerve just to the right side of her spine was damaged, causing severe pain; and her right eardrum was perforated. Although suffering from shock and pain, Kate crawled to the side of her wounded colleague who was clearly dying. It soon became apparent that she herself was badly wounded, but even after she had been persuaded by her fellow nurses to lie down on a stretcher she continued to direct their work, refusing to allow anyone to treat her until all other patients and wounded staff had been assessed. After initial surgery, she was moved down the line to base and then back to Britain.

For her courage and endurance on 21 March, Kate was awarded the Military Medal. Her citation, published in the *London Gazette* on 4 June 1918, praised her 'gallantry and conspicuous devotion to duty', adding that 'although suffering severe pain, she showed an example of pluck and endurance which was inspiring to all'.[5]

Three other professional nurses who were at Lillers on 21 March, 1918, were also awarded the Military Medal: Marie Daw Lutwick 'who crossed the open, bomb swept ground alone to procure help'; Dorothy Penrose Foster, who assisted with the loading of patients onto the ambulance train; and Mary Agatha Brown, who 'worked devotedly for many hours, under conditions of great danger'.

Kate Maxey's commanding officer at No. 58 CCS, J. Graham Martin, was later to write a confidential report on her work:

> This lady's professional work was of the highest quality, she had a splendid knowledge of nursing and had a special gift of imparting it to other Nursing Sisters and orderlies. Her administration was exceedingly good as she watched over the health of all under her as

well as their duties. I found that Maxey could get the orderlies to carry out all their duties thoroughly and cheerfully even under the most trying and heavy conditions; this was due to her personality and skill. Miss Maxey's tact, zeal for work and influence for good are of the highest. On the night of 21/3/18 when lying wounded, she still directed nurses, orderlies and stretcher bearers and refused aid until others were seen to first. I have the greatest pleasure in giving this testimony to one of the finest Nursing Sisters I have ever met.

On the same report, Maud McCarthy, Matron-in-Chief of the British Expeditionary Force in France and Flanders, inserted her own view: 'Miss Maxey was a first rate Theatre Sister and in addition an able manager and administrator. She managed her CCS, which was a difficult one, with great skill.'

Kate Maxey was evacuated from Lillers on 24 March, and was eventually moved to Millbank Military Hospital in London for further treatment. In April, she received a letter, signed by all members of the sergeants' mess at No. 58 CCS, offering her their

most hearty congratulations on the occasion of your being awarded the MILITARY MEDAL, and [we] sincerely hope that you will soon have recovered from your wounds, and be able to carry on the good work you have so nobly commenced, which, whilst you were at this Hospital, was so much appreciated by both patients and personnel.

Among Kate's letters of congratulation none was more valued than this, and Kate preserved it carefully among her private papers. About two weeks later, she also received a letter of congratulation and concern from the Matron-in-Chief of the TFNS, Sidney Browne, to which she replied: 'I thank you. I am pleased to say my wounds are healing splendidly.'

Kate may have been taking a stoical stance. Her condition was reviewed by a medical board in August 1918, which declared that, although the disability caused by her wounds was 'to some extent permanent', she would be able to return to nursing work following six weeks' leave. Anxious to return to front-line service, she wrote to Sidney Browne that 'my wounds are quite better and I feel perfectly strong again. As this is my first sick leave, I trust you will allow me to return to France.' But the matron-in-chief decided that over four years almost continuous active service overseas was enough for anyone, and she ordered Kate to report for duty at the 2nd Northern General in Leeds. Four years later Kate was still experiencing some problems from her injuries, though she was also still making light of them. In response to a letter from Maud McCarthy in 1922, she commented: 'I am pleased to say I am quite strong again, only rarely having the slightest pain from any of my old wounds.'

On 21 March, as the German advance was breaking through the Allied lines, new U.S. surgical teams were being rapidly deployed to the front lines. As part of one of these, Sister Isabella Stambaugh was sent to the Somme front. She and colleagues joined No. 32 CCS, where a thousand wounded were waiting for assessment, treatment and evacuation. Soon afterwards, they were moved to No. 42 Stationary Hospital at Amiens, where, during a bombing raid, all were injured. A large piece of shrapnel-shell casing tore a hole in Isabella Stambaugh's leg, and she was rapidly evacuated to Abbeville and then to Millbank Hospital in London.

The German breakthrough was a direct and immediate threat to CCSs and stationary hospitals along large sections of the Western Front. Nurses were being hustled into ambulances and driven west, sometimes less than one mile ahead of advancing German troops. Catherine Black was with No 41 British Stationary hospital at Sailly-Laurette on the River Somme when the Germans broke through. 'There was not time even to think of our equipment,' she wrote later. 'We snatched up what drugs and necessities we could and flung them into the waggons.' As she struggled to fix a splint onto the leg of a man with a compound fracture, she was almost left behind. It was only with the help of a German prisoner-patient that she managed to get the wounded man to the convoy: 'I wanted to thank him as he turned away, but I could not for he knew no English and I no German. But I waved to him as he stood there, smiling shyly. And suddenly I knew that there was no such person as the enemy ... only the people of one nation obeying orders to fight the people of another.'[6]

In late March, the staff of U.S. Base Hospital No. 10 – which was already full to capacity – received a convoy of 320 severely wounded men. Somehow they selected 300 of their existing patients for evacuation to England. Many of these were desperately badly wounded, some were even on the 'dangerously ill' list, with relatives from Britain sitting beside their beds. Margaret Dunlop was later to comment:

> The fortitude and bravery of the severely wounded coming down, the patient, uncomplaining attitude of the sick men suddenly taken

from their beds and sent upon a journey, the efficient handling of the numbers of patients by the officers, men and nurses, the quiet, repressed, controlled attitude of the friends of the dying – these will never be forgotten.

At the end of March, the entire hospital was evacuated piecemeal, nurses and patients being divided between several base hospitals in Rouen. Two weeks later, it became apparent that the German army was not going to reach the coast of Picardy, and the Le Treport unit re-opened. From then onwards, Base Hospital No. 10 came under greater pressure than ever before, taking in as many as 600 patients per day. The work was made even harder by an outbreak of dysentery. As a specialized infectious-diseases unit, the hospital took large numbers of sufferers, and its dietician, Miss Bettman, was kept busy supervising the preparation of special starch feeds. Air raids in the area meant that trenches had to be dug, and all hospital huts were sandbagged but, much to Margaret Dunlop's relief, the bombing raids never reached as far as Le Treport. By July, hospital staff were beginning, for the first time, to receive their own compatriots, as American soldiers from the desperate battles on the Somme and the Marne were brought down the line. Alongside them were increasing numbers of German prisoner-patients.

At Rousbrugge, during the March retreat, Mobile Surgical No. 1 was hurriedly evacuated. Its surgeons remained with a unit serving the 36ième Corps, but its nurses were moved well back behind the now rapidly changing front lines. Their new location was Forge-les-Eaux, about mid-way between Amiens and Rouen. Here, even though the war seemed very distant, the retreat was producing massive numbers of Allied casualties.

Closer to the front lines, the surgeons were working under chaotic conditions, performing both surgical and nursing duties. Under the pressure of the retreat, their practice had regressed to something resembling Crimean-War surgery. The unit was moving quickly just ahead of the German advance, narrowly escaping capture. Operations were being performed on patients who still lay on their stretchers, sometimes with no anaesthetic. One of her former surgeon colleagues wrote to Agnes Warner, begging her to bring her nurses back to the unit, which was now serving 'Ambulance 16/21'. Lives were being lost, he declared, for want of good nursing care. Agnes wrote, at once, to her Red Cross committee, asking for permission to take a small unit of nurses to Ambulance 16/21, but it was July before she and four colleagues were given permission to move back up the line. By this time it was becoming clear that the Allies had held back the German advance. Soon they began to push eastwards, and the ambulance was almost overwhelmed by wounded from the so-called 'One Hundred Days Advance'. That month, French forces succeeded in pushing the German forces back from the River Marne. Then, on 8 August, a further decisive Allied victory at Amiens forced the German army to retreat back towards its strongest fortifications on the so-called Hindenburg Line. The staff of Ambulance 16/21 became accustomed to travelling light, packing rapidly and moving fast in order to keep up with the advancing French troops. They established makeshift hospitals in schools, ruined châteaux, or – where no shelter was available – in what tents they were able to carry with them. On 26 September Hilda Loxton and Minnie Hough, who were still in Forge les Eaux, received a letter from Agnes Warner inviting them to join the ambulance. Hilda noted sadly in her diary that 'it was very hard to decide not to go, but I was not in good health, so Minnie with her usual common sense strongly urged that it was wiser for us both to return home, before we really broke down, as she was also feeling the strain'.[7] The 'Bluebirds' began their homeward voyage on 11 October.

At 2.30 a.m. on 28 September, Sir Herbert Plumer's Second Army finally broke out of the Ypres Salient in a decisive attack against a thinly defended German front. The ground over which so much blood had already been spilt was taken in a decisive advance that was given the name 'the Fourth Battle of Ypres'. It is believed that this collapse of his army in Flanders was what finally convinced German military leader, General Erich Ludendorff to persuade the German high command to sue for peace. Meanwhile, Allied armies on all parts of the Western Front continued to press eastwards.

Mobility was becoming one of the greatest assets of a military field hospital. In September 1918, American Base Hospital No. 10 was asked to supply a large mobile unit that could move rapidly, following the advancing Allied armies through eastern France towards Germany. The unit – Mobile Hospital No. 8 – which was modelled on the French *autochirs*, had twenty nurses, under the supervision of chief nurse, Marie Eden. The hospital had over forty trucks, among which were an X-ray truck, a 'Dodge touring car', two laundry units and a sterilizer.

Catherine Black, with British CCS No. 50 was at Bohain where, at one point, the CCS was located right on the front lines. Shells passed over the hospital tents, and Catherine was later to remark in her memoir that

> I never expected to see the dawn again, but I was too sleepy to care
> very much. As soon as I went off duty I lay down on my bed, with
> the somewhat inadequate protection of a tin hat tied firmly on

my head and an enamel basin strapped over my tummy. What I expected to achieve by that I cannot imagine, but at the time it gave me a ridiculous sense of security.[8]

Nurses of all nations were joining the advance. As they crossed the devastated terrain over which armies had fought for four years, they were shocked by the desolation they witnessed. Where once there had been rural villages, farms, châteaux and arable or pastoral farmland, there were now only piles of rubble and a great deal of mud. As they moved further east beyond the former 'zone of the armies', they were treated as liberators, greeted with joy by people who had lived under foreign occupation for four years. Along with the wounded men being evacuated from the still-advancing front lines, they were now also caring for returning prisoners of war many of whom were emaciated and close to starvation, some with festering wounds. For the first time, they also found themselves taking in large numbers of civilians: men, women and children who had been wounded during the fighting or damaged by disease and starvation.

As the advance continued a new enemy emerged, one that was more insidious and ultimately far more destructive than any army. Cases of the so-called 'Spanish influenza' had been noticed earlier in the year, but by August 1918 it was becoming clear that the medical services were fighting a disease outbreak of epidemic proportions. It was only later that the 1918/19 influenza outbreak came to be recognized as a global pandemic. War had created the conditions under which the 'flu' virus could thrive: vast numbers of debilitated, malnourished and enervated men, whose immune systems were unable to combat the virus, were living in conditions of squalor and overcrowding which enabled the rapid airborne spread of the disease from person to person. The Spanish influenza was very ugly: initial symptoms of fever, sore throat, coughing and exhaustion, soon gave way to total collapse. As patients' lungs became congested with fluid, they began to drown, becoming so starved of oxygen that their skin turned blue, grey or black. They gasped for air and, even in hospitals where oxygen was available, its administration made little difference as the toxins created by the infection ravaged the bodies of sufferers.

In the autumn, Base Hospital No. 10 began to take in large numbers of patients suffering from influenza. These, the nurses agreed, were worse than the mustard-gas-poisoned cases they had received the previous year. Many nurses and orderlies contracted the disease. All of the nurses recovered, but four corpsmen died, and were buried alongside their compatriots in military cemeteries. The Philadelphia nurses were lucky. In hospitals throughout the lines of evacuation nurses were dying from the disease. Working as closely as they did to their patients, offering fundamental nursing care, they were highly vulnerable to infection.

CCS were now leap-frogging each other as they moved east, racing to keep up with the rapidly advancing Allied armies. A unit would be placed close to the fighting lines, only to find itself, a few days later, in a 'back area' – left behind by the advance, and having to pack up and move once more. Convoys of wounded poured into the hospitals; they were a more complex group now than they had ever been. Alongside the Allied soldiers with combat injuries, there were newly released prisoners suffering from a range of illnesses, German prisoner-of-war patients, wounded civilians, and large numbers of individuals of all nationalities with influenza. Surgical teams were, once again, working sixteen-hour shifts. At No. 38 CCS, American Sister Julia Ravenel was caring for large numbers of former Allied prisoners of war. Her colleague, surgeon John Flick, described one American patient brought to the hospital from an advanced German war hospital in eastern France. His condition was 'wretched'. He was

> very septic and emaciated. He had a disarticulation at the left knee-joint, the articular surface was covered with granulations and bathed in pus and he had a compound fracture of the other leg and several flesh wounds elsewhere. He said that the German hospital had been under-staffed and without adequate supplies; that the prisoners had suffered from want of food and attention.[9]

The 'disarticulation' and 'granulations' on this patient's knee joint indicated that the knee had been left to heal without having been adequately re-aligned and without the wound having been kept clean or properly dressed. Infection had clearly set in and was spreading. The patient was lucky to have survived.

At 11 a.m. on 11 November 1918, the guns fell silent across the Western Front. As the war ended, spontaneous, jubilant celebrations erupted in towns and cities across Allied nations. But many nurses spent that day and the night that followed at the bedsides of men for whom peace had come too late. The accumulation of patients with 'Spanish flu' and the continuing care and treatment of men who had been wounded just before the Armistice – some of whom were slowly dying – meant that it was several weeks before workloads began to ease.

Margaret Brander had served with the Territorial Force Nursing Service throughout the war. She had been mentioned in despatches twice: on 31 May 1915 and on 7 November 1917. She had served with No. 5 British CCS for much of 1917. In December that year, the sister-in-charge, K. C. Todd, had written in her official report that

> Sister Brander has worked under me for 10 months – as Ward Sister, Night Sister, and as a Theatre Sister. She has at all times fulfilled her duty with the utmost zeal and conscientiousness. Her general professional ability is well above the average. She is a most capable administrator – especially in the operating theatre – thoroughly understands the training of orderlies, and has a marked power of initiative.

The officer commanding the CCS added that Margaret was 'a lady of marked ability, in whom I have the utmost confidence'. On 1 January 1918, Margaret was awarded the Royal Red Cross (Second Class).

From 21 February to 29 August 1918, Margaret served as sister-in-charge of a special operating hut at No. 26 General Hospital, Etaples, where her skill in operating theatre work soon came to be very highly regarded by her medical and nursing superiors. Then, in September 1918, she was invited to train as an anaesthetist, and was posted first to No. 2 Canadian General Hospital at Le Treport, and then to No. 45 British CCS at Bailleuleval, near Arras, where she completed her training and was declared 'very satisfactory as an anaesthetist'. Having learned how to administer chloroform, ether and nitrous oxide, she was to serve in operating teams in CCSs until well after the Armistice.

Margaret was with No. 44 British CCS from 17 December 1918 to 3 March 1919, moving east between Namur and Cologne. On 14 April, her matron, Minnie Wood wrote in her annual confidential report that 'she was absolutely reliable, most capable, had plenty of initiative and self-confident; good disciplinarian and ward manager. Very good nurse either medical or surgical ... Able to train and instruct orderlies, and had good influence amongst other members of staff.' Matron-in-chief Maud McCarthy concurred, adding to the report her opinion that Margaret was an 'Excellent sister and ward manager. Dedicated to her work and her patients.'

In Le Treport, the work was easing. From November onwards, American Base Hospital No. 10 received smaller and smaller convoys of patients. Margaret Dunlop commented that this was the most difficult period of service for her nurses. The war was over, and 'the longing for home grew intense'. Base Hospital No. 10 was eventually dismantled in early February 1919, and the nurses were sent to the picturesque town of Vannes in Brittany, before embarking on the liner *Rotterdam* for their return voyage to New York, this time without accompanying destroyers. They were demobilized at Camp Dix, New Jersey on 22 April 1919. Margaret would never forget her experience in France:

> The hours of worry, the hours of work followed by the equally difficult hours of leisure, the feeling of living in but not *of* a country, the nearness to and daily familiarity with such intense suffering, bravely borne; the close contact with the friends and relatives of the dying soldier; the seeing the quiet repressed sorrow with which they carried their burdens; these impressions are serious and lasting.[10]

# Epilogue

As the German forces were breaking through the lines at Ypres, in March 1918, May Tilton was on board the hospital ship *Kenilworth Castle*, taking convalescent troops, many with permanent disabilities, home to Australia. She felt 'like a deserter'. Yet she had been tested to the limit, working sixteen-hour shifts in one of the most advanced CCSs on the most difficult part of the Western Front. All passengers on board the *Kenilworth Castle* wore life-belts for most of the journey, eventually disembarking in Melbourne on 22 May, where they processed through the streets to the cheers of an admiring crowd. Yet May always felt that 'the best part of me will always remain in [the] Passchendaele area where lie many of the friends I loved best'.[1] Nine months later, the war she had been so anxious to participate in was over. But the Armistice did not end the work of nurses. The war-damaged and seriously ill continued to pour into their CCSs, and it would be many months before most were demobilized.

On 21 December 1918, a parade was held for all the orderlies and stretcher-bearers of Ambulance 16/21 attached to the 36ième Corps of the French army. The unit had reached a 'little straggling village' well east of the Hindenburg Line. The general of the 36ième Corps arrived for a special ceremony at which the nurses who had shown such loyalty to the corps were to be awarded the Croix de Guerre. By now, only four of the original nurses from Mary Borden's Mobile Surgical No. 1 still remained with the unit: Canadian nurses Agnes Warner and Helen McMurrich and British nurses Annie Hanning and Mabel Jones. Their citations were carefully composed to emphasize the resilience and determination they had shown.

The first to receive her Croix de Guerre was Agnes Warner, who had been in the *formations sanitaires* of the French army for four years. The general solemnly and slowly read aloud: 'she is well known as a model of enduring energy, of disinterestedness and of devotion; spent day and night attending to gassed and severely wounded cases, regardless of fatigue and bombardments. Has commanded the admiration of all.' Of English nurse Annie Hanning he declared that having since the outbreak of hostilities, hastened to the help of the French Armies, [she] fell in the hands of the enemy. As soon as she was liberated [she] resumed the task of charity and devotion in the advanced 'formations sanitaires' giving proof in every circumstance of an astonishing activity and of perfect competence. Has preserved under several bombardments a most admirable composure and has continued to show proof of the same qualities in the course of the operations of the last two months.

Helen McMurrich, Agnes Warner's close friend, was said to have 'helped many precious lives in the struggle against death, never allowing herself to be vanquished either by bombardment or by fatigue', while Mabel Jones was similarly declared to have 'toiled without ceasing for four years as insensible to hard work as to bombardment'.[2]

Eventually, war service did end, and many of the nurses who had lived such extraordinary lives behind the Ypres Salient moved quietly back into civilian nursing practice. Professional nurse Kate Luard returned to her previous job as matron of a tuberculosis sanatorium before moving to other senior civilian nursing positions. Her last professional role was as 'lady matron' of Bradfield Boys' School in Berkshire. Eventually, a back complaint forced her to retire, and she spent the rest of her life in rural Essex, living with two of her sisters. Catherine Black also moved back into civilian practice, although she did take on a highly unusual role, becoming private nurse to George V.

Other nurses found that they were unable to return quietly to civilian life. Violetta Thurstan continued to travel and seek adventure. In December 1917, she had joined the Scottish Women's Hospitals, and travelled to Macedonia as matron to a hospital in Ostrovo, returning home in August 1918. After the war, she joined the Women's Royal Air Force, before becoming an adviser with the Bedouin Industries in Egypt in the interwar period, working with the Universities Ambulance during the Spanish Civil War, and for Naval Intelligence, advising the Merchant Marine during the Second World War. Eventually, she retired to Cornwall to focus on her interests of spinning, weaving, and novel-writing. She died at Penryn on 13 April, 1978, at the age of 99; at her own request, she was buried with her eight medals, among which were awards for service and bravery from Belgium, Russia and Britain.

Mary Borden went on to write numerous best-selling novels, while her colleague at Mobile Surgical No. 1, Ellen La Motte, also continued to pursue a writing career. She travelled to the Far East and became a campaigner against the opium trade. Agnes Warner, who had been Borden's head nurse at

Adinkerke and Rousbrugge, returned home to Saint John, New Brunswick, Canada to a heroine's welcome, but died just a few years later from breast cancer, at the age of fifty-four.

Kate Maxey worked at Beckett's Park Hospital in Leeds until well after the end of the war. In June 1919, following her demobilization, she set up a nursing home – 'Heathroyde' – in Halifax, with her friend, Assistant Matron Anne Simpson, eventually retiring from both the home and the TFNS in 1931. In addition to her Military Medal, Kate also received the Royal Red Cross (on 3 June 1918), the 1914–15 Star, the British War Medal and the Victory Medal. In 1920 she was awarded the highest honour for nurses, the Florence Nightingale Medal, by the International Society of the Red Cross.

The St John Ambulance Brigade and Nursing Division in Kate's home town of Spennymoor presented her with a silver set of salts and spoons, and even though she spent much of her retirement living in a flat in Muswell Hill in North London, she retained a life-long affection for her home town. She died in 1969, at Bishop Auckland, just six miles from where she had been born. She is still remembered by her great-nieces as a formidable lady with smooth, white hair, who always stood to attention when the national anthem was played.

Some nurses continued to serve with the Queen Alexandra's Imperial Military Nursing Service – as if the First World War were just one, particularly challenging, episode in a larger career. Minnie Wood was awarded the Order of the British Empire on 1 June 1919, and was mentioned in despatches for a third time in July that year. She served with the Army of the Rhine from August to October 1919, although she was forced to take sick leave due to 'debility' and 'anaemia' in September. She served in England, Malta and Ireland in the 1920s, before resigning from the army in 1924 for private reasons 'concerning family affairs'. On her retirement, she wrote to Anne Beadsmore-Smith, matron-in-chief of the QAIMNS: 'I have had a particularly happy time during my period of service, and feel very sad to be giving it up.'

Margaret Brander was still on the Western Front, serving at No. 44 British CCS in April 1919, but was asking to be released so that she could resume her duties at the Arbroath Infirmary. She was permitted to return home, arriving at Folkestone on 4 April – the day she was officially demobilized. In 1926, she was awarded the Médaille de la Reconnaissance Francais en Bronze by the French government 'for services rendered to French civilians' during the war. In 1936, Margaret was promoted to matron of the Arbroath

Infirmary, a position she retained until her retirement in September 1947. She died the following March. In a tribute, the Chair of the Board of Hospital Directors declared that 'Nursing was to her a calling ... it came first and for 24 hours every day.' He added that, from her 'there flowed unerringly a selfless service that our pound-for-pound, penny-for-penny world today cannot match nor fully appreciate'.[3]

Madeleine Jaffray was fitted with a prosthetic foot, and was able to gain employment again as a nurse. After the war, she worked at the Dominion Orthopedic Hospital on Christie Street in Toronto, Many of her patients were amputees – men like those she had cared for in Flanders. She joined the Amputations Association of the Great War – its only female member in Canada – and, in 1926, at a convention held by the association, she met fellow amputee, Byron Morrison, a watchmaker from Edmonton who had lost a leg at the battle for Vimy Ridge. The 'two fragments', as they were affectionately named, married on 23 September 1927 at an association convention in Hamilton; fellow amputees formed an 'arch' of crutches and walking sticks, through which the couple walked.[4] Following her marriage, Madeleine worked as a district nursing sister for the Victorian Order of Nurses, and continued to serve the War Amputees of Canada as a volunteer. She died on 23 July 1972.

Colonel Richard Harte – one-time commander of Pennsylvania Base Hospital No. 10 – returned to civilian practice. In 1921, he wrote of his 'thanks and unbounded gratitude to all the members of the Unit – the officers, nurses, and enlisted personnel – for their magnificent loyalty and devotion to duty under the most trying conditions; at all times both day and night, through rain and snow, they vied with one another in trying to make the work of the Unit conspicuous for efficiency'.[5] On the subject of his retreat from Dozinghem in the middle of August 1917 with Helen Fairchild, he remained silent. The reason for their sudden return to base will probably never be known. It may simply be that their tour of duty was over. Helen's sister, Christine, always remembered that, after the war, a man came to her parents' house to tell them about Helen's illness. He said that one night, during her time at British CCS No. 4, Helen had given her gas mask to a soldier, thus exposing herself to drifting toxins from gas shells landing close to the unit. He believed that this deliberate act of self-sacrifice had meant that the stomach ulcer, which was already making her very ill, had become more acute. The story was passed down within the Fairchild family: for descendants who never knew her, Helen was both a war hero and a compassionate humanitarian.

In an eighteen-month period from 13 June 1917 to 31 December 1918, American Base Hospital No. 10 admitted 47,811 patients to its site at Le Treport, only 3,012 of whom were American soldiers. Most were Britons, Australians, New Zealanders and Canadians. Three thousand seven hundred and thirty-six operations were performed, and there were 538 deaths.

At the end of the war, Helen Fairchild's body was moved to the United States Military Cemetery at Bony, on the Somme, in France. Her name is registered at the Women in Military Service for America Memorial at Arlington National Cemetery, Virginia, USA. Helen Fairchild's brother, Ned, and his wife, Phoebe, had three children. They named their first daughter Helen. Their youngest, Nelle, was born on 23 May 1930 in Watsontown, Delaware Township. When she was in fourth grade at school her teacher asked the class if any of them had a relative who had served in the Great War, and Nelle proudly named her Aunt Helen, only to be told by the boys in her class that, as a woman, Helen 'did not count'. From that moment, Nelle became determined to tell her aunt's story, accumulating evidence for a book and website, and campaigning vigorously for the recognition of Helen Fairchild's sacrifice. Nelle believes that her aunt – already in fragile health when she travelled to France – died as a result of overwork and exposure to mustard gas, both at CCS No. 4 and at Base Hospital No. 10. Her extensive tribute to her aunt reproduces every shred of evidence that can be mobilized to substantiate the claim that Helen Fairchild died, as the chaplain of Base Hospital 10 said, 'as a result of her work at the front'.

Many patients survived because of the care and treatment they received at CCSs, on ambulance trains and at general hospitals behind the Western Front. Sidney Beldam, the 18-year-old with severe facial wounds who had somehow lived after having lain for three days and nights in no man's land near Passchendaele, spent most of the last ten months of the war at the Queen's Hospital, Sidcup, undergoing operation after operation to repair his devastated face. While he was there, he met Winifred Winkworth, a professional pianist who had been asked to come into the hospital to play for the patients. She was later to declare that she fell in love with Sidney 'at first sight' – because his smile 'lit up the room'. Sidney's ordeal was not over: he was to undergo more than forty further operations and every time he caught a cold he would experience an agonizing inflammation of his scarred nasal passages. His seventy-two hours in a shell hole at Passchendaele had left him with a phobia of rats and cockroaches that lasted for the rest of his life. Yet Sidney considered himself lucky. Many of the patients who were discharged from the Queen's Hospital were unable to find their way back into 'normal' life. Some died of illnesses associated with their injuries. Others committed suicide. Sidney and Winifred had a happy marriage. Their granddaughter, Marilyn, was later to write: 'I thought all granddads looked like mine, and honestly never thought twice about it … of all people his was the lap I always sought and found.'

The price that was paid by nurses and other medical workers for securing the survival of men like Sidney was a high one. Many became physically or emotionally ill as a result of their front-line work. Some suffered both wounding and shell-shock. Very few received compensation in the form of a war pension. And there was very little reporting of the real nature of their work, or of the dangers they had faced. The wounding and death of nurses at front-line hospitals would have been a difficult form of propaganda for early-twentieth-century governments to manage and control. Such news could easily have led to recrimination with the question, 'Why place women so close to danger?' Nurses *did* receive high praise after the war, and, in Britain, they were rewarded by the passing of the Nurses Registration Act, in December 1919, which recognized their professional status. But somehow the reality of nurses' work and the nature of the risks they took were never fully known. Among the many voices of their generation, theirs were mostly silenced. Although many memoirs, diaries and letters were carefully preserved in archives and libraries across the world, these were rarely consulted by historians, who were mostly searching for 'mainstream', masculine histories of the First World War. Only recently has the faintest whisper of nurses' experiences been heard, as a few tenacious descendants, inspired by the war's centenary, have published their grandmothers' or great-aunts' diaries and memoirs.

Today, beside a war-cemetery near Westvleteren, there stands a memorial, an ethereal image of a nurse in the blue uniform of the American Red Cross. Helen Fairchild seems to be looking across the rows of white monuments towards the stillness of the Belgian landscape. Where once the air was sprayed with shrapnel splinters from 'daisy-cutter bombs', now there is only a tranquil, fertile landscape. It is almost as if war's horrors have been erased, leaving only the white sentinels of the grave-markers and the serene image of the nurse.

# Notes on material used in the text

O
ne of the main aims of this book is to capture the perspectives of nurses. My research therefore drew heavily on their memoirs and other personal writings. Although at times I paraphrase or summarize those writings, I also, sometimes, quote them in order to give voice to the nurses themselves. Where I have directly quoted the writings (published or unpublished) of nurses or other eyewitnesses, I have given a reference to my source in an endnote. Full references for all published material consulted for this book can be found in the bibliography. Unpublished materials, along with the most significant published sources are discussed below.

Helen Fairchild's letters home to her family (along with their letters to her, and a large amount of other correspondence) are available at the U.S. Army Medical Department at Fort Sam Houston, Texas, USA and can be found at: Helen Fairchild; fire-safe 3-B-2, AMEDD Center of History and Heritage, Archival Repository, JBSA Fort Sam Houston, TX 78234. Complete transcripts of Helen's letters home are provided in a book written by her niece, Nelle Rote: Nelle Fairchild Hefty Rote, *Nurse Helen Fairchild WW1 1917–1918* (Lewisburg, PA, Nelle Rote, 2004). Ellen La Motte's letters to Amy Wesselhoeft von Erdberg can be found in the Ellen La Motte Collection, the Alan Mason Chesney Archives of the Johns Hopkins Medical Institutes, Baltimore. Margaret Brander's diary is lodged in the archives of the Imperial War Museum, London (Personal Papers: 13190). Australian nurse Effie Garden's account of her experiences is also at the Imperial War Museum ('Australian Army Nursing Services during the First World War', including an account by Mrs Effie Fussell (née Garden); Misc 47, item 790). The First World War diaries of Violetta Thurstan can be accessed at the Liddle Collection, the Brotherton Library, Leeds, UK (WW1/WO/116). The writings of Philip Clayton are in the archives of Talbot House, Poperinge. The letters of Annie Wright to the parents of Glynne Morris are in the Nottinghamshire Archives, UK (DD/873/18, 19, 20, 22, 23, 26, 27, 29, 34). Kate Maxey's personal papers are held in a private collection by her great-niece, Maureen Defty. These, along with material from her War Office file, have been summarized by historian John Banham. His paper can be found at: http://www.durhamatwar.org.uk/story/11260/. The story of Sidney Beldam was reconstructed from papers and photographs in the private collection of Marilyn McInnes, and also from Marilyn's own memories of her grandparents. The Gillies British patient file of Sidney Beldam, MS0513/1/1/ID133, is reproduced by kind courtesy of Marilyn McInnes and with the permission of The Archives at the Royal College of Surgeons of England.

The 'Nurses Narratives' held as part of the Butler Collection at the Australian War Memorial, Canberra, were an important source for the experiences of Australian nurses. Of particular value to this project were:

Emma Cuthbert, 'Narrative'; AWM41/958
Ellen McClelland, 'Narrative'; AWM41/1000
Nellie N.C. Morrice, 'Narrative'; AWM41/1013
Violet Minnie Payne, 'Narrative'; AWM41/1021

A number of published nurses' memoirs allowed me to gain a vivid – if patchy – perspective on life close to the front lines in Belgium. Sister Kate Luard's long, journalistic letters home to her family were published in book form: Anonymous [Kate Luard], *Diary of a Nursing Sister on the Western Front* (Edinburgh, William Blackwood & Sons, 1915); Kate Luard, *Unknown Warriors* (London, Chatto & Windus, 1930). May Tilton's memoir, *The Grey Battalion* (Angus & Robertson, Ltd., 1933) was particularly important in enabling me to better understand the experiences of nurses at the Brandhoek casualty clearing stations, as well as in a number of other locations on the Western Front. Elsie Knocker's original diary is available at the Imperial War Museum, London, UK (Personal Papers 9029). Her memoir was published much later as: Baroness de T'Serclaes, *Flanders and Other Fields* (London, George Harrap & Co. Ltd., 1964). Violetta Thurstan's first memoir, *Field Hospital and Flying Column* (London, G.P. Putnam's Sons, 1915) is a valuable source of information for her earlier wartime experiences in Belgium. Several of her books are listed in the bibliography.

Much information relating to U.S. Base Hospital No. 10 was obtained from Paul Hoeber's *History of the Pennsylvania Hospital Unit (Base Hospital No. 10 USA) in the Great War* (Paul B. Hoeber, 1921). Hoeber brought together a number of writings by key members of staff at the hospital, including Matron Margaret Dunlop. Other eyewitness testimony has been drawn from the writings of surgeons, notably George Crile's

*An Autobiography* (Philadelphia and New York, J. B. Lippincott Co., 1947) and Harvey Cushing's *From a Surgeon's Journal, 1915–1918* (Boston, Little, Brown & Co., 1936).

The official *War Diaries* of casualty clearing stations (CCSs) are available at the British National Archives, Kew, London. Photographs of the pages from the *Diaries* for CCSs at Remy Siding are on display at the Lijssenthoek Cemetery Visitor Centre, Poperinge. Information on the careers and wartime postings of British QAIMNS and QAIMNSR nurses was obtained from their War Office records at the British National Archives, Kew, London. The following were of particular value:

Catherine Black WO 399/660
Margaret Allan Brander WO 399/9967
Kate Luard WO 399/5023
Kate Maxey WO 399/13235
Nellie Spindler WO 399/7850
Minnie Wood WO 399/9206

Information on the backgrounds of nurses can also be found in the Register of Nurses of the Royal British Nurses Association at RBNA 4/1 King's College Archives, London, UK. Information on the work and experiences of nurses can be obtained from the *British Journal of Nursing,* which is available online via the Royal College of Nursing Archives, Edinburgh: http://www2.rcn.org.uk/development/library_and_heritage_services. Two of the most valuable resources for the history of the official British nursing services during the war are the 'Scarlet Finders' and 'Fairest Force' websites, which were created by Sue Light: http://www.scarletfinders.co.uk, and http://www.fairestforce.co.uk/. Information on nurses' medals and awards was obtained from the *London Gazette,* which is available online at: www.thegazette.co.uk.

Memoirs of Mobile Surgical No. 1 provide a range of perspectives on the work of the hospital. See:

Mary Borden, *The Forbidden Zone* (London, William Heinemann, 1929).

Ellen La Motte, *The Backwash of War* (New York, G.P. Putnam's Sons, The Knickerbocker Press, 1916).

Ellen La Motte, 'Under Shell-Fire at Dunkirk', *The Atlantic Monthly,* 116 (November 1915).

Anonymous [Agnes Warner], *My Beloved Poilus* (Saint John, New Brunswick, N. B. Barnes, 1917).

Maud Mortimer, *A Green Tent in Flanders* (New York, Doubleday, Page & Co., 1918).

Alongside these published memoirs, two archived collections of personal papers were of great value in reconstructing events during the later period at Mobile Surgical No. 1:

Hilda Mary Loxton, Diary; 2DRL/1172; Private Record; Australian War Memorial, Canberra, Australia.

Madeleine Jaffray, newspaper interviews and other documents relating to her experiences: Madeleine Morrison Fonds; PAA-8298; Provincial Archives of Alberta, Edmonton, Canada.

Information on individual French soldiers who were nursed at Mobile Surgical No. 1 has been obtained from the following Ministry of Defence website: Ministère de la Défense, Memoires des Hommes: www.memoiredeshommes.sga.defense.gouv.fr. Information was also obtained from Archives Nationales, Paris, France and from MemorialGenWeb: www.memorialgenweb.org. These documents contain information about the full name, date and place of birth, date and place of conscription, previous occupation and date of death for each former patient. I matched information on the documents to the narratives of Borden, Mortimer, Warner and La Motte. Borden generally anonymized the identities of the patients she wrote about. Mortimer used names very similar to patients' actual names. La Motte and Warner used actual names (though Warner used these very sparingly). These were easily matched with Mortimer's slightly adapted pseudonyms, permitting me to identify each patient and then source the information available on him at 'Memoires des Hommes'. I was greatly assisted in this process by Dirk Claerhout.

This book draws upon insights gained during work on my three monographs (although material in these books is not directly reproduced):

Christine E. Hallett, *Containing Trauma: Nursing Work in the First World War* (Manchester University Press, 2009).

Christine E. Hallett, *Veiled Warriors: Allied Nurses of the First World War* (Oxford University Press, 2014).

Christine E. Hallett, *Nurse Writers of the Great War* (Manchester University Press, 2016).

There is a vast body of literature on the Ypres campaigns (see bibliography). In researching this book I found the following texts particularly useful:

Robin Prior and Trevor Wilson, *Passchendaele: The Untold Story* Third Edition (New Haven, Yale University Press, 2016 [first published 1996]).

Nigel Steel and Peter Hart, *Passchendaele: The Sacrificial Ground* (London, Cassell, 2000) (narratives relating to Lieutenant M. L. Walkinton and Driver Rowland Luther were obtained from this text; the original papers are lodged in the Imperial War Museum, London).

Peter Barton, *Passchendaele* (London, Constable, in association with Imperial War Museum, 2007) (Letters relating to the death of Glynne Morris were first published in this book).

# Bibliography

Anonymous [Kate Luard], *Diary of a Nursing Sister on the Western Front* (Edinburgh, William Blackwood & Sons, 1915).

Anonymous, 'Nursing at La Panne', *British Journal of Nursing* (10 March 1917): 169.

Anonymous, 'Care of the Wounded', *British Journal of Nursing* (14 April 1917): 253.

Anonymous [Agnes Warner], *My Beloved Poilus* (Saint John, New Brunswick, Barnes & Co., 1917).

Anonymous, *A War-Nurse's Diary: Sketches from a Belgian Field Hospital* (New York, Macmillan, 1918).

Anonymous (ed.), *Reminiscent Sketches, 1914 to 1919 by Members of Her Majesty Queen Alexandra's Imperial Military Nursing Service* (London, John Bale, Sons & Danielsson, Ltd, 1922).

Atkinson, Diane, *Elsie and Mairi Go To War: Two Extraordinary Women on the Western Front* (London, Preface Publishing, 2009).

Barton, Peter, *Passchendaele* (London, Constable, in association with Imperial War Museum, 2007).

Bassett, Jan, *Guns and Brooches. Australian Army Nursing from the Boer War to the Gulf War* (Melbourne, Oxford University Press, 1992).

Biddle, Major Charles J., *The Way of the Eagle* (New York, Charles Scribner's Sons, 1919).

Black, Catherine, *King's Nurse – Beggar's Nurse* (London, Hurst & Blackett Ltd, 1939).

Black, J. Elliot, Glenny, Elliot T., and McNee, J. W., 'Observations on 685 Cases of Poisoning by Noxious Gases Used by the Enemy', *The British Medical Journal* (31 July 1915): 165-7.

Borden, Mary, *The Forbidden Zone* (London, William Heinemann Ltd, 1929).

Borden, Mary, *The Forbidden Zone* (London, Hesperus Press, 2008).

Bowser, Thelka, *The Story of British VAD Work in the Great War* (London, Imperial War Museum, 2003 [1917]).

Bradshaw, Ann, *The Nurse Apprentice, 1860–1977* (Aldershot, Ashgate, 2001).

Brown, Malcolm, *1918 Year of Victory* (London, Pan Books with Imperial War Museum, 1998).

Butler, Arthur G., *Official History of the Australian Army Medical Services, 1914–1918*, Vol. II, *The Western Front* (Australian War Memorial, Canberra, 1940).

Butler, Arthur G., *Official History of the Australian Army Medical Services, 1914–1918*, Vol. III, *Special Problems and Services* (Australian War Memorial, Melbourne, 1943).

Byerly, Carol R., *Fever of War: The Influenza Epidemic in the U.S. Army during World War I* (New York, Viking, 1991).

Clayton, Ann, *Chavasse Double VC.* (Barnsley, Pen & Sword Books, 2008 [1992]).

Conway, Jane, *Mary Borden: A Woman of Two Wars* (Chippenham, Munday Books, 2010).

Cooter, Roger, Harrison, Mark & Sturdy, Steve (eds.) *War, Medicine and Modernity* (Stroud, Sutton Publishing, 1998): 125-148.

Cowen, Ruth (ed.) *War Diaries. A Nurse at the Front. The Great War Diaries of Sister Edith Appleton* (London, Simon & Schuster, 2012).

Crile, George, *An Autobiography*, Edited, with Sidelights by Grace Crile, Volume 1 (Philadelphia & New York, J. B. Lippincott Co., 1947).

Cushing, Harvey, *From a Surgeon's Journal, 1915–1918* (Boston, Little, Brown & Co., 1936).

Darrow, Margaret, 'French Volunteer Nursing and the Myth of War Experience in World War I', *American Historical Review*, 101, 1 (1996): 80-106.

Das, Santanu, *Touch and Intimacy in First World War Literature* (Cambridge, Cambridge University Press, 2005).

de Munck, Luc and Vandeweyer, Luc, *Het Hospital van de Koningin: Rode Kruis, L'Ocean en De Panne* (De Panne, Gemeetebestuur De Panne en de auteurs, 2012).

Ellison, Grace, 'Nursing at the French Front', in Stone, Gilbert (ed.) *Women War Workers. Accounts contributed by representative workers of the work done by women in the more important branches of war employment* (London, George G. Harrap & Co. 1917): 155-80.

Fell, Alison S. and Hallett Christine (eds.), *First World War Nursing: New Perspectives* (New York, Routledge, 2013): 1-14.

Ferro, Marc, *The Great War 1914–1918*, transl. Nicole Stone (London, Routledge, 2002 [1973]).

Fitzgerald, Gerard, 'Chemical Warfare and the Medical Response during World War I', *American Journal of Public Health*, 98 (4) (April 2008): 611-625.

Freedman, Ariela, 'Mary Borden's *Forbidden Zone*: Women's Writing from No-Man's Land', *Modernism/modernity*, 9: 1 (2002), 109-24.

Fussell, Paul, *The Great War and Modern Memory* (Oxford, Oxford University Press, 2000 [1975]).

Gibbs, Philip, *The Soul of the War* (New York, A. L. Burt Co., 1915).

Gillespie, H. S., 'McCarthy, Dame (Emma) Maud (1858–1949), in *Oxford Dictionary of National Biography* (Oxford, Oxford University Press, 2004–13).

Gooding, Norman G., *Honours and Awards to Women: The Military Medal* (London, Savannah Publications, 2013).

Goodnow, Minnie, *War Nursing: A Text-Book for the Auxiliary Nurse* (Philadelphia & London, W. B. Saunders Co., 1917).

Grayzel, Susan, *Women's Identities at War: Gender, Motherhood, and Politics in Britain and France during the First World War* (Chapel Hill, NC, University of North Carolina Press, 1999).

Gregory, Adrian, *The Last Great War* (Cambridge, Cambridge University Press, 2008).

Groom, W. H. A., *Poor Bloody Infantry: The Truth Untold* (New Malden, Picardy Publishing Ltd., 1983; first published 1976).

Haldane, Elizabeth S., *The British Nurse in Peace and War* (London, John Murray, 1923).

Hallett, Christine E., *Containing Trauma: Nursing Work in the First World War* (Manchester, Manchester University Press, 2009).

Hallett, Christine E., 'Portrayals of Suffering: Perceptions of Trauma in the Writings of First World War Nurses and Volunteers', *Canadian Bulletin of the History of Medicine*, 27 (1) (2011): 65-84.

Hallett, Christine E. and Cooke, Hannah, *Historical Investigations into the Professional Self-Regulation of Nursing and Midwifery: Volume I, Nursing* (London, Nursing & Midwifery Council, 2011); available at the Archives of the Nursing & Midwifery Council, 23, Portland Place, London.

Hallett, Christine E., 'Nursing, 1840–1920: Forging a Profession', in Borsay, Anne and Hunter, Billie (eds.) *Nursing and Midwifery in Britain since 1700* (London, Palgrave Macmillan, 2012): 46-73.

Hallett, Christine E., '"Emotional Nursing": Involvement, Engagement, and Detachment in the Writings of First World War Nurses and VADs', in Fell, A. S. and Hallett, C. E. (eds.), *First World War Nursing: New Perspectives* (New York, Routledge, 2013): 87-102.

Hallett, Christine E., '"Intelligent interest in their own affairs": The First World War, the *British Journal of Nursing* and the pursuit of nursing knowledge', in d'Antonio, P., Fairman, J. and Whelan, J. (eds.) *Routledge Handbook on the Global History of Nursing* (London & New York, Routledge, 2013): 95-113.

Hallett, Christine E., *Veiled Warriors: Allied Nurses of the First World War* (Oxford, Oxford University Press, 2014).

Hallett, Christine, E., '"This fiendish mode of warfare": nursing the victims of gas poisoning in the First World War', in Brooks, Jane and Hallett, Christine (eds.) *One Hundred Years of Wartime Nursing Practices* (Manchester, Manchester University Press, 2015).

Hallett, Christine E., *Nurse Writers of the Great War* (Manchester, Manchester University Press, 2016).

Harris, Kirsty, *More than Bombs and Bandages: Australian Army Nurses at Work in World War I* (Newport, NSW, Big Sky Publishing, 2011).

Harrison, Mark, *The Medical War: British Military Medicine in the First World War* (Oxford, Oxford University Press, 2010).

Hoeber, Paul H., *History of the Pennsylvania Hospital Unit (Base Hospital No. 10 USA) in the Great War* (Paul B. Hoeber, New York, 1921).

Holmes, Richard, *Tommy: The British Soldier on the Western Front, 1914–1918* (London, HarperCollins, 2004).

Jensen, Kimberly, *Mobilizing Minerva: American Women in the First World War* (Urbana & Chicago, University of Illinois Press, 2008).

Johnson, Niall, *Britain and the 1918–19 Influenza Pandemic* (London, Routledge, 2006).

Keegan, John, *The First World War* (London, Hutchinson, 1999 [1998]).

Kramer, Alan, *Dynamic of Destruction: Culture and Mass Killing in the First World War* (Oxford, Oxford University Press, 2007).

La Motte, Ellen, 'Under Shell-Fire at Dunkirk', *Atlantic Monthly*, 116 (November 1915): 692-700.

La Motte, Ellen N., *The Backwash of War: The Human Wreckage of the Battlefield as Witnessed by an American Hospital Nurse* (New York, G. P. Putnam's Sons, The Knickerbocker Press, 1916).

Leed, Eric J., *No Man's Land: Combat and Identity in World War I* (Cambridge, Cambridge University Press, 1979).

Leese, P. J., *Shell Shock: Traumatic Neurosis and the British Soldiers of the First World War* (London, Palgrave Macmillan, 2002).

Lewis, Thomas, *The Soldier's Heart and the Effort Syndrome* (London, Shaw & Sons, 1918).

Liddle, Peter, *Captured Memories: 1900–1918. Across the Threshold of War* (Barnsley, Pen & Sword Military, 2010).

Light, Sue, 'British Military Nurses and the Great War: A Guide to the Services', *The Western Front Association Forum*, 7 February, 2010: 4; sourced at: www.westernfrontassociation.com (date downloaded: 20/10/2016).

Louagie, Jan, *A Touch of Paradise in Hell, Talbot House Poperinghe – Everyman's Sanctuary from the Trenches* (Helion & Co., 2015).

Luard, Kate E., *Unknown Warriors: Extracts from the Letters of Kate Lard, RRC, Nursing Sister IN France, 1914–1918* (London, Chatto & Windus, 1930).

Luard, Kate, *Unknown Warriors: The Letters of Kate Luard, RRC and Bar, Nursing Sister in France 1914–1918* New Edition (Stroud, The History Press, 2014).

Macdonald, Lyn, *They Called it Passchendaele* (London, Penguin, 1978).

Macdonald, Lyn, *The Roses of No Man's Land* (London, Penguin, 1993 [1980]).

Macfie, A. B. S., *The Curious History of Toc H Women's Association. The First Phase, 1917–1928* (London, Toc H Women's Association, Crutched Friars House, 1956).

Maclean, Hester, *Nursing in New Zealand – History and Reminiscences* (Wellington, NZ, Tolan Printing Co., 1932).

Macpherson, Sir William Grant, *History of the Great War Based on Official Documents by Direction of the Historical Section of the Committee of Imperial Defence. Medical Services: General History*, Volumes 1, 2 & 3 (London, Macmillan, 1921, 1923, 1924).

Medical Research Committee, *Report on the Anaerobic Bacteria and Infections: Report on the Anaerobic Infections of Wounds and the Bacteriological and Serological Problems Arising Therefrom* (London, HMSO, 1919).

Mitchell, T. J. and Smith, G. M., *History of the Great War Based on Official Documents: Medical Services* (Uckfield, West Sussex, The Naval & Military Press Ltd with the Imperial War Museum; facsimile of book first published in 1931).

Mitton, G. E. (ed.), *The Cellar-House of Pervyse: A Tale of Uncommon Things from the Journals and Letters of the Baroness De T'Serclaes and Mairi Chisholm* (London, A. & E. Black, 1916).

Mortimer, Maud, *A Green Tent in Flanders* (New York, Doubleday, Page & Co., 1918).

Ouditt, Sharon, *Fighting Forces, Writing Women: Identity and Ideology in the First World War* (London, Routledge, 1994).

Oxford, M. N., *Nursing in Wartime: Lessons for the Inexperienced* (London, Methuen & Co., 1914).

Pelis, Kim, 'Taking Credit: The Canadian Army Medical Corps and the British Conversion to Blood Transfusion in World War I', *Journal of the History of Medicine and Allied Health Sciences*, 56 (2001): 238-77.

Phillips, Howard and Killingray, David, *The Spanish Influenza Pandemic of 1918–19: New Perspectives* (London, Routledge, 2003).

Poynter, Denise J., '"The Report on her Transfer was Shell-Shock". A Study of the Psychological Disorders of Nurses and Female Voluntary Aid Detachments who served alongside the British and Allied Expeditionary Forces during the First World War, 1914–1918', unpublished PhD thesis, University of Northampton, 2008.

Prior, Robin Prior and Wilson, Trevor, *Passchendaele: The Untold Story*, 3rd edition (New Haven, Yale University Press, 2016 [first published 1996]).

Quinn, Shawna M., *Agnes Warner and the Nursing Sisters of the Great War* (Fredericton, New Brunswick, Goose Lane Editions, 2010).

Rae, Ruth, *Scarlet Poppies: The Army Experience of Australian Nurses during World War One* (Burwood, NSW, College of Nursing, 2004).

Rae, Ruth, *Veiled Lives. Threading Australian Nursing History into the Fabric of the First World War* (Burwood, NSW, College of Nursing, 2009).

Rogers, Anna, *While You're Away. New Zealand Nurses at War, 1899–1948* (Auckland, Auckland University Press, 2003).

Roper, Michael, *The Secret Battle: Emotional Survival in the Great War* (Manchester University Press, Manchester, 2009).

Rote, Nelle, *Nurse Helen Fairchild: WW1 1917–1918* (Lewisburg, PA, Nelle Rote, 2004).

Sarnecky, Mary T., *A History of the U.S. Army Nurse Corps* (Philadelphia, University of Pennsylvania Press, 1999).

Schultheiss, Katrin, *Bodies and Souls. Politics and the Professionalization of Nursing in France, 1880-1922* (Cambridge, MA, Harvard University Press, 2001).

Scotland, Thomas and Heys, Steven (eds.) *War Surgery 1914–18* (Solihull, Helion & Co. Ltd., 2012): 178-211.

Sheffield, Gary, *Forgotten Victory: The First World War: Myths and Realities* (London, Headline Book Publishing, 2002 [2001]).

Shephard, Ben, *A War of Nerves: Soldiers and Psychiatrists, 1914–1994* (London, Pimlico, 2002 [2000]).

Smith, Angela, *The Second Battlefield: Women, modernism and the First World War* (Manchester, Manchester University Press, 2000).

Smith, Angela, *Women's Writing of the First World War* (Manchester, Manchester University Press, 2000).

Sondhaus, Lawrence, *World War I: The Global Revolution* (Cambridge, Cambridge University Press, 2011).

Steel, Nigel and Hart, Peter, *Passchendaele: The Sacrificial Ground* (London, Cassell, 2000).

Stephenson, David, *1914–1918: The History of the First World War* (London, Allen Lane, 2004).

Stone, Norman, *World War One. A Short History* (London, Penguin, 2008 [2007]).

Stuart, Denis, *Dear Duchess: Millicent Duchess of Sutherland (1867-1955)* (Newton Abbot, David & Charles, 1982).

Strachan, Hew, *The First World War* (London, Pocket Books, 2006 [2003]): 60-63.

Summers, Anne, *Angels and Citizens: British Women as Military Nurses, 1854–1914* (London, Routledge & Kegan Paul, 1988).

Sutherland, Millicent, Duchess of, *Six Weeks at the War* (London, The Times, 1914).

T'Serclaes, Baroness de, *Flanders and Other Fields* (London, George G. Harrap & Co. Ltd., 1964).

Taylor, A. J. P., *The First World War* (London, Penguin, 1966 [1963]).

Telford, Jennifer Casavant, 'American Red Cross Nursing during World War I: Opportunities and Obstacles', Unpublished PhD thesis, University of Virginia, 2007.

Thurstan, Violetta, *Field Hospital and Flying Column* (London, G. P. Putnam's Sons, 1915).

Thurstan, Violetta, *The People Who Run* (London, G. P. Putnam's Sons, 1916).

Thurstan, Violetta, *A Text Book of War Nursing* (London, G. P. Putnam's Sons, 1917).

Thurstan, Violetta, *The Hounds of War Unleashed* (St Ives, United Writers, 1978).

Tilton, May, *The Grey Battalion* (Sydney, Angus & Robertson Ltd., 1933).

Todman, Dan, *The Great War: Myth and Memory* (London, Hambledon Continuum, 2005).

Toman, Cynthia, '"Help us, serve England": First World War Military Nursing and National Identities', *Canadian Bulletin of Medical History*, 30, 1 (2013): 156-7.

Tylee, Claire, *The Great War and Women's Consciousness. Images of Militarism and Womanhood in Women's Writings, 1914–64* (Houndmills, Macmillan 1990).

Van Bergen, Leo, *Before My Helpless Sight: Suffering, Dying and Military Medicine on the Western Front, 1914–1918*, transl. Liz Waters (Farnham, Surrey, 2009).

Van Emden, Richard, *The Trench: Experiencing Life on the Front Line, 1916* (London, Corgi Books, 2002).

Van Schaick, John Jr. *The Little Corner Never Conquered: The Story of the American Red Cross War Work for Belgium* (New York, The Macmillan Co., 1922).

Watson, Janet S. K., 'Wars in the Wards: The Social Construction of Medical Work in First World War Britain', *Journal of British Studies*, 41 (2002): 484-510.

Watson, Janet S. K., *Fighting Different Wars: Experience, Memory and the First World War in Britain* (Cambridge, Cambridge University Press, 2004).

Williams, Caroline H., *Lives in Letters: A New England Family, 1870–2000* (Caroline H. Williams, 2016).

Winter, Jay, *Sites of Memory, Sites of Mourning: The Great War in European Cultural History* (Cambridge, Cambridge University Press, 1995).

Yule, Peter (ed.), *Sergeant Lawrence Goes to France* (Melbourne, Melbourne University Press, 1987).

Zeiger, Susan, *In Uncle Sam's Service: Women Workers with the American Expeditionary Force, 1917–1919* (Philadelphia, University of Pennsylvania Press, 1999).

# Notes

## Chapter Two: Fight for Freedom

1. Baroness de T'Serclaes, *Flanders and Other Fields* (London, George C. Harrap & Co., 1964): p 23.
2. Mary Borden, *The Forbidden Zone* (London, William Heinemann Ltd., 1929): pp 47-8.
3. Ellen La Motte to Amy Wesselhoeft von Erdberg; Letter dated 14 March 1915; Ellen La Motte Collection; the Alan Mason Chesney Archives of the Johns Hopkins Medical Institutions, Baltimore, USA. On the life of Amy Wesselhoeft, see: Caroline H. Williams, *Lives in Letters: A New England Family, 1870–2000* (Caroline H. Williams, 2016).
4. Anonymous [Kate Luard], *Diary of a Nursing Sister on the Western Front* (Edinburgh, William Blackwood & Sons, 1915): pp 1-32.
5. The experiences of this nurse are recounted in: Anonymous, *A War-Nurse's Diary: Sketches from a Belgian Field Hospital* (New York, Macmillan, 1918).
6. Baroness de T'Serclaes, *Flanders and Other Fields* (London, George C. Harrap & Co., 1964): pp 62-3.

## Chapter Three: 'Second Ypres' and Other Assaults

1. Margaret Allan Brander, *Diary*, Volume I; Personal Papers; Documents 13190; Imperial War Museum, London: p 7.
2. Anonymous, *Diary of a Nursing Sister on the Western Front* (Edinburgh, William Blackwood & Sons, 1915).
3. Ibid.
4. Ibid.
5. Margaret Allan Brander, *Diary*, Volume I: pp 22-3.
6. Peter Liddle, *Captured Memories, 1900–1918: Across the Threshold of War* (Barnsley, Pen & Sword, 2010): Chapter 19: Brigadier Sir John Smythe: pp 265-78.
7. Anonymous, *A War Nurse's Diary*.
8. Margaret Allan Brander, *Diary*, Volume I: p 31.
9. Anonymous, *Diary of a Nursing Sister*.
10. Ibid.
11. Margaret Allan Brander, *Diary*, Volume I: p 33.
12. Margaret Allan Brander, *Diary*, Volume II: p 34.
13. Ibid: p 2.

14. Anonymous [Agnes Warner] *My Beloved Poilus* (Saint John, New Brunswick, Barnes & Co., 1917): pp 10–11.
15. Ellen La Motte, 'Under Shell-Fire At Dunkirk', *The Atlantic Monthly*, 116 (November 1915): pp 692–700.
16. Mary Borden, *The Forbidden Zone*: pp 1–4.
17. Ibid: pp 26–7.
18. Ibid: pp 34–5.
19. Ibid: pp 51–66.
20. Catherine Black, *King's Nurse – Beggar's Nurse* (London, Hurst & Blackett Ltd, 1939): p 87.

## Chapter Four: Supporting the Salient

1. Margaret Allan Brander, *Diary*, Volume II: p 10.
2. For further information on work and life at No. 1 British General Hospital, see: Ruth Cowen (ed.) *War Diaries. A Nurse at the Front: The Great War Diaries of Sister Edith Appleton* (London, Simon & Schuster, 2012).
3. Kate Luard, *Unknown Warriors* (London, Chatto & Windus, 1930): p 7.
4. Philip Gibbs, *The Soul of the War* (New York, A. L. Burt Co., 1915): pp 198–99.
5. Anonymous, *My Beloved Poilus*: pp 10–11.
6. Maud Mortimer, *A Green Tent in Flanders* (New York, Doubleday, Page & Co., 1918).
7. Information about soldiers who died at Mobile Surgical No. 1 has been obtained from the following French Ministry of Defense website: Ministère de la Défense, Memoire des Hommes; sourced at: www.memoiredeshommes.sga. defense.gouv.fr [date downloaded: 17/07/2016]. I am deeply indebted to Dirk Claerhout, who drew my attention to these documents. Further information is available at: Archives Nationales, Paris, France; and at MemorialGenWeb: www.memorialgenweb.org.
8. Ibid [date downloaded: 17/07/2016].
9. Maud Mortimer, *A Green Tent*.
10. Ministère de la Défense, Memoire des Hommes [date downloaded: 17/07/2016].
11. Maud Mortimer, *A Green Tent*: p 165.
12. Ibid: p 169.
13. Ellen La Motte, *The Backwash of War*: p 31.
14. Ibid, *The Backwash of War*: pp 49–59.
15. Ministère de la Défense, Memoire des Hommes [date downloaded: 17/07/2016].
16. Ellen La Motte, *The Backwash of War*: pp 56–7.
17. Maud Mortimer, *A Green Tent*.
18. Ibid.
19. Ibid.
20. Ibid: p 226.

21. Ibid: pp 240-42.
22. Ellen La Motte to Amy Wesselhoeft.
23. Richard H. Harte, 'Organization of the Unit', in Paul H. Hoeber (ed.), *History of the Pennsylvania Hospital Unit (Base Hospital No. 10 USA) In the Great War* (Paul B. Hoeber, New York, 1921): pp 22-3.
24. Helen Fairchild; *Letters*; fire-safe 3-B-2, AMEDD Center of History and Heritage, Archival Repository, JBSA Fort Sam Houston, TX 78234. Material relating to Helen Fairchild in this book (including transcripts of the letters) has been reproduced by kind courtesy of Fairchild's niece, Nelle Rote, and is from her private collection, which was published in 2004 as: Nelle Rote, *Nurse Helen Fairchild: WW1 1917–1918* (Lewisburg, PA, Nelle Rote, 2004). The reference to the 'crazy stuff' written by Christine is on p 16.
25. Ibid: p 47.
26. Kate Luard, *Unknown Warriors*: pp 83-4.
27. Ibid: p 88.
28. Ibid: p 89.

**Chapter Five: Prelude to the 'Big Push'**

1. Hilda Mary Loxton; *Diary*; 2DRL/1172; Private Record; Australian War Memorial, Canberra, Australia.
2. Transcript of a speech made by Madeleine Jaffray to the Monroe County Nurses Association: unidentified newspaper clipping, Madeleine Morrison Fonds; PAA-8298; Provincial Archives of Alberta, Edmonton, Canada.
3. Hilda Loxton; *Diary*.
4. Ibid.
5. Ibid.
6. Ibid.
7. Violetta Thurstan, *Field Hospital and Flying Column* (London, G. P. Putnam's Sons, 1915).
8. Violetta Thurstan, *The People Who Run* (London, G. P. Putnam's Sons, 1916).
9. Violetta Thurstan, *A Text Book of War Nursing* (London, G. P. Putnam's Sons, 1917).
10. Jan Louagie, *A Touch of Paradise in Hell, Talbot House Poperinghe – Everyman's Sanctuary from the Trenches* (Helion & Co., 2015).
11. A. B. S. Macfie, *The Curious History of Toc H Women's Association. The First Phase, 1917-1928* (London, Toc H Women's Association, Crutched Friars House, 1956): pp 6-7.
12. Philip Clayton, *Letter*, dated 17 August, 1915, to his mother; Archives of Talbot House, Poperinge, Belgium.
13. From an account by Philip Clayton, quoted in: Jan Louagie, *A Touch of Paradise in Hell. Talbot House, Poperinge – Every-Man's Sanctuary from the Trenches* (Solihull, Helion, 2015): p 335.

14. Philip Clayton, *Letter* dated 1 May 1917; Archives of Talbot House. The text of this letter was kindly forwarded to me by Jan Louagie.
15. A. B. S. Macfie, *The Curious History*.
16. Transcript of a speech made by Madeleine Jaffray to the Monroe County Nurses Association: unidentified newspaper clipping, Madeleine Morrison Fonds.
17. 'Canadian Nurse tells of German Air Raids ...': unidentified newspaper clipping, Madeleine Morrison Fonds.
18. Hilda Loxton; *Diary*.
19. Ibid.
20. Ibid.
21. Ibid.
22. Agnes Warner; letter to Mr Jaffray re-printed in an unidentified newspaper clipping; Madeleine Morrison Fonds.

## Chapter Six: Moving 'Up the Line'

1. Helen Fairchild; *Letter*; Nelle Rote, *Nurse Helen Fairchild*: pp 25-6.
2. Ibid: p 28.
3. Ibid: pp 31-2.
4. Quotation taken from: Margaret A. Dunlop, 'History of the Nursing Corps of Base Hospital No. 10 USA', in Paul H. Hoeber (ed.), *History of the Pennsylvania Hospital Unit*: pp 76-102.
5. Helen Fairchild; *Letter*; Nelle Rote, *Nurse Helen Fairchild*: p 46.
6. Margaret A. Dunlop, 'History of the Nursing Corps', in Paul H. Hoeber (ed.), *History of the Pennsylvania Hospital Unit*: pp 76-84.
7. Helen Fairchild; *Letter*; Nelle Rote, *Nurse Helen Fairchild*: p 65.
8. Ibid: p 78.
9. Margaret A. Dunlop, 'History of the Nursing Corps', in Paul H. Hoeber (ed.), *History of the Pennsylvania Hospital Unit*: pp 84-5.
10. Paul H. Hoeber (ed.), *History of the Pennsylvania Hospital Unit*: p 67.
11. Head Sister Nellie N. C. Morrice, 'Narrative'; AWM41/1013; Butler Collection; Australian War Memorial, Canberra, Australia.
12. Catherine Black, *King's Nurse – Beggar's Nurse*: p 91.
13. George Crile, *An Autobiography*, Edited, with Sidelights by Grace Crile, Volume 1 (Philadelphia & New York, J. B. Lippincott Co., 1947): pp 284-7.
14. Violet Minnie Payne, 'Narrative'; AWM41/1021; Butler Collection; Australian War Memorial, Canberra, Australia: pp 6-7.
15. May Tilton, *The Grey Battalion* (Sydney, Angus & Robertson Ltd., 1933): pp 198-9.
16. Anonymous, 'Australia Army Nursing Services During the First World War', undated; including an account by Mrs Effie Fussell (née Garden); Misc 47, item 790; Imperial War Museum, London.

## Chapter Seven: Edge of Hell

1. May Tilton, *The Grey Battalion*: p 203.
2. George Crile, *An Autobiography*: p 291.
3. Violetta Thurstan, *Diaries*; WW1/WO/116; The Liddle Collection, The Brotherton Library, Leeds.
4. Letter written by Helen McMurrich, reproduced in unidentified newspaper clipping; Madeleine Morrison Fonds.
5. Kate Luard, *Unknown Warriors*: p 192.
6. May Tilton, *The Grey Battalion* : p 214.
7. Kate Luard, *Unknown Warriors*: p 194.
8. George Crile, *An Autobiography*: p 300.
9. Ibid: p 311.
10. May Tilton, *The Grey Battalion*: p 217.
11. Kate Luard, *Unknown Warriors*: pp 196-8.
12. Lieutenant M. L. Walkinton, 24th Machine Gun Company; quoted in: Nigel Steel & Peter Hart, *Passchendaele: The Sacrificial Ground* (London, Cassell, 2007): p 112.
13. Driver Rowland Luther, 92nd Brigade, Royal Field Artillery, 'The Poppies are Blood Red', typescript memoir, IWM, Department of Documents; quoted in Nigel Steel & Peter Hart, *Passchendaele*: pp 125-6.
14. George Crile, *An Autobiography*: pp 301-2.
15. Violet Minnie Payne, 'Narrative': p 7.
16. May Tilton, *The Grey Battalion*: p 255.
17. Violet Minnie Payne, 'Narrative': p 8.
18. Margaret A. Dunlop, 'History of the Nursing Corps', in Paul H. Hoeber (ed.), *History of the Pennsylvania Hospital Unit*: p 85.
19. Hilda Loxton; *Diary*.
20. May Tilton, *The Grey Battalion*: p 219.
21. Kate Luard, *Unknown Warriors*: pp 201-2.
22. Ibid: p 203.
23. Ibid: p 211.

## Chapter Eight: August Raids

1. May Tilton, *The Grey Battalion* : pp 222-3.
2. Kate Luard, *Unknown Warriors*: p 217.
3. May Tilton, *The Grey Battalion*: pp 227.
4. Ibid: pp 229-30.
5. Kate Luard, *Unknown Warriors*: pp 226.
6. Ibid: pp 228-9.
7. Margaret A. Dunlop, 'History of the Nursing Corps', in Paul H. Hoeber (ed.), *History of the Pennsylvania Hospital Unit*: p 86.
8. Helen Fairchild; *Letter*; Nelle Rote, *Nurse Helen Fairchild*: pp 134-5.

9. Harvey Cushing, *From a Surgeon's Journal 1915–1918* (Boston, Little Brown & Co., 1936): p 186.
10. Major Charles J. Biddle, *The Way of the Eagle,* (New York, Charles Scribner's Sons, 1919): pp 62-3. This description can also be found in: Paul H. Hoeber (ed.), *History of the Pennsylvania Hospital Unit*: pp 142-4.
11. The War Diaries for the CCSs at Remy Siding are on display at the Lyjssenthoek Military Cemetery Visitor Centre. All the original War Diaries are held at the National Archives, Kew, UK.
12. George Crile, *An Autobiography*: p 305.
13. The War Diary is on display at the Lyjssenthoek Military Cemetery Visitor Centre.
14. George Crile, *An Autobiography*: pp 311-12.
15. John H. Gibbon, 'Two months at Casualty Clearing Station No. 61', in Paul H. Hoeber (ed.), *History of the Pennsylvania Hospital Unit*: pp 147-52.
16. Ibid: pp 147-52; quotation in p 151.
17. *London Gazette*, 17 October, 1917. An amendment had been made to the Royal Warrant on 21 June 1916, to permit the Military Medal to be awarded to women. For a full list of British nurses who were awarded the medal during the First World War, see: http://www.scarletfinders.co.uk.
18. May Tilton, *The Grey Battalion*: p 236.
19. *London Gazette*, 17 October 1917.
20. May Tilton, *The Grey Battalion*: p 235.
21. *London Gazette*, 17 October 1917.
22. This text is taken from a Yorkshire newspaper cutting, a copy of which is available in: Nelle Rote, *Nurse Helen Fairchild*: p 50.
23. Harvey Cushing, *From a Surgeon's Journal*: pp 192-3.
24. Ellen McClelland, 'Narrative'; AWM41/1000; Butler Collection; Australian War Memorial; Canberra, Australia.
25. Kate Luard, *Unknown Warriors*: p 236.
26. Hilda Loxton; *Diary*.
27. Violetta Thurstan, *Diary*; Liddle Collection, The Brotherton Library, Leeds; WW1/WO/116; entry for Monday 27 August.
28. The account is taken from the citation recommending that Violetta Thurstan should receive the Military Medal, and is quoted by: Norman G. Gooding, *Honours and Awards to Women: The Military Medal* (London, Savannah Publications, 2013): pp 149-50.
29. Violetta Thurstan, *Diary*.
30. Helen Fairchild; *Letter*; Nelle Rote, *Nurse Helen Fairchild*: p 169.
31. Hilda Loxton; *Diary*.

## Chapter Nine: Battle for Lives

1. Robin Prior & Trevor Wilson, *Passchendaele: The Untold Story* Third Edition (New Haven, Yale University Press, 2016): p 119. On the Battle of the Menin

Road see pp 113-23; on Polygon Wood, see pp 125-31. All casualty figures cited in this chapter are taken from Prior's and Wilson's book.

2. This and other letters of Annie Wright are in: Letters relating to Glynne Morris: DD/873/18,19,20,22,23,26,27,29,34, Nottinghamshire Archives, UK. Full text of the letters written by Annie Wright can be found in: Peter Barton, *Passchendaele* (London, Constable, in association with Imperial War Museum, 2007): pp 226-7.

3. I am indebted to Jeremy Banning for drawing my attention to Annie Wright's letters. The figure quoted is from: Peter Barton, *Passchendaele*: p 227.

4. Catherine Black, *King's Nurse – Beggar's Nurse*: p 95.

5. Ibid: p 96.

6. May Tilton, *The Grey Battalion*: p 249.

7. Ibid: p 251.

8. Hilda Loxton; *Diary*.

9. Ibid.

10. Ibid.

11. Emma Cuthbert, 'Narrative'; AWM41/958; Butler Collection; Australian War Memorial, Canberra, Australia: p 20.

12. Helen Fairchild; *Letter*; Nelle Rote, *Nurse Helen Fairchild*: p 174.

13. Ibid: p 185.

14. May Tilton, *The Grey Battalion*: p 261.

15. Ibid: pp 262-3.

16. Robin Prior & Trevor Wilson, *Passchendaele*: p 119.

17. *London Gazette*, 29 January 1918.

18. *London Gazette*, 19 November 1917, p 11961.

19. Figures are quoted from: Robin Prior & Trevor Wilson, *Passchendaele*: p 195.

**Chapter Ten: End of Days**

1. Margaret A. Dunlop, 'History of the Nursing Corps', in Paul H. Hoeber (ed.), *History of the Pennsylvania Hospital Unit*: p 88.

2. Nelle Rote, *Nurse Helen Fairchild*: p 216.

3. Ibid: p 224.

4. Baroness de T'Serclaes, *Flanders and Other Fields*: pp 99-100.

5. *London Gazette*, 4 June 1918.

6. Catherine Black, *King's Nurse – Beggar's Nurse*: p 107.

7. Hilda Loxton; *Diary*.

8. Catherine Black, *King's Nurse – Beggar's Nurse*: p 121.

9. John B. Flick, 'Casualty Clearing Station Team No. 23', in Paul H. Hoeber (ed.), *History of the Pennsylvania Hospital Unit*: p 170.

10. Margaret A. Dunlop, 'History of the Nursing Corps', in Paul H. Hoeber (ed.), *History of the Pennsylvania Hospital Unit*: p 99.

## Epilogue

1. May Tilton, *The Grey Battalion*: p 275.
2. The citations for all four nurses, translated into English, can be found in the *British Journal of Nursing*, 4 January 1919.
3. Margaret Allan Brander, Personal Papers; Documents 13190; Imperial War Museum, London.
4. 'Brave War Nurse attends Amputations Association Convention...': unidentified newspaper clipping, Madeleine Morrison Fonds.
5. Richard H. Harte, 'Organization of the Unit', in Paul H. Hoeber (ed.), *History of the Pennsylvania Hospital Unit*: p 29.

# Index